THE
REASSESS
YOUR CHESS
WORKBOOK

THE
REASSESS YOUR CHESS
WORKBOOK
HOW TO MASTER CHESS IMBALANCES

by IM Jeremy Silman

SILES PRESS LOS ANGELES

First Edition

13 12 11 10

Library of Congress Cataloging-in-Publication Data

Silman, Jeremy.
The reassess your chess workbook / by Jeremy Silman. -- 1st ed.
p.cm.
1. Chess—Handbooks, manuals, etc.
2. Chess—Collections of games.
I. Title.
GV1449.5.S56 2001   794.1—dc21   2001020473

ISBN: 1-890085-05-7

Cover design by Heidi Frieder

Printed and bound in the United States of America

SILES PRESS

a division of Silman-James Press, Inc.
www.silmanjamespress.com
info@silmanjamespress.com

Dedicated to Sri Nisargadatta Maharaj (who offers us truth), Kali (my patron saint), Zev (my favorite cluster lizard), Stan (yet another idiot), 790 (look at my head!), Kai (dead and loving it), Khu (teeth, claws, fur, and brains), Pa'u Zotoh Zhaan (who makes me want to immerse myself in botany), Hans Baruch (IQ, IQ, IQ), John Watson (who somehow puts up with my phone ravings), and John Donaldson (the only one who will know what all of this means).

CONTENTS

W hen my book, *How to Reassess Your Chess*, first came out, I never guessed how popular it would ultimately become. Since that time, I've received hundreds of requests for more on this same theme (i.e., the art of thinking in chess). This led to *The Amateur's Mind*, a very personal look into a player's head and thinking habits. The flow of mail didn't stop, though, and requests for a third volume arrived in even greater numbers than before.

It was clear that many players liked the thinking technique I expounded, rallying around my system because it allowed them to understand various chess subtleties in a way that was easy and made sense. In fact, many students of the game felt they had mastered the "system," though a talk with them quickly demonstrated that this wasn't the case. This realization showed me what had to be done: I needed to write a book that would enable a player to test himself and see how much he really understood about planning.

This book is divided into three parts. Part One: A Look at a System, explores my method of chess thought. In Thinking Techniques, I start with a discussion of modern thinking techniques describing a few attempts by well-known chess thinkers to clarify how chess positions should be looked at and how individual moves should be found. My own system of thinking is then compared to those previously discussed.

In Imbalances: a Crash Course, I discuss the seven inbalances that form the basis of my system. Each of these imbalances are explained in detail, and examples are given that teach the student how to use them to their advantage as well as how to play against them. In fact, this part of the book is the key to solving the problems that follow. All the problems in this book are designed to see how well you can form a plan and recognize the imbalances in each phase of the game.

Part Two is composed of 131 positional/strategic and tactical problems from the opening, the middlegame, and the endgame, plus a section on self-annotations. Though the problems are presented in these four basic ways, I purposely avoided any continuity of theme or idea. As in real play, it's up to you to find and understand these things without help from an invisible voice ("White to mate in two" appears in books, but we often miss the mate in real play because nobody is giving us this enormous clue). I've also designed the problems to have a huge range of difficulty, usually from 1200 to the much higher 2100 level. In fact, some of the tests will be challenging to players with ratings of 2500 and up!

Even if you are unfamiliar with the material from my previous books, the solutions to the problems, given in Part Three, are laid out in such depth that the positions in question will be filled with new and exciting meaning. Fresh ways of looking at the game will be served to you on a platter, and your knowledge of chess as a whole should go through a major revolution.

The Reassess Your Chess Workbook can be used as a serious testing device or as a straightforward book of instruction:

✦ You can make a serious effort to solve all the problems. An excellent way to do this is to place your answers (given in as much detail as you can manage) in a notebook. Only look at the solutions when you've gone through all the questions. This will allow you to form an honest idea of how knowledgeable you really are. (Many players feel they already know this material. This is your chance to see if you are wise or deluded!) This method of studying *The Reassess Your Chess Workbook* should prove very rewarding.

✦ You can look at a problem, try to solve it, and then immediately look at the answer.

✦ Instead of trying to solve the problems, you can skip that section of the book, jump to the solutions, and simply study what's given. In this way, you will be using the book in a purely instructional manner.

This book fills a void in chess literature. Most problem books tend to ask lots of questions, but give pathetically sparse answers—they don't really teach you anything at all. It is my hope that *The Reassess Your Chess Workbook* will prove to be both entertaining and highly instructive, and the student should garner many hours of pleasure from it.

As always, I welcome readers with corrections, observations, or comments to email me at jsilman@earthlink.net.

!	=	excellent move.
!!	=	brilliant move.
!?	=	interesting move.
?!	=	dubious move.
?	=	poor move.
??	=	blunder.

SYMBOL LEGEND

SILMAN

SMYSLOV
SOVIET UNION

JOHN NUNN AND JUDIT POLGÁR

Thirty years ago, the English translation (from the original Russian) of a now classic book appeared that offered a detailed discussion on how to improve your powers of analysis. This book, *Think Like a Grandmaster*,[1] by Alexander Kotov, strove to show the serious student how to become a fast and accurate calculator. In his introduction, Mr. Kotov gave the following qualities as being the building blocks that form a "real" chess player:

1) He must be well up in modern opening theory.

2) He must know and keep in his memory the principles behind typical middlegame positions learned both from his own games, and from those of other players. The more a player knows and remembers the easier it is for him to find a 'precedent', i.e., a position which has occurred before and which is similar to his own present position.

3) A grandmaster must be able to assess a position accurately and correctly.

4) No less important is the ability to hit upon the right plan—a plan that meets the demands of the given position.

5) A grandmaster must be able to calculate accurately and quickly those variations which might arise in the subsequent course of play.

---

[1] Alexander Kotov, *Think Like a Grandmaster* (Dallas: Chess Digest, Inc., 1971).

THINKING TECHNIQUES

Later in the book, Kotov goes on to discuss his method of calculation: (The following wording is mine. I hope I've captured Kotov's true meaning!) List the candidate moves (i.e., all the moves you are seriously considering) and then analyze each one thoroughly to the end, without jumping back and forth between them. For example, if you are looking at three possible moves (36.Rg6, 36.Qg6 and 36.Ne5), you would first take a deep look at 36.Rg6 until you were sure you had figured out its "truth." Next on the agenda would be another deep analysis, this time of 36.Qg6. At this point, even if you decide that 36.Qg6 is a great move, you must still follow the same detailed procedure with your final candidate move, 36.Ne5. Once you have analyzed them all, then and only then is it time to decide which move to actually play (and, at times, that decision may turn out to be a matter of taste).

Kotov makes a compelling point when he says that, though some players have an innate talent for speedy calculation, most have to work very hard to improve in this area. Unfortunately, he's right! The vast majority of chess hopefuls will indeed have to invest hours and hours of intense labor if they want to calculate at a high level.

I have no argument with Kotov's views. However, after I read his book and thought about what he had said, I became worried about one extremely important question: *How* is the poor chess player supposed to figure out the correct candidate moves? Kotov likes telling us what to do once we know what the candidate moves are in a given position, but he doesn't bother telling us how to find those candidates in the first place! His comment is not too helpful: "How then does a chessplayer choose which move to play in a given position? There is no easy answer; each player goes about choosing in his own way."

Gee thanks, Alexander, that's useful! A later comment by Kotov did nothing to illuminate the darkness: "How many candidate moves then does a grandmaster examine? As must be clear, there is no standard answer to this question; in each position he examines as many as seem necessary in the given circumstances."

Ultimately, Kotov's advice comes up short for most players, simply because they will never be able to calculate like a grandmaster, nor do they have any real expectations of doing so. Nevertheless, wouldn't these same people still be able to play a very strong game of chess if they could find a proper plan and come up with a logical series of candidate moves to actualize it? I was positive this was the case, but how could an Expert, Class A (1800-1999) or even a Class B (1600-1799), C (1400-1599), or D (1200-1399) find these hidden plans and candidates?

Before looking at my attempt to solve this problem, let's see how other chess thinkers tackled the concept of planning. Grandmaster John Nunn, one of the world's most respected chess writers, is the first on our list. The following planning tips come from his excellent book, *Secrets of Practical Chess*.[2]

> There comes a point in the vast majority of games when your acquired knowledge will be exhausted and you will have to rely on your own resources. This point normally arises in the early middlegame. The next step is to formulate a plan.

Cutting to the chase (and skipping a few sentences), Nunn then goes on to say:

> In some positions, for example, those with a blocked center, it may be appropriate to construct a long-term plan which may require ten or twenty moves to execute. More likely, your plan will be much shorter-range, lasting perhaps five moves. This applies particularly in relatively open positions.

Nunn offers the student the following three steps:

1) Make sure your plan is beneficial. There is no point aiming for a target that does not actually enhance your position. Typical misguided plans are: attacking on the wrong part of the board; aiming for the exchange of the wrong pieces; committing yourself to weakening pawn advances.

2) Make sure your plan is realistic. There is no point in embarking on a five-move plan if your opponent can wait for the first four moves, and then stop your plan by playing one move himself.

3) Make sure your plan is not tactically flawed. Even if what you are aiming for is worthwhile, this will not help if your opponent can mate you while you are executing it.

---

[2] John Nunn, *Secrets of Practical Chess* (London: Gambit Publications LTD, 1998).

Nunn later points out that you should be ready to change your plan or, at the very least, make adjustments to it:

> If your opponent has blocked Plan A, but at the cost of creating a weakness elsewhere on the board, it would be foolish to stick to your original intention, ignoring the new situation.
>
> Most games are like this: the players formulate a series of mini-plans and strike a balance between forwarding their own plans and interfering with those of the opponent.

The good doctor gives useful advice, but it really doesn't answer my earlier question about finding that hidden plan and its candidate moves. In other words, he assumes a fairly high degree of chess skill from the reader of his book, and much of what he says is over the head of Class C and B players.

Having failed to find enlightenment from world class grandmasters (they just don't share the pain of us guys in the trenches!), let's see if a "normal" grandmaster might prove to be more helpful. American-born Jonathan Tisdall, who now resides in Norway, wrote an incredibly good book called *Improve Your Chess Now*.[3] Let's take a peek at a small bit of what he had to say on our subject:

- **Talk to yourself** – not out loud, of course! – that's against the rules, and chess players have a shaky enough reputation already.
- **Try to determine your next move by examining one principal variation.** This variation may either be the one that first or most strongly appeals, or which you feel seems to fit the strategic demands of the position.
- **Process the concrete variations calculated,** into themes and positional factors and use them to determine what moves are likely to be relevant. *Use* the information gathered on your calculation, and try to render it in verbal form that makes it useful for further searches. Describe your findings.
- **If your primary variation is unsatisfactory,** calm down, lean back, and make a thorough list of possible candidates with fresh eyes.
- **The times for a conscious listing of candidate moves are quite logical:** when one pauses naturally due to an obvious wealth of alternatives, or when one's preliminary calculations have not achieved the desired result.

---

[3] Jonathan Tisdall, *Improve Your Chess Now* (London: Cadogan, 1997).

In sharp, tactical positions it is extremely important to make a comprehensive list at these times.

- **Have faith in your calculations.** You may be wrong, but you have only yourself to trust. If you are often wrong, it just means that you need to improve this ability, but when you use it, you must trust it.
- **In predominantly strategic games,** the search process is similar, but the calculation of concrete variations will be less important than the internal discussion of positional elements.

All this is very interesting, but it's still over the head of a average class player. It seems that we have to move even further down the food chain in an attempt to find a writer who actually remembers what it's like to be confused about things that most masters take for granted.

Our next "guest speaker" was pondering our question about plans and candidate moves way back in the 1930's, long before I was born! Cecil Purdy (winner of the World Championship of Correspondence Chess in 1953) was an Australian player and teacher who created one of the most detailed systems for finding a plan ever devised. Written mainly for amateurs, his work was forgotten (or ignored) by players in this part of the world until his writings were collected in *The Search For Chess Perfection: The Life, Games, and Writings of C.J.S. Purdy.*[4]

Even I wasn't aware of the scope of Purdy's work until a few students of mine demanded that I take a look at the aforementioned book. After spending a couple of hours with it, I had to agree that Purdy was that very rare author who understood the suffering of the typical amateur. Having noticed their disease, Purdy then devised a "cure" in simple, easy to understand language.

The following is Purdy's recommended thinking technique. It's been cut and reshaped by me (his actual format and language is, at times, rather ponderous) for clarification (my comments appear in bold), so if you wish to see the original, buy the book!

I. MY TURN TO MOVE.

    1. What are all the moves I have to consider?

        Purdy points out that this question may be unanswerable at this stage, but will become clear after ques-

---

[4] C.J.S. Purdy, *The Search for Chess Perfection: The Life, Games, and Writings of C.J.S. Purdy* (Davenport: Thinkers' Press, Inc., 1997).

tion five. So why ask this question so quickly? Because, in some cases, there may be only one or two obvious possibilities and you can then save time by ignoring the rest of the system.

2. How has his last move changed the position? What are his threats? What are his objectives?

> **Always keep the position "up to date" by demanding to know how, and to what extent, your opponent's move has changed things.**
>
> It is vital to be aware of any threats!
>
> When you see a threat, your first reaction should not be to search for a defense to it but rather for a way of ignoring it.

3. Complete your search if not already done.

a. Material. **Notice such things as two Bishops, Bishops of opposite colors, pawn majorities, etc.;**

b. King positions. **Is one of the Kings exposed? Always note if there is a lack of flight squares;**

c. Weaknesses and strengths. **Weak pawns, weak squares, confined pieces, lack of space;**

d. Development. **Purdy considers the value of a tempo to be a quarter to a third of a center pawn, and up to half a flank pawn;**

e. Where could either side break through? After 1.e4 e6 2.d4 d5 3.e5, White's breakthrough point is f5, while Black's are on c5 and f6.

4. Have I a good combination? To help in this, look for possible combination motifs.

a. geometrical;

b. nets;

c. jump moves;

d. zugzwang (applies only to an endgame);

e. stalemate (applies only to an endgame).

5. If not satisfied that the answer to 4 is yes, what is my best plan (for this, use the reconnaissance)?

> How can I best exploit his weaknesses, establish my strengths, eliminate my weaknesses and reduce his strengths. **Now, when you consider the first question, *What are all the moves I have to consider?* again, the answer should be far easier to discover.**

II. I AM CONSIDERING A CERTAIN MOVE.

1. Visualize the move as though made, firmly

2. Does it leave me vulnerable to any combination?

III. IT IS HIS TURN TO MOVE.

1. Make a reconnaissance, as described in I, to be completed when he has made his move.

2. Visualize the position after this or that likely move, and proceed as in I.

I was shocked to see how similar Purdy's recommendations were to my own! His "When you see a threat, your first reaction should not be to search for a defense to it but rather for a way of ignoring it" is a particular rave of mine with students. I'm always telling them to try their best to ignore enemy threats by making sure that a "threat" is real and not imagined. I see so many games where a player "threatens" something and his opponent (usually a student of mine) weakens his position to stop it. Closer examination, though, shows that the so-called threat would have failed completely. In other words, my student went out of his way to stop his opponent from losing the game!

As I just mentioned, my own thinking technique (given in great detail in my books, *How to Reassess Your Chess*[5] and *The Amateur's Mind*[6]) is similar to Purdy's in many ways, though I like to think of mine as being more concise and to the point. In particular, my concept of IMBALANCES considerably simplifies the work an amateur has to do. What is an imbalance? An imbalance is any difference between the White and Black positions. My system of thought, quite simply, calls for the student to:

✦ Take note of the differences in the position (i.e., all the imbalances that exist, not being partial to one side or the other).

✦ Figure out the side of the board you wish to play on (queenside, center, or kingside). You can only play where a favorable imbalance or the possibility of creating a favorable imbalance exists.

---

[5] Jeremy Silman, *How to Reassess Your Chess: The Complete Chess Mastery Course, Expanded 3rd Edition* (Los Angeles: SIles Press, 1993).

[6] Jeremy Silman, *The Amateur's Mind: Turning Chess Misconceptions into Chess Mastery* (Los Angeles: Siles Press, 1999).

✦ Find all the candidate moves (back to Kotov!) that allow your side to make use of a major imbalance, or a series of imbalances. This improves on Kotov, who didn't tell us *how* to find candidate moves. A candidate move should always be directed at your positive imbalances unless you're being forced to play a purely defensive move.

✦ Finally, calculate the candidate moves you've chosen.

I've long held that a player can be guided to the correct move by simply listing the imbalances for both sides—of course, a basic understanding of how to use these imbalances must also exist. Once he "hears" the language of these imbalances (first noting what imbalances exist and then trying and find a way to nurture them), the correct move, or, at the very least, a few logical candidates, will virtually jump out and bite him on the nose!

For example, let's say you are playing a game and note that your opponent's position is not too threatening and that he has a weak pawn on b6. You also see that the b- and g-files are half open and that all other files are closed.

Two things are of great importance here:

✦ your opponent has a weakness on b6.

✦ Rooks belong on open or half-open files.

So what kind of moves should you look for? What would the candidate moves be? Clearly, you must get your Rooks into the battle, and you must also try and generate pressure against your opponent's weakness on b6.

Thus, the only moves you would address should have something to do with these key points. Though we are playing without a position in mind, I would say that you'd almost certainly want to double Rooks on the b-file (the g-file has nothing to do with the weakness on b6), because that mixes both plusses at the same time (playing on a file and attacking b6). In other words, any candidate move would have to begin this doubling operation.

Note that this imaginary position allowed us to make easy use of the four points listed on the previous page: we listed the imbalances; we decided to play on the side of the board where our favorable imbalances resided; we were able to find the proper candidate moves (moves designed to make use of the imbalances); we were only ready to calculate after we verbalized the positions possibilities.

Now that I've demonsrated how simple this method of thought is, it's time to gain a deeper understanding of the various imbalances.

MIKHAIL TAL

An IMBALANCE in chess denotes any difference in two respective positions. Of course, most players don't think about imbalances, they prefer to concentrate on attacking the enemy King. However, to think that the game of chess is solely devoted to checkmating the opposing King is much too simplistic. The correct way to play chess is to create an imbalance and try to build a situation in which it is favorable for you. An actual checkmate will follow once your opponent is helpless, or if the imbalances insist that an early kingside attack is the correct course. A deeper understanding of this statement shows that an imbalance is not necessarily an advantage. It is simply a difference. It is the player's responsibility to turn that difference into an advantage.

A study of this chapter should enable you to immediately make the most of each imbalance you create, as well as allow you to look at the upcoming problems in a way that might not have been possible before digesting this information.

List of Imbalances

> **Superior Minor Piece** — the interplay between Bishops and Knights (trying to make one superior to the other).

> **Pawn Structure** — a broad subject that encompasses doubled pawns, isolated pawns, backward pawns, passed pawns, etc.

➤ **Space** — the annexation of territory on a chessboard.

➤ **Material** — owning pieces of greater value than the opponent's.

➤ **Control of a key file or square** — files, ranks, and diagonals act as pathways for your pieces, while squares act as homes. Whole plans can center around the domination of a file, or the creation of a weak square in the enemy camp.

➤ **Development** — a lead in development gives you more force in a specific area of the board. This is a temporary imbalance because the opponent will eventually catch up.

➤ **Initiative** — dictating the tempo of a game. This can also turn out to be a temporary imbalance.

If one side owns a Bishop while the other has a Knight, that's an important imbalance. If one side has the superior pawn structure while the opponent owns more space, then that, too, is an imbalance. You must always try and make your imbalance beat the opponent's! Whole plans can and should be created around this idea. In fact, these plans can often be found with little or no calculation.

Take a look at the diagram and see if you can spot White's proper path.

(1)

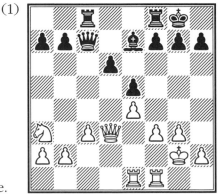

White to move.

Can you list the imbalances? If you noticed the weakened d5-square, the backward d6-pawn, and the fact that White owns a Knight while Black has a Bishop, you did really well!

How can you make use of these imbalances? What move addresses these factors? Let's consider the following bits of chess wisdom:

> A Knight needs an advanced, permanent home if it wants to prove itself superior to an enemy Bishop.

> A weak square tends to make an excellent home for your pieces!

> A backward pawn can't always be attacked immediately. However, it's important to fix it in place so that it becomes an immobile target (it's easy to hit things that can't run away!).

With this information in mind, we should be able to surmise that White would like to improve the position of his Knight in order to make it better than Black's Bishop. How would you do this? 1.Nb5 pushes the Knight forward, but is b5 a permanent home? No, it's not. Black can move his Queen to safety and then kick White's Knight off b5 with ...a7-a6.

The dream square for the White Knight is actually d5. Once it sits there, nothing can chase it away! How can the Knight reach that square (all this internal talk brings to mind Tisdall's recommendation that we should learn to talk to ourselves during play)? Once you see that the goal is domination and occupation of d5, there is really only one candidate move that makes sense: 1.Nc2 when either 2.Nb4 and 2.Ne3 (both take you to d5) followed by 3.Nd5 allows White to fulfill all his imbalance-oriented dreams: The Knight dominates the Bishop, White owns the d5-square, and the d6-pawn isn't going anywhere (all this was done with no calculation!).

Now that you realize how helpful an understanding of the imbalances can be, it's time to address the particulars of each situation.

Superior Minor Pieces

The battle between Bishops and Knights is one of the most subtle and important in chess. A good player will invariably end up with a powerful Knight over a poor Bishop (or a powerful Bishop over a poor Knight) against his lower-rated opponent. Then, when he plays someone stronger than himself, he will find that the situation is reversed and his minor piece is inferior to whatever his opponent owns. You will discover that this "food chain" lacks any kind of mercy; only a deep understanding of the needs of both the Bishop and the Knight will allow you to keep your head above water in this turbulent fight.

If you are already familiar with this information (as many of you will be), skip this chapter and jump right into chapter two.

The Bishop

There are three basic types of Bishop:

➤ **Good** — A Bishop is considered good when its central pawns are not on its color and thus are not obstructing its activity.

➤ **Bad** — A Bishop is considered bad when its central pawns are on its color and thus block it.

➤ **Active** — An active Bishop can be either good or bad; it's called active simply because it serves an active function.

Personally, I can't stand the "good" and "bad" labels. Insisting that your Bishop serves some kind of active function is all you really need to do.

(2)

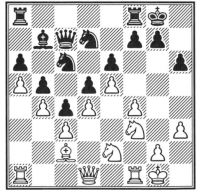

White's Bishop is good,
Black's is bad.

(3)

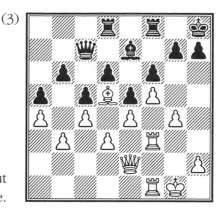

Two "bad" Bishops, but
White's is very active.

In diagram (2) White has a good Bishop that also happens to
be very active. Black's, on the other hand, is bad and also completely inactive.

Our next diagram (3) shows two bad Bishops. However,
White's is so active that it virtually dominates the game.

**Bishop Rule 1 — Bishops are long-range pieces and
love wide-open positions that are free of central
pawns.**

**Bishop Rule 2 — In the endgame, Bishops are great
at stopping enemy pawns, which they can often do
from the other side of the board.**

(4)

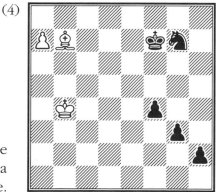

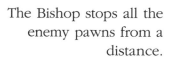

The Bishop stops all the
enemy pawns from a
distance.

In diagram (4) the Bishop's long-range ability crushes the
enemy Knight.

Bishop Rule 3 — If you are unfortunate enough to possess a bad (and inactive) Bishop, you are usually well advised to do one of three things:

➤ Trade the offending piece off for an enemy Bishop or Knight.

➤ Make it good by moving the central pawns off the color of your Bishop.

➤ Get your Bishop outside the pawn chain. Many games have been won by turning an impotent bad Bishop into a "bad" but active piece.

(5)

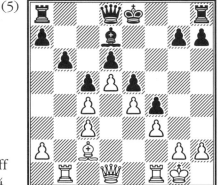

White to play will trade off his horrible Bishop by 1.Ba4.

In diagram (5) White's Bishop is clearly inferior to Black's. Because of this, trading it off by 1.Ba4 makes good sense.

(6)

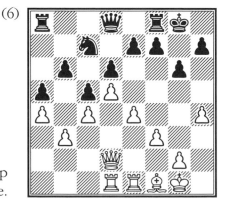

Bring White's Bishop back to life.

In diagram (6) White's Bishop again seems to be a loser. However, by 1.g3 followed by 2.Bh3 (1...Qd7 2.Kh2 still gets the Bishop to the golden square) the calcified piece suddenly finds a new lease on life.

> **Bishop Rule 4 — If a player gets the two Bishops versus a Bishop and Knight or Two Knights, he usually wants to retain them because, working together, the Bishops control squares of both colors. If your opponent has two Bishops, trade one of them off and leave yourself with a more manageable Knight versus Bishop or Bishop versus Bishop scenario.**

The Knight

Knights are the only pieces that have the ability to jump over other men. This makes them very effective in closed positions, but vulnerable to Bishops in situations with no support points and wide-open diagonals (Steinitz said that the best way to beat Knights was to take away all their advanced support points).

> **Knight Rule 1 — Knights need advanced support points if they are going to compete successfully with Bishops.**
>
> **A support point (i.e., an advanced square that can't be controlled by an enemy pawn) on the sixth rank is ideal, while a Knight on the fifth is usually better than a Bishop. A Knight on the fourth is a very strong piece, but we see a case of diminishing returns if you place it on the third, second, or first ranks. The first and second ranks in particular are not good homes for a Knight and should only be used as a path to greener pastures.**

(7)

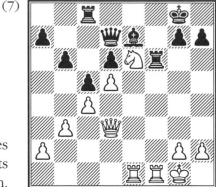

The horse dominates
the game from its
sixth-rank perch.

Knight Rule 2 — Knights tend to be superior to Bishops in closed positions. A wall of pawns will completely shut a Bishop down, but a Knight will just jump over this wall and continue on its way.

(8)

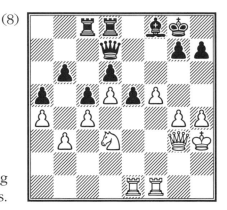

The nimble Knight is king
of closed positions.

White's Knight, in diagram (8), is flexible and happy. It will dominate the game after Nd3-f2-e4 where it eyes the d6-pawn, blocks Black's passed e-pawn, helps White's kingside majority advance, and also envisions possibilities like Ne4-g5-e6.

Knight Rule 3 — Knights are the best blockaders of passed pawns. A Knight can stop an enemy passer in its tracks and still remain active due to its ability to jump over other units.

(9)

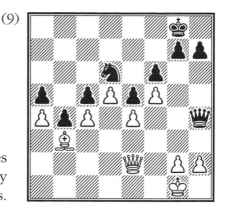

Both sides' minor pieces
are blocking enemy
passed pawns.

In diagram (9), White's Bishop is blocking Black's passed pawn but it has virtually no activity or scope. On the other hand, Black's Knight is not only blocking White's passed pawn, it is also attacking the enemy pawns on e4 and c4. After 1.Bc2 (defending e4) 1...Qf4, Black's Queen will penetrate into the enemy position and cause White all sorts of trouble.

> **Knight Rule 4 — Knights are usually superior to Bishops in endings with pawns on only one side of the board. Such a position makes light of a Bishop's long-range powers, while the Knight's ability to go to either color (a Bishop is forever stuck on one color complex) becomes extremely valuable.**

Pawn Structure

In the 1700s, Andre Philidor said, "Pawns are the soul of chess." This simple statement tells us that a particular pawn structure dictates what plan(s) to adopt, when to seek an endgame, and when to realize that a position has some sort of static inferiority.

Since pawn chains ("Always attack a pawn chain at its base.") and my "pawn pointing theory" will be studied within the confines of the problems, I will only present the basics of doubled pawns, isolated pawns, backward pawns, and passed pawns here.

Doubled Pawns

Though despised by most players, doubled pawns are not all bad, and can often be an actual advantage.

Doubled Pawns Rule 1 — A doubled pawn gives its owner an extra open file for his Rooks.

Doubled Pawns Rule 2 — If the pawns are central, double pawns allow for coverage of critical squares that would not be possible if the pawns were undoubled and "healthy."

(10)

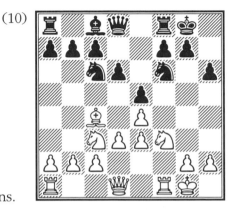

Useful doubled pawns.

In diagram (10) White's doubled pawns give him control over d5, f5, d4, and f4. The half-open f-file is another perk that this structure offers.

Doubled Pawns Rule 3 — Doubled pawns can turn out to be inflexible and, in the worst case scenario, simply weak. In general, the lead pawn turns out to be the target.

(11)

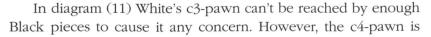

White's c4-pawn is
vulnerable to attack.

In diagram (11) White's c3-pawn can't be reached by enough Black pieces to cause it any concern. However, the c4-pawn is within range of the Black army, and it will feel a lot of heat after Black plays ...Nb8-c6-a5 followed by ...Ba6.

Isolated Pawns

An isolated pawn results when no other "friendly" pawn is on an adjacent file. This lonely guy can't be touched or defended by any of his brothers and, as a result, he becomes vulnerable to attack by enemy pieces.

Most players feel that an isolated pawn is always a weakness. However, nothing could be further from the truth!

Isolated Pawn Rule 1 — An isolated pawn might be an unstoppable passer.

Isolated Pawn Rule 2 — It might be centrally placed, which means that it may guard important squares.

Isolated Pawn Rule 3 — You might be able to use an isolated pawn as a battering ram that will slam into, and subsequently fragment, the enemy's "superior" structure.

Isolated Pawn Rule 4 — Even if your isolated pawn isn't going anywhere, your Rooks might become more active than the opponent's thanks to the two half, or fully, open files on either side of it.

(12)

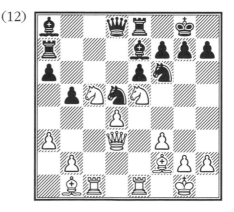

The isolated d-pawn gives White control over the c5- and e5-squares.

(13)

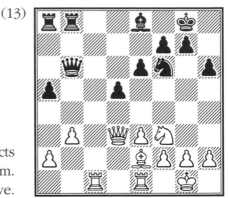

The isolated a-pawn acts
as a battering ram.
Black to move.

In diagram (13) Black plays 1...a4, gets rid of his isolated battering ram and, after making a pawn trade via ..axb3, turns White's "healthy" queenside majority into a weak isolated pawn.

Isolated Pawn Rule 5 — If your opponent ends up with an isolated pawn, make sure you control the square directly in front of it. Aside from stopping the pawn in its tracks, the square will turn out to be an excellent home (support point) for one of your pieces.

(14)

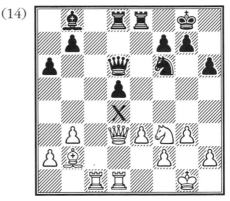

White's control over d4 stops the isolated d-pawn and gives White's Knight a very nice home.

Isolated Pawn Rule 6 — An advanced isolated pawn (i.e., a White pawn on d4 or a Black pawn on d5) gains space and makes its army's pieces active.

Isolated Pawn Rule 7 — The side playing against the isolated pawn should (ideally) exchange all the minor pieces (they can't get active if they're not on the board!), place a Rook in front of the pawn, immobilizing the poor thing, and put the Queen behind it, doubling on the pawn and putting a lot of pressure on it.

(15)

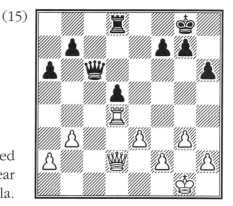

White wins the isolated pawn by following a clear formula.

In diagram (15) White has followed all the key steps: he has taken control of the square in front of the pawn; he has exchanged off all the minor pieces; and he has doubled on it and forced the remaining Black units to take up a defensive stance.

White now wins this pawn by 1.e4 when the pin along the d-file doesn't give Black a way to escape his fate.

Backward Pawns

A backward pawn is a pawn that has fallen behind its brother pawns and can't be guarded by them. It also can't safely move side by side with them.

Backward Pawn Rule 1 — If the backward pawn sits on a half-open file it might be weak. If it isn't on a half-open file, the pawn probably won't become a significant weakness.

Backward Pawn Rule 2 — A well-defended backward pawn, even if it's sitting on a half-open file, can often shrug off many kinds of attacks.

Backward Pawn Rule 3 — Often of more importance than the potential weakness of a backward pawn is the weakness of the square directly in front of it. If the square is adequately guarded by pieces, then the pawn might not be a problem.

Backward Pawn Rule 4 — A backward pawn often serves a useful purpose by guarding a pawn that has gone ahead of it.

Backward Pawn Rule 5 — Often a backward pawn is backward in name only. If it can safely advance at will, then the label of "backward" should be punted out of one's mind.

(16)

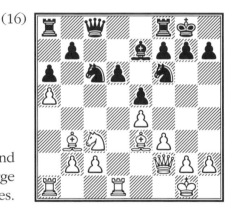

Backward pawns on b7 and d6 leave White in charge of two weak squares.

In diagram (16) the backward pawn on b7 isn't weak at all since it doesn't stand on a half-open file. However, the weakness of the b6-square is obvious. Black's backward pawn on d6 does stand on a half-open file and needs to be defended. Of greater consequence, though, is the gaping hole on d5 which will prove to be a fine home for White's pieces.

(17)

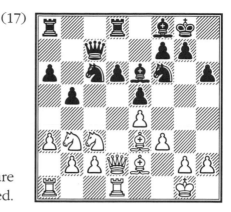

Both d6 and d5 are
well defended.

In diagram (17) the backward pawn on d6 is well defended, as is the d5-square. Since the pawn threatens to advance to d5 at any moment, one can't call d6 or d5 weak.

Passed Pawns

Most players take it for granted that passed pawns are an advantage. Though often true, especially in the endgame, passed pawns can also be a disadvantage!

Passed Pawn Rule 1 — If both sides have play elsewhere that has nothing to do with the passer, a passed pawn, even one that isn't playing a dynamic role, can prove useful as an endgame insurance policy.

Passed Pawn Rule 2 — When one side owns a passed pawn, the most important square on the board, for *both* players, is usually the square directly in front of the passer.

Passed Pawn Rule 3 — If the passed pawn can be firmly blockaded, then the pawn may end up as a traitor; its very existence may block files and diagonals and thus limit its own Bishops and Rooks, giving the opponent access to a key square (the one in front of the passer) that wouldn't be available if the pawn were not there.

(18)

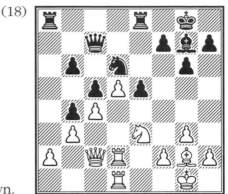

A bad passed pawn.

The passed pawn in diagram (18) is firmly blocked by Black's Knight. If Black hadn't taken control of the all-important d6-square, then White could have advanced his pawn by d5-d6, when the "goat" in the diagram suddenly turns into a winning possession! To make matters worse, the traitorous pawn severely limits the scope of White's Rooks, his Bishop, and his Knight!

> **Passed Pawn Rule 4 — If a passed pawn can't be blockaded, the pawn can run down the board and cause panic in the enemy's ranks. The defender will usually be in for a hard ride if the pawn gets safely past the fifth rank.**

> **Passed Pawn Rule 5 — In general, the owner of a passed pawn would like to trade off all the minor pieces, thus getting rid of the most useful blockaders. He would also prefer to retain the Queens and at least one Rook. Keeping the Queens on the board scares the defender's King and stops it from taking on the duties of a blockader.**

(19)

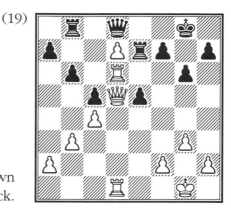

The White passed pawn
is torturing Black.

Space

When we own property, we usually map out our territory by building a fence. In chess, we also build fences, but in place of timber we use pawns.

> **Space Rule 1 — Extra space is advantageous for one simple reason: the more space we possess, the more room our pieces have to move about in.**

> **Space Rule 2 — The side with more space should avoid exchanges since this would give more room to the boxed-in enemy.**

> **Space Rule 3 — The side with less territory should actively seek trades since that will transform his cramped quarters into something a bit easier to tolerate.**

(20)

White's pawns give him a
huge space advantage.

Material

A material advantage is a wonderful thing to have because it influences all phases of the game. In the opening and middlegame, the side with extra wood has a larger army. In the endgame, the side with the material deficit usually goes into a deep depression. In fact, this endgame nightmare is often felt in the middlegame because the material-down defender is basically giving endgame odds and this severely limits his options.

Material Rule 1 — Most endgames are in your favor. This means that trading pieces is an option that your opponent won't enjoy.

Material Rule 2 — If you can make your extra unit of force an active participant in the battle, then do so!

Material Rule 3 — If you can't make immediate use of your material plus, don't worry. An extra pawn will act as endgame insurance, threatening your opponent's endgame chances for the rest of the game.

Material Rule 4 — When you employ a plan that nets you some extra wood, immediately shore up your weak points and bring all your pieces to squares where they work together. Don't keep lashing out if your army is off balance!

Material Rule 5 — If you are behind in material, you must seek out some kind of compensation to justify the deficit. Some common forms of compensation are active pieces, a lead in development, possession of the initiative, and extra space.

(21)

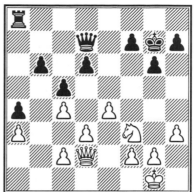

Black is up an Exchange
for a pawn.
Black to move.

In diagram (21) White has a Knight and a pawn for a Rook. Black is obviously much better, but his material advantage won't amount to much if he can't create an open file for his Rook. Thus 1...b5! rips open the b-file and allows the Rook to eventually penetrate on that newly-opened road.

(22)

Black's lead in development and control over the hole on d4 gives him ample compensation for the sacrificed pawn.

Control of a Key File

Rooks belong on open files. We have all heard this on many occasions but, for some reason, few players are able to get the most out of these pieces.

Rooks are extremely powerful, no doubt about it. But if that's true, why do they sit around doing nothing for so long? The answer lies in the movements of the other pieces. A Knight just leaps over its pawns and boom, it's active! A Bishop doesn't even have to move; the d-pawn lunges forward and suddenly the lazy c1-Bishop is patrolling the c1-h6 diagonal.

Rooks have a much harder time finding a way into the enemy position. However, when they do enter the fray, their enormous strength becomes obvious.

Rook Rule 1 — Your Rooks will be useless unless you can create an open file for their use.

Rook Rule 2 — An open file is only worth bothering with if a Rook can use it to penetrate into the enemy position. If no penetration points exist, then the file is useless.

Rook Rule 3 — Usually an open file won't be handed to you on a platter. It's your responsibility to crack open a file; turn your Rook's need into a reality!

Rook Rule 4 — An open file will often be equally contested by opposing Rooks. This will usually lead to massive trades. Unfortunately, such things can't be avoided because stepping away from the file would hand it over to the opponent.

Files, ranks, and diagonals act as pathways for your pieces, while squares act as homes. An entire plan can center around the domination of a file, or the creation of a weak square in the enemy camp.

(23)

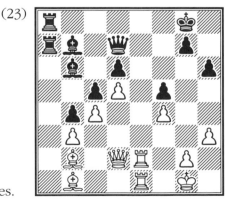

Two files.

In diagram (23) the open a-file offers no penetration points for the Black Rooks (a1, a2, a3, and a4 are all controlled by White's pieces and pawns). The open e-file is another matter: here White's Rooks have access to e6, e7 and, in some cases, e8.

Control of a Key Square

Playing for dominance of one single square is a hard concept for many amateurs to understand. Nevertheless, the idea of fighting for squares instead of material or attack is extremely important and must be appreciated if the student wishes to improve his game.

> **Square Rule 1 — The reason one plays for control of a key square (such a square is also known as a "hole") is that it will usually prove to be an excellent home for a Knight or a Bishop, though other pieces can also gain from laying claim to it.**

> **Square Rule 2 — Once your piece reaches a hole, it will inevitably be more valuable than its counterpart on the other side of the board.**

> **Square Rule 3 — Often entire plans are based on the acquisition of such squares.**

(24)

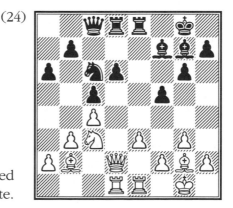

The square on d5 is owned by White.

In diagram (24) it's clear that a White Knight on d5 will be more valuable than Black's Knight on c6.

(25)

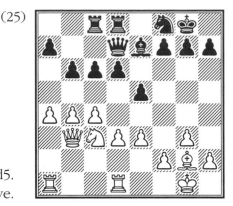

White fights to dominate d5.
White to move.

In diagram (25) White forces the "win" of the d5-square by 1.b5, destroying the defending c-pawn's ability to cover d5. After 1...c5 (1...cxb5 2.axb5 allows White's Rook to eye Black's backward a-pawn) White would have complete control over the juicy d5-square.

Development

It is important to develop your *whole* army. Note the word "whole." Some players get a few pieces out and launch an attack. The correct way to play chess is to develop each and every piece (chess is a team game!), get your King safely castled, and only then begin more aggressive maneuvers.

On occasion, a player will fall significantly behind in development, giving his opponent the opportunity to make use of the greater force that he has in play. To get maximum use of this imbalance, you will have to kick things into high gear (called fast-play) so that some gain can be made before the enemy catches up and nullifies the edge you once possessed.

> **Development Rule 1 — A lead in development is a temporary advantage (structural and material plusses are considered to be long-term or permanent advantages). The opponent will catch up if you don't make immediate use of it.**

> **Development Rule 2 — If the center is closed, rapid development is not necessarily a priority**

because the enemy pieces won't be able to break into your position.

Development Rule 3 — If the center is open (meaning that open files and diagonals penetrate into your camp), rapid development takes on greater significance.

(26)

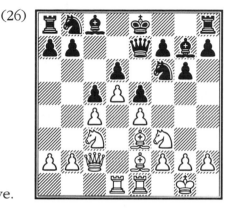

White to move.

In diagram (26) White has a huge lead in development, but the closed center makes it a non-issue.

(27)

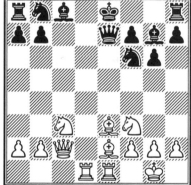

White to move.

This position, diagram (27), is the same as the previous one, except that the center pawns have been removed, leaving us with an open center. Now White's lead in development gives him a winning advantage. White would fast-play the position (not giving Black the time to castle and get some pieces out) by 1.Bb5+ Kf8 (or 1...Nc6 2.Bc5, winning the house) 2.Bc5! Qxc5 3.Rd8+ Ne8 4.Rdxe8 mate.

Initiative

The side that forces an opponent to react to his ideas is said to have the initiative. This control over a position can be based on dynamic or static considerations. If you are attacking a weak pawn and your opponent is busy defending it, you have an initiative based on a static advantage. This means that you can often play in a slow or calm manner because a static plus is long lasting. If you are using a lead in development to play for mate, you have the initiative based on a dynamic advantage. Here you play for immediate effect since dynamic pluses often dissipate with the passage of time.

The concept of initiative is a very important one in top-flight chess, and both sides struggle for possession of it right out of the starting blocks. Gambits can be used to obtain it, though the price often turns out to be too high. A sudden attack can claim it, or simple positional pressure can grab hold of it for the duration of the game.

Initiative Rule 1 — You should always try to impose your will on the character of the game.

Initiative Rule 2 — Never mindlessly react to every threat, perceived or real, that your opponent throws your way. This will give him a firm initiative and will leave you passively reacting to his ideas.

Initiative Rule 3 — Like a lead in development, the initiative can fade away if you don't make good use of it.

(28)

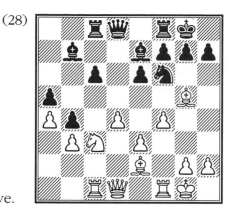

White to move.

In diagram (28) Black is fighting to carry out the freeing ...c6-c5 which would activate his b7-Bishop and place pressure on White's center. A normal move by the threatened Knight, like 1.Nb1, would allow Black to do this. However, instead of caving in to his opponent's desires, White can grab the initiative by 1.Bxf6! gxf6 (1...Bxf6 2.Ne4 gives White permanent control over c5) 2.Ne4 when Black's plan of ...c6-c5 has been nipped in the bud. Occupation of the c5-square (Nc5), followed by placing pressure against the potential targets on c6 and a5, will leave White firmly in control of the game.

BENT LARSEN

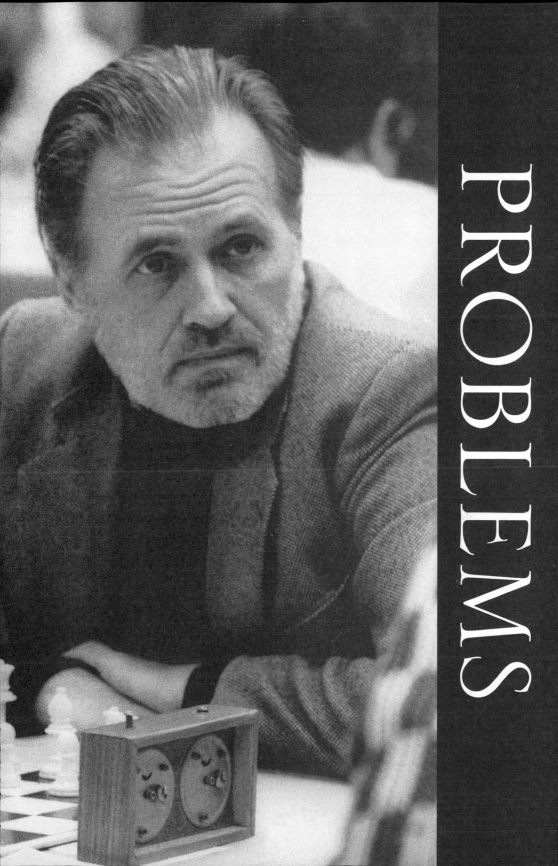

PROBLEMS

JEREMY SILMAN

In this modern age, the opening phase of a chess game has gotten a bad rap. Huge databases, a seemingly endless array of opening books, and the sheer volume of variations that, apparently, must be memorized, make even the bravest chessplayers want to run and hide.

Beginner's books paint a somewhat less intimidating picture of opening play: "Get your pieces out quickly," "Use your pawns to gain space and control the center." The platitudes go on and on. If only the realities of opening mastery were as simple as this.

Thanks to these basic books, most players think that the opening revolves around the development of both side's armies. While true in a limited sense, this is actually a view that misses the big picture. The *real* purpose of the opening is to create a difference, or series of differences, in the respective positions and then develop your pieces around these facts so that, hopefully, these differences (imbalances) will eventually favor you.

For example, if you, as White, get to advance your pawns to d4 and e4 while your opponent places his pawns on d6 and e6, you will enjoy a spatial plus. You would then develop your forces in such a manner as to highlight this advantage.

Another typical example centers around Black playing ...Bc8-g4x(Kt)f3 or ...Bf8-b4x(Kt)c3. These common exchanges create an imbalance of Bishop versus

Knight. As soon as this appears on the board, White should place his pieces and pawns on squares that highlight the powers of his Bishop(s). Black, on the other hand, should play for a closed position (which is known to usually favor Knights) and try hard to create advanced support points that will ultimately enable his horses to become equal or superior to the enemy Bishops.

This view of opening play will enable amateurs to figure out new situations in an intelligent manner (okay, at a higher level at least some memorization is still necessary!). It will allow them to create a plan, verbalize a goal, and then make sure that every pawn advance and piece development caters to the imbalances that you've created in the first few moves.

In this section you will see many different opening situations. Once you grasp that everything is geared, in one way or another, to this idea of opening imbalances, the solutions will be easier to find or, at the very least, far easier to understand when you turn to Part Three: Solutions.

Problem 1

(29)

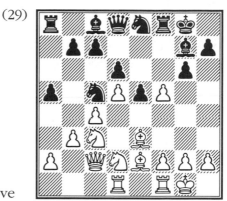

Black to move

Black, whose ...f7-f5 was answered by exf5, has to recapture his pawn on f5. What's the best way to do this?

Problem 2

(30)

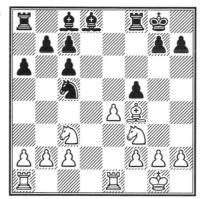

White to move.

This position arose after 1.e4 e5 2.Nf3 Nc6 3.Bb5 a6 4.Ba4 Nf6 5.0-0 Be7 6.Bxc6 dxc6 7.Re1 Nd7 8.d4 exd4 9.Qxd4 0-0 10.Bf4 Nc5 11.Qxd8 Bxd8 12.Nc3 f5. How should White react to this advance of Black's f-pawn?

Problem 3

After 1.e4 e5 2.Nf3 Nc6 3.Bb5 a6 4.Ba4 Nf6 5.0-0 Be7 6.Qe2 b5 7.Bb3 0-0 8.c3 d6 9.d4 Bg4 10.Rd1 exd4 11.cxd4 d5 12.e5 Ne4 13.a4 bxa4 14.Bxa4 Nb4 15.h3 Bh5 16.Nc3 Bg6 17.Be3 Rb8, we reach a position that was once thought to be all right for Black.

However, a new move was unveiled that cut to the heart of the position and showed that White is actually clearly better. How would you play the White position?

(31)

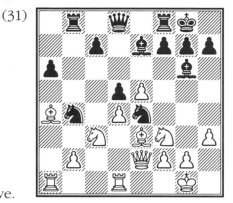

White to move.

Problem 4

What do the following two fairly well-known opening systems have in common? The answer lies in the meaning of Black's ...g7-g5 advance.

1.e4 c5 2.Nf3 Nc6 3.d4 cxd4 4.Nxd4 g6 5.c4 Bg7 6.Be3 Nf6 7.Nc3 Ng4 8.Qxg4 Nxd4 9.Qd1 Ne6 10.Rc1 Qa5 11.Bd3 b6 12.0-0 g5.

(32)

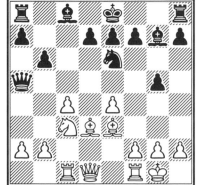

White to move.

1.e4 c5 2.Nf3 d6 3.d4 cxd4 4.Nxd4 Nf6 5.Nc3 a6 6.Bg5 e6 7.f4 Be7 8.Qf3 Qc7 9.0-0-0 Nbd7 10.Bd3 h6 11.Bh4 g5.

(33)

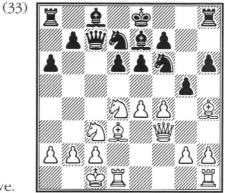

White to move.

Problem 5

After 1.d4 Nf6 2.Bg5 Ne4 3.Bh4 c5 4.Qd3, we arrive at an interesting position.

(34)

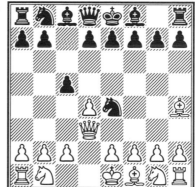

Black to move.

Black's Knight is attacked and he has to decide how this threat should be dealt with. What is the correct decision here?

Problem 6

After 1.e4 d5 2.exd5 Nf6 3.c4, is 3...c6 a good idea?

(35)

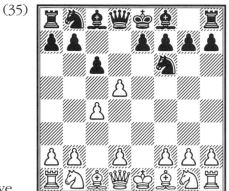

White to move.

Problem 7

After 1.d4 f5 2.Nf3 Nf6 3.Bf4 e6 4.e3 b6 5.Bd3 Bb7 6.Nbd2 Be7 7.0-0, how should Black play this position?

(36)

Black to move.

Problem 8

Take a look at the position that arises after 1.d4 Nf6 2.c4 c5 3.d5 e5 4.Nc3 d6 5.e4 Be7 6.Bd3 0-0 7.Nge2.

(37)

Black to move.

If you had to choose between 7...Bg4, 7...Nbd7, 7...Na6, 7...Ne8, 7...g6, and 7...h6, which would you play?

Problem 9

(38)

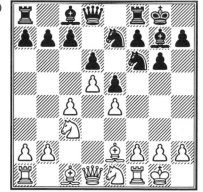

Black to move.

This popular main line position of the King's Indian Defense, reached after 1.d4 Nf6 2.c4 g6 3.Nc3 Bg7 4.e4 d6 5.Be2 0-0 6.Nf3 e5 7.0-0 Nc6 8.d5 Ne7 9.Ne1, is a good test to see if you understand what's expected when a closed position is reached in the opening. Black has only two logical moves here. Can you list them? To find the answer, you will have to understand the nature of the position as a whole.

Problem 10

In a skittles game, after 1.e4 g6 2.d4 Bg7 3.Nf3 d6, White played 4.h3 and said, "Strengthening d4 and e5." Does this make sense, or did he have too much to drink before the game?

(39)

Black to move.

Problem 11

After 1.e4 g6 2.d4 Bg7 3.Nf3 d6 4.h3 Nf6 5.Nc3 c6, White often plays 6.a4, stopping Black from gaining queenside space with ...b7-b5 and, in many lines, threatening to play a4-a5 with a clear spatial plus in that sector. Black can now reply with 6...a5. What are the pros and cons of this move?

(40)

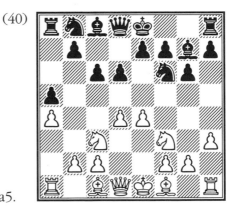

Black has just played 6...a5.

Problem 12

After 1.c4 e5 2.Nc3 Nc6 3.Nf3 g6 4.g3 Bg7 5.d3 d6 6.Bg2 f5 7.0-0
Nf6, White usually plays for a b2-b4 advance. Why is this advance
important, and should he prepare it with 8.Rb1 or 8.a3?

(41)

White to move.

Problem 13

Analyze these moves: 1.d4 d6 2.c4 e5 3.d5 Nf6 4.Bg5 Be7 5.Nc3
0-0 6.e4 Nbd7 7.Nge2 Qe8 8.Ng3. Do they make sense? Who
stands better? Did either player make any major mistakes?

Problem 14

(42)

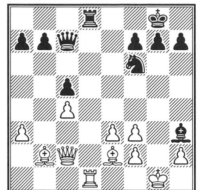

White to play.

This position, reached from a once-popular Nimzo-Indian line after 1.d4 Nf6 2.c4 e6 3.Nc3 Bb4 4.e3 c5 5.Nf3 d5 6.Bd3 0-0 7.0-0 Nc6 8.a3 Bxc3 9.bxc3 dxc4 10.Bxc4 Qc7 11.Be2 e5 12.Bb2 Rd8 13.Qc2 Bg4 14.dxe5 Nxe5 15.c4 Nxf3+ 16.gxf3 Bh3 17.Rfd1 Rxd1+ 18.Rxd1 Rd8, is very interesting from the point of view of opening imbalances. List the imbalances and, from that, deduce White's correct plan and his best move.

Problem 15

After 1.e4 c5 2.Nf3 Nc6 3.d4 cxd4 4.Nxd4 Nf6 5.Nc3 d6 6.Be2, is 6...e5 a reasonable move for Black? Whether it is or isn't, what are its ramifications?

(43)

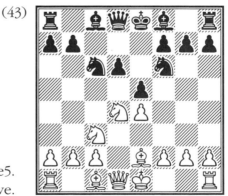

Black just played 6...e5.
White to move.

Problem 16

(44)

White to move.

This common type of position and the plans that come out of it was first brought to world attention in the game Botvinnik-Capablanca, AVRO 1938 which White won brilliantly. Though this position isn't quite the same as the Botvinnik-Capablanca game, the ideas are identical and have been used in many guises.

See if you can spot White's most effective plan, and Black's best counter to it.

Problem 17

(45)

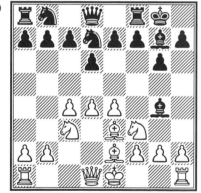

White to move.

After 1.d4 Nf6 2.c4 g6 3.Nc3 Bg7 4.e4 d6 5.Nf3 0-0 6.Be2 Bg4 7.Be3 Nfd7, figure out Black's plan (you can't play properly in the opening if you don't know what your opponent is trying to do) and then tell me which of the following White moves appear to be most threatening to the second player: 8.h3, 8.d5, 8.Qc2, 8.Qb3, 8.Ng1, 8.Nd2.

Problem 18

(46)

White to move.

If you had to choose between 1.Be3, 1.Bd2, or 1.Na4, which would you play?

Problem 19

True or false: In the Silman thinking system, the idea of the opening is to develop your pieces as quickly as possible.

Problem 20

After 1.d4 Nf6 2.c4 e6 3.Nc3 Bb4 (the Nimzo-Indian Defense), 4.e3 c5 5.Nf3 Nc6 6.Bd3 Bxc3+ 7.bxc3 d6 8.e4, Black plays 8...e5. What is his strategic justification for playing in this way?

(47)

White to move.

Problem 21

After 1.d4 f5 2.Nc3 d5 3.Bf4 Nf6 4.e3 e6 5.Nf3 Bb4 6.Bd3 c5, how should White handle this position?

(48)

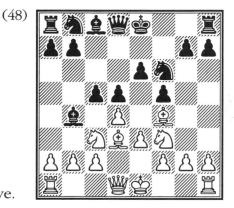

White to move.

Problem 22

After 1.e4 e5 2.Nf3 Nc6 3.Bb5 (the Ruy Lopez) 3...a6 4.Ba4 Nf6 5.0-0 Be7 6.Re1 b5 7.Bb3 d6 8.c3, Black usually castles when White can, and almost always does, play 9.h3, stopping ...Bg4 and preparing for central gains by d2-d4. Why shouldn't Black anticipate this and toss in 8...Bg4 while he has the chance?

(49)

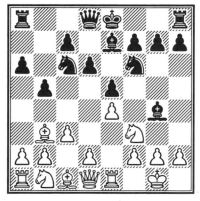

Black just played 8...Bg4.
Is this a good idea?
White to move.

Problem 23

After 1.e4 e5 2.f4 (the King's Gambit) 2...Bc5 3.Nf3 d6 4.c3 a6?! 5.d4 exd4 6.cxd4 Ba7, (1700 vs. 1900), both sides should instantly see the strategy they are going to pursue and develop accordingly. What is White's correct strategy? What is Black's?

(50)

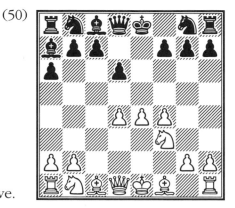

White to move.

Problem 24

After 1.c4 g6 2.g3 f5 3.d4 Bg7 4.Bg2 d6 5.d5 c5, would White do better to develop the g1-Knight to the center by 6.Nf3 or should he place it on the rim via 6.Nh3?

(51)

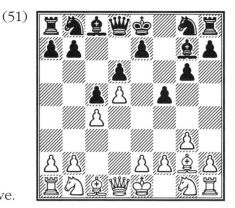

White to move.

Problem 25

After 1.e4 c6 (the Caro-Kann) 2.d4 d5 3.exd5 cxd5, commonly seen moves at the amateur level are 4.Nc3, 4.c4, and 4.Bd3. What one of these is simply incorrect?

(52)

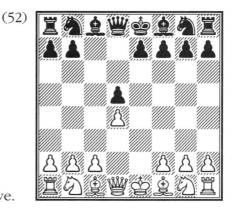

White to move.

Problem 26

After 1.e4 c5 2.c3, the popular Alapin Variation against the Sicilian Defense where White hopes to play d2-d4 with a full pawn center, 2...d5, White almost never plays 3.d3, a move once recommended by Grandmasters Hort and Lombardy. Why has 3.d3 been tossed into the rubbish bin?

(53)

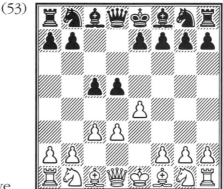

Black to move.

Problem 27

After 1.d4 Nf6 2.c4 e6 3.Nf3, Black often plays 3...b6 (the Queen's Indian Defense). What's the logic behind this move?

(54)

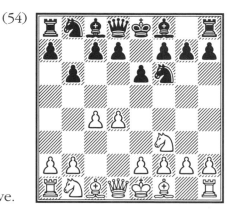

White to move.

Problem 28

After 1.d4 d5 2.Nf3 Nf6 3.e3 e6 4.Nbd2 c5 5.c3 Nc6 6.Bd3 Be7 7.0-0, we reach a common position in the ever-popular (on the amateur level) Colle Opening. At this point, two moves that might be considered are 7...c4 and 7...cxd4. What do you think of these two possibilities?

(55)

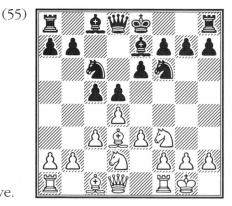

Black to move.

Problem 29

(56)

Black to move.

If you had 1...e6, 1...Bf5, and 1...Bg4 to choose from, what would you play?

Problem 30

After 1.c4 c5 2.b3 Nf6 3.Bb2 g6, should White be tempted by 4.Bxf6?

(57)

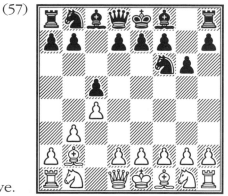

White to move.

Problem 31

(58)

White to move.

White's system has left him with a hole on d4. How serious is this? Also, would you label the White position flexible or inflexible?

Problem 32

(59)

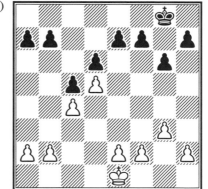

In diagram (59), the bare bones structure should tell you what Black is aiming for.

(60)

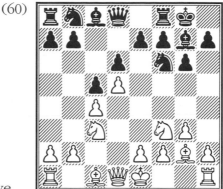

Black to move.

Moving on to diagram (60), we can't help but notice that we have the same basic structure as in the previous position, except now we have to determine where to place our pieces. How would you develop your forces if you had the Black position?

Problem 33

(61)

White to play.

Black has just played ...Bb7. Break this position down and explain the respective plans for both sides. An exact move or series of moves isn't important.

Problem 34

After 1.Nf3 d5 2.d4 Nf6 3.c4 c6 4.Nc3 e6 5.e3 Nbd7 6.Qc2 Bd6 7.Bd3 0-0 8.0-0 Qe7, we have a common position in the Semi-Slav Defense. White has tried many moves here: 9.e4, gaining central space, and 9.b3, preparing to fianchetto the c1-Bishop and also giving White the chance to meet ...dxc4 with bxc4, both make sense. How would you judge the aggressive 9.c5?

(62)

Black has just played
8...Qe7.
White to move.

Problem 35

(63)

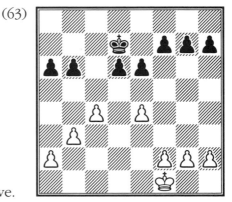

Black to move.

This bare bones illustration of a Hedgehog structure, typically found in the English Opening and the Sicilian, allows us to illustrate Black's two main plans. Do you know them?

Problem 36

After 1.d4 Nf6 2.c4 e6 3.Nf3 b6 4.a3 (the Petrosian System in the Queen's Indian Defense) 4...Ba6 5.Qc2 Bb7 6.Nc3 c5 7.e4 cxd4 8.Nxd4 Nc6 9.Nxc6 Bxc6 10.Bf4 Nh5 11.Be3, take a look at 11...Bd6 and then describe its good and bad points.

(64)

White to move.

Problem 37

(65)

Black to move.

What would you do in this position?

JAY WHITEHEAD

For players who can't stand the memorization that the openings demand, and who become bored when faced with endgames, the middlegame is what "real" chess is all about. Of course, to become a chess master, you must become proficient in all three phases of the game. Nevertheless, the middlegame's possibilities have captured the imaginations of millions of players over the centuries, and this is where most amateurs firmly plant their attention. At this level, attacks and combinations (exciting, beautiful, yet also holding a certain air of mystery) sound their siren call to chess lovers everywhere. At higher levels, too, this phase of the game has many pleasing characteristics: primal kingside attacks are created, subtle strategic plans are put into motion, and preparations for the endgame are quietly, sometimes secretly, begun.

Many games don't get past the middlegame. A checkmate ends matters in no uncertain terms, huge material losses convince experienced players to resign the contest in disgust, and the specter of a lost endgame can also lead a player to tip his King over in a gesture of defeat.

The problems in this section run the gamut from quiet positional maneuvering to attacking in earnest. It's up to you to feel the ebb and flow of the position, to understand whether static or dynamic play is called for, and to make use of the imbalances at all

PROBLEMS / THE MIDDLEGAME

times. Without these things you won't be able to find the correct solutions. Certain general bits of knowledge are also needed to correctly answer the true-false questions.

Problem 38

Answer the following questions. No moves are necessary:

1. What is an imbalance?

2. Name the seven main imbalances.

3. What are the main components of the "Silman Thinking Technique?"

4. What is a plan?

5. What is the difference between a static and dynamic advantage or imbalance?

6. What is the difference between a good and bad Bishop?

7. Can an active Bishop also be bad?

8. What are the three cures for a bad Bishop?

9. What do Knights need to reach their full power?

10. Explain Steinitz's rule on how to beat Knights.

11. If your opponent has two Bishops, what should you do?

12. Why are two Bishops usually superior to two Knights?

13. Why is extra territory a good thing?

14. What should the side with less space do to make the situation more acceptable?

15. Why is a full pawn center a good thing to have?

16. How can a player make use of a full pawn center?

17. What must you do if your opponent creates a full pawn center?

18. Are doubled pawns always bad? If not, what are their good points?

19. How does one make use of an isolated d-pawn and how does one play against it?

20. Do Rooks always stand well on open files?

21. When you triple on an open file with two Rooks and a Queen which takes up the rear, what is this called?

22. A static plus usually calls for slow play while a dynamic plus usually calls for fast play (often fast play leads to the creation of a static, long-lasting advantage). With this in mind, figure out if you must play fast or slow when you possess:

    a. A lead in development.

    b. An isolated d-pawn.

    c. Play against your opponent's backward pawn.

    d. The initiative.

    e. A material advantage.

    f. A superior minor piece.

    g. Play against a weak square in the enemy camp.

    h. An advantage in space.

23. True or false:

    a. It's better to be behind in material than to have a position that's devoid of activity.

    b. A Bishop should usually be considered as slightly better than a Knight.

    c. Bishops enjoy open positions.

    d. A Rook reaches the zenith of its power on the eighth rank.

    e. A Rook on the seventh rank is often worth a pawn.

    f. Two Rooks on the seventh are known as "roving eaters."

    g. An attack against the enemy King is the most effective plan in chess.

    h. Knights are most effective on the eighth rank.

    i. A protected passed pawn is always a good thing to have.

Problem 39

A systematic pawn advance designed to knock aside the opponent's pawn fortifications is known as a pawn break. Name some advantages that this kind of pawn advance might bring.

Problem 40

In positions with locked centers, should you attack on the wings with pieces or pawns?

Problem 41

(66)

White to move.

In this position, White played 1.Kh1 Qd7 2.Rg1 Rad8 3.Ne4 Qf7 4.g4. Odd-looking moves to be sure, but in our next game, something similar seems to occur over a hundred years earlier!

(67)

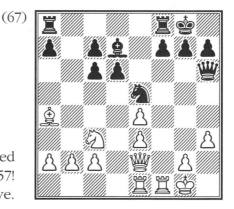

A position that occurred
in 1857!
Black to move.

Here Black played 1...Kh8 2.Nd1 g5 3.Nf2 Rg8.

What is the point of the plans chosen in both games, and was the plan used in the first game emulating the plan used in the second?

Problem 42

(68)

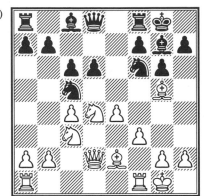

Black to play.

Name the tactical theme that Black employs in this game.

Problem 43

(69)

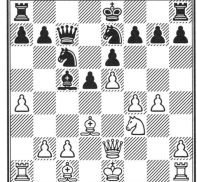

Black to play.

Black can make use of a thematic idea. It won't sit around forever, so you better take notice and make a grab for the brass ring.

Problem 44

(70)

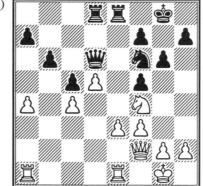

White to play.

White appears to stand better due to his pressure against d5, the possibility of a central advance by c2-c4, and the hole on c6. What's the best way to make use of these plusses? Does White actually have the better game?

Problem 45

(71)

Black to move.

Would 1...a5 be a reasonable choice for Black?

Problem 46

(72)

White to move.

White's Bishop is threatened and he only has three squares to choose from. What is his proper move and, more importantly, what's the proper evaluation?

Problem 47

(73)

White to play.

White obviously has a significant advantage due to Black's backward pawn on c7. What's the best way to proceed?

Problem 48

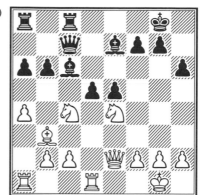

(74)

White to play.

Annotate the following moves:

1.a5 dxc4 2.Qxc4 Rf8 3.axb6 Qxb6 4.Nd6 Bb5 5.Nxb5 axb5 6.Qd5 Rxa1 7.Rxa1.

Problem 49

(75)

Black to play.

Let's consider three moves for Black: 1...Qc7, 1...0-0, and 1...a6. Two of these moves are perfectly reasonable, while one is a major error. Which one of these moves would you label with a question mark?

Problem 50

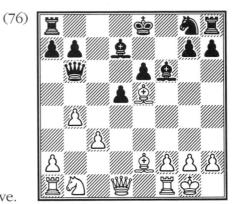

(76)

White to move.

Black threatens to chop off White's Bishop on e5. How would you deal with this obvious but bothersome fact?

Problem 51

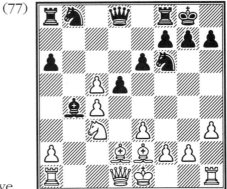

(77)

Black to move.

What's happening and how should Black continue?

Problem 52

(78)

Black to play.

Black played 1...c6. Is this a good move? If not, what would you recommend?

Problem 53

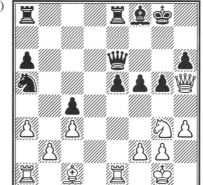

(79)

Black to move.

What do you think of 1...f4 in this position?

Problem 54

The position we're interested in occurred after:

1.e4 e5 2.Nf3 Nc6 3.Bb5 Nge7 4.c3 a6 5.Ba4 d6 6.d4 Bd7
7.h4!? h6 8.h5 exd4 9.Nxd4 Nxd4 10.cxd4 d5 11.e5 Bxa4 12.Qxa4+
Nc6 13.Be3 Qd7 14.Nc3 Bb4 15.Qc2 0-0 16.0-0-0 Bxc3 17.Qxc3 f6
18.f4. What would you play for Black at this point?

(80)

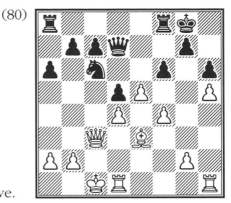

Black to move.

Problem 55

(81)

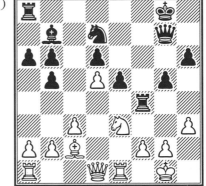

White to move.

White played 1.a4. Does this make any sense, and if it doesn't,
what would you suggest?

Problem 56

(82)

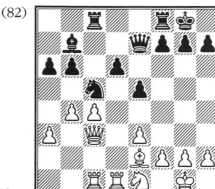

Black to move.

In Problem 85 I discuss the technique of asking, "What wonderful thing does this move do for my position?" before playing any individual move. Annotate the following moves and explain what wonderful things both sides' choices do for their cause. 1...Ne6 2.Qd3 Rfd8 3.Bf3 Bxf3 4.Nxf3 g6 5.Nd2 Nc7 6.Ne4.

Problem 57

(83)

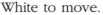

White to move.

While there's no doubt that White has the better game, turning this into something concrete is quite another matter. If you had to choose between 1.c3, 1.Nec5, 1.Nbc5, 1.Nxf6+, 1.Bxf6, or 1.c4, what would you pick?

Problem 58

After 1.c4 e5 2.g3 Nf6 3.Bg2 c6 4.d4 exd4 5.Qxd4 d5 6.cxd5 cxd5
7.Nf3 Nc6 8.Qa4 Bc5 9.0-0 h6 10.Ne5 Qb6 11.Nc3 0-0 12.Nd3 d4
13.Nxc5 Qxc5 14.Qb5 Qe7 15.Nd5 Nxd5 16.Bxd5 a6 17.Qc4 Nb4,
we come to an important position.

(84)

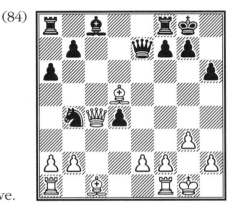

White to move.

Would you choose 18.Bf3, 18.Qxd4, 18.Rd1, 18.Re1, or 18.e3
here?

Problem 59

(85)

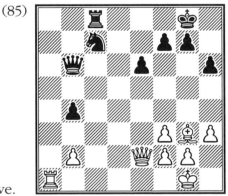

White to move.

This position doesn't appear to be very exciting. Will it be a
draw, or does White have a way to generate some play?

Problem 60

(86)

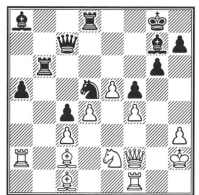

Black to move.

This position is filled with imbalances. How would you rate Black's chances? What should he do?

Problem 61

(87)

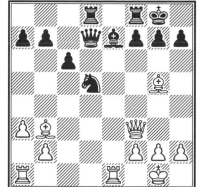

White to move.

White has just blundered and is now a pawn down with little, if anything, to show for it. Should he just throw his arms in the air and give up, should he slap his opponent's face and demand that a draw be agreed upon, should he kick the pieces across the room to show his displeasure (I've seen grandmasters use this trick on more than one occasion!), or is there a way to put up real (legal) resistance?

Problem 62

(88)

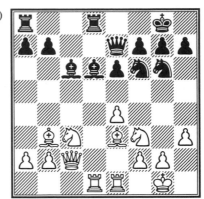

Black to move.

Black has achieved a comfortable position and now must find a plan. In the actual game, Black played the very odd 1...Rdc8. What is the point of this move, and is it any good? If the Rook move isn't correct, what would you prefer?

Problem 63

(89)

White to move.

Consider the following possibilities: 1.Nxc6, 1.Nxg4, 1.f4, 1.Bb5, 1.Qa4, 1.h3.
    Which one of these moves is best?

Problem 64

(90)

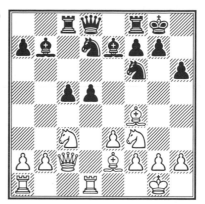

White to move.

A common position has been reached. White usually tries to place pressure against the "hanging pawns" on c5 and d5. Black relies on his extra space (which those "weak" pawns supply) and his active pieces to turn the game in his favor. White wanted to make use of the f5-square via 1.Nh4 with the intention of Nf5. Unfortunately, 1...g5 picks up material. Since this doesn't work, he hatches an original idea designed to take away key queenside squares from the Black forces. Do you see what White found?

Problem 65

(91)

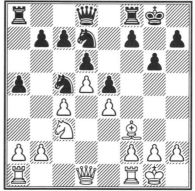

White to move.

Is 1.a3 a good move?

Problem 66

(92)

White to move.

What thematic idea should White implement in this position?

Problem 67

(93)

White to move.

Discuss this position and then annotate the following moves:
1.Nxf6+ gxf6 2.Rxd2 h5 3.Rg1 hxg4 4.fxg4 Bc4 5.b3 Bxf1 6.Rxf1.

Problem 68

(94)

White to move.

Black has just played ...e5, gaining central space and threatening White's pawn on d4. How should White react to this?

Problem 69

(95)

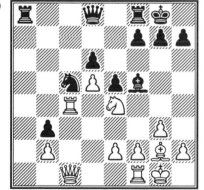

Black to move.

Break this position down and assess it. Who, if anyone, is better, and by how much? After figuring this out, show me Black's best move (i.e., the move that highlights the plusses you've found).

Problem 70

(96)

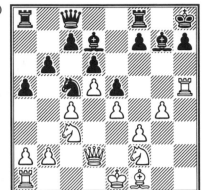

White to move.

White's enormous superiority is obvious. How would you continue if you were blessed with this position?

Problem 71

(97)

Black to move.

White threatens to win a pawn by Qxd6. How should Black deal with this threat?

Problem 72

(98)

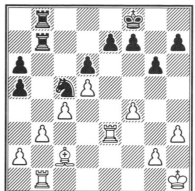

Black to move.

List the imbalances and form a plan based on them and/or on the creation of new plusses.

Problem 73

(99)

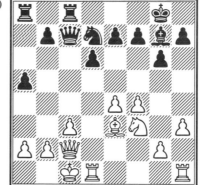

Black to move.

Black's move is so natural that it should be so obvious to all tournament players. What is it?

Problem 74

(100)

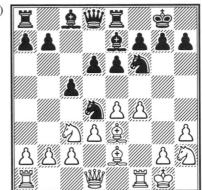

Black to move.

Black played 1...Nxe2+. Was this a good move? If it is, what is the follow up? If it's poor, please explain why.

Problem 75

(101)

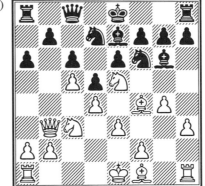

Black to move.

In the game, Black played the odd-looking 1...Bd8. Is this any good? If not, what would you have preferred?

Problem 76

(102)

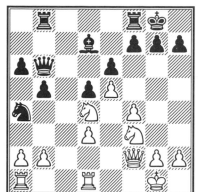

White to move.

A glance at the position's main imbalances will make White's first move easy to understand. List the imbalances and your interpretation of White's correct move.

Problem 77

(103)

Black to move.

How would you read this position? Once you list all the imbalances, what move best serves whatever plusses Black may have?

Problem 78

(104)

Black to move.

Whose position do you like and why?

Problem 79

(105)

White to move.

From the diagram, play continued: 1.b4 h4 2.Be2 hxg3 3.hxg3 Kh7 4.Rf1 Rh8 5.Nb3 Bh6 6.Bxh6 Kxh6. Annotate these moves (maybe they make sense, maybe some of them are bad, maybe all of them are suspect) and then tell me what you think of the final position.

Problem 80

(106)

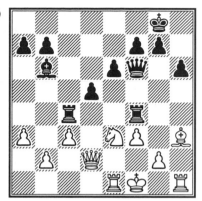

N.Wong-Elizabeth de la
Torre, Knoxville 1997.
Black to move.

Elizabeth, a 10 year-old girl rated 1359, had played a fine game and reached this very interesting position. How would you assess the situation and what do you think Black's best plan is?

Problem 81

(107)

Black to move.

Things look bad for Black. White has more central space and is preparing a central advance by Nf3 and e4-e5. White also has good chances against the Black King because all of White's pieces are aiming in that direction, while nothing much is happening on the queenside. To say that the queenside is equal and the center and kingside favor White, speaks for itself. What is Black going to do about this state of affairs? His Rook is under attack and a swap would give White control of the open b-file.

Problem 82

(108)

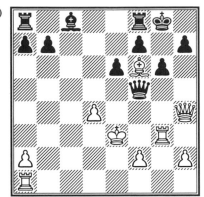

Black to move.

White appears to have a strong attack. His immediate threat is Rf3 when the Black Queen is attacked, the White Bishop is guarded, and Qh6 will lead to mate. Can Black defend this position?

Problem 83

(109)

Black to move.

This is a game between two 1600 players. White's position looks pretty good, though his King can't castle. It has already moved to f1 and then back to e1! He has control over the important e5-square, White's Bishop is much better than Black's Bishop, his Knight is very well placed on d4 and the pawn on e6 is backward and weak.

How would you handle the "unfortunate" Black position?

Problem 84

(110)

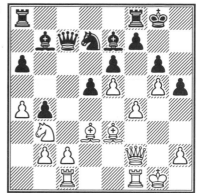

Grefe-Bellin,
World Open 1973.
Black to move.

White, 1973 U.S. Champion John Grefe, seems to be doing very well. He has lots of kingside and central space, he has a firm grip on the important d4-square, pressure against a6 and possibilities of opening the c-file by c2-c3. It's also important to note how bad the b7-Bishop is. International Master Bellin of England was Black. Grefe was clearly the superior player. Will the negative aspects of his position and fear of his powerful opponent make Black crack? What would you do?

Problem 85

(111)

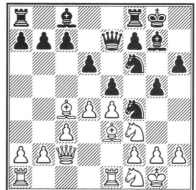

White to move.

We all make errors in chess. However, a logical move that turns out to be a tactical mistake or a simple case of flawed judgment are far cries from moves that do more for our opponents than for us. Self-destructive ideas come up in almost every amateur game I have seen and, after lots of thinking, the closest thing to a cure I have found is the following: Whenever you are about to play a move in chess, always ask: "What wonderful thing does this move do for my position?"

As simple as this may sound, I have never had a student who could follow this advice. Why? I honestly don't know. Perhaps the fire of battle blinds us to lessons of the past. Perhaps this verbal inquiry into a move's usefulness leaves a bad taste in one's mouth.

In this game White, who was worried about ...exd4 with threats to his e-pawn, played 1.d5, gaining central space. Was this a wise thing to do? What wonderful thing does this move to for White's position?

Problem 86

(112)

Black to move.

How would you handle the Black position?

Problem 87

(113)

White to move.

If you had a choice between 1.Ra7, 1.Nd1, 1.Nc2, 1.g4, or 1.e5, which would you play?

Problem 88

Take a look at the following exciting but error-filled moves: 1.e4 e6 2.d4 d5 3.Nc3 Bb4 4.e5 c5 5.a3 Ba5 6.b4 cxb4 7.Nb5 bxa3+ 8.c3 Bc7 9.Bxa3 Ne7 10.Bd6 Ba5 11.Bxe7 Kxe7 12.Qb3 Bc7 13.Qb4+ Ke8 14.Rxa7 Nc6 15.Qc5 Bb6 16.Nd6+ Kd7 17.Qxc6+ Kxc6 18.Bb5+ Kc7 19.Rxa8 Qg5 20.Ne2 Qe7 21.0-0 Rf8 22.Rb1 f6 23.Nf4 fxe5 24.dxe5 g5 25.Nd3 Qg7 26.Ra2.

How would you judge White's 17th move (17.Qxc6+), the position after 19.Rxa8, and White's 26th move (26.Ra2)?

(114)

Position after Black's
16th move.
White to move.

(115)

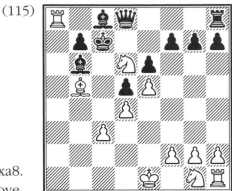

Position after 19.Rxa8.
Black to move.

(116)

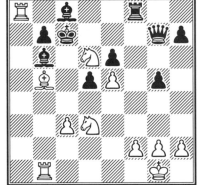

Position after Black's
25th move.
White to move.

Problem 89

(117)

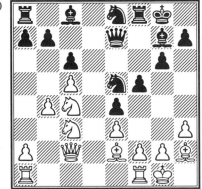

Black to move.

In this seemingly simple position, Black played 1...Nxc4. After 2.Bxc4+, which side would you prefer to play?

Problem 90

(118)

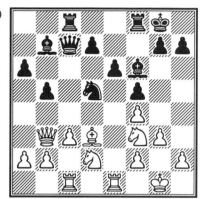

Black to move.

White just moved his Queen from c2 to b3. What plan(s) should Black consider in this position, and what was the point of White's last move?

Problem 91

(119)

Black to move.

In the game, Black played the calm 1...Bxd2+ 2.Qxd2 Qc7. White died a horrible death after 3.Qd3? exf4 4.gxf4 Qxf4 5.Nd2 Ne5 6.Qd4 Bg4 7.h3? Rad8 8.Qc3 Nxd3+! 9.cxd3 Qe3+ and mates.

White was rightfully punished for leaving his King in the center. However, instead of playing 1...Bxd2+, Black could have tried a sharper continuation which he saw and rejected. Was he correct in passing up possible glitter for the more secure and patient course he actually chose?

Problem 92

After 1.d4 Nf6 2.Nf3 g6 3.Bf4 Bg7 4.e3 0-0 5.Be2 d6 6.h3 c5 7.0-0 Qb6 8.Nbd2 cxd4 9.exd4 Nc6 10.c3 Nd5 11.Nc4 Qc7 12.Bg5 f6 13.Ne3 Nxc3, should White play 14.Bc4+ or 14.bxc3?

(120)

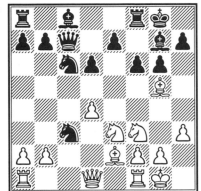

Position after 13...Nxc3.
White to move.

Problem 93

(121)

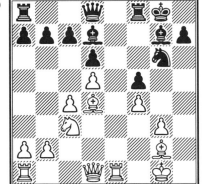

Black to move.

White enjoys the superior position. Do you see why White's game is better? Can Black improve his situation with correct play? How?

Problem 94

(122)

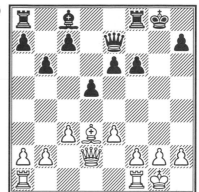

White to move.

What would you do if you were White?

Problem 95

(123)

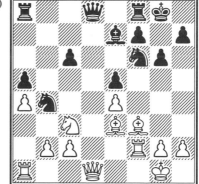

White to play.

How would you play this position? Be ready to discuss its secrets in detail.

Problem 96

(124)

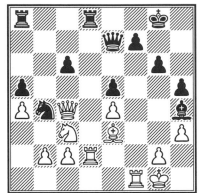

Karpov-Spassky,
Leningrad 1974.
White to play.

White has a clear advantage, but making this statement and improving your position are two very different things. In fact, it's often in this kind of situation that one's edge, visually so clear, begins to evaporate with each and every move.

What should White do to increase his superiority?

Problem 97

(125)

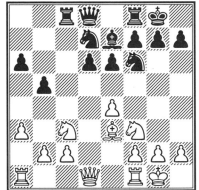

Black to move.

Black has a very comfortable Sicilian position and he can handle this situation in several different ways. There's one move that a good player would choose instantly. However, a less experienced player might never even consider it.

Problem 98

(126)

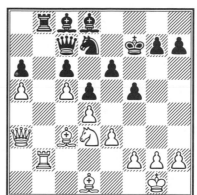

White to play.

White is much better, but it's very hard to break through and force a win. How would you handle this position?

Problem 99

(127)

Black to play.

Black has a big lead in development and pressure against d4. White has more central space but his King is strangely posted. Who stands better?

Problem 100

Some grandmasters pull madly on a locket of hair while pondering their moves. Others shake in their seats or contort their faces in frightful ways. Why are they doing this? Do they have lice? Are they terrified? Do they suffer from delirium tremens?

Viswanathan Anand and Vladimir Kramnik

Most players study the opening to get a quick, positive start to the game—sort of a fast-food solution to chess strength. Others wisely push the opening books to the side and put more time into middlegame play. Very few, though, take time out to explore the complicated and largely unknown world of the endgame.

I guess there are good reasons why the endgame is ignored:

➤ Some players *constantly lose before that phase is ever reached!* This, of course, is a bad excuse. An understanding of the endgame will significantly strengthen your middlegame play.

➤ Some feel that *the endgame is too subtle for players below the expert rank.* Wrong again! Endgame basics are easy to pick up and will reward you with victories throughout your chess career.

➤ *Endgame books are dry and turn chess study into a form of torture.* Well, I must admit that this is the case with many books. However, there are exceptions that contain interesting prose, fun examples, and rules of endgame conduct that guarantee an enjoyable and educational read.

It might seem improbable, but a firm knowledge of endgame basics, giving you a 2100 endgame rating, won't take more than four or five hours to study and assimilate. For example, a thorough knowledge of the opposition for King and pawn endgames, taking all of fifteen minutes to learn, is extremely important. Rook endgame basics like the Lucena and Philidor positions are also something that a serious player can't do without. Both these positions can be fully understood in ten minutes.

The fact of the matter is, once you've mastered this kind of basic endgame material, you can use these themes to work out more complex endgames that would have previously been out of your reach. If you don't know the basics, which are easily found in any one of dozens of endgame manuals, you'll be like a blind man trying to wend his way through a maze.

The problems in this section are a mix of both very complicated and very basic endgame situations. Hopefully, they will make you ralize just how fascinating this final phase of the game can be.

Problem 101

(128)

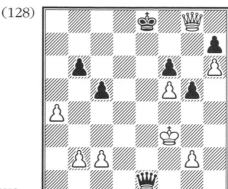

Black to move.

I had been in agony the whole game (White had missed at least one instant win), and the creation of various perpetual check themes was my last line of defense. After offering my opponent several bottles of free beer which he refused, seemingly intent on winning the game, we reached the position in the diagram.

Black has a choice between two legal moves: 1...Kd7 and 1...Ke7. Is there any real difference between the two? If so, what?

Problem 102

(129)

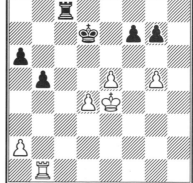

White to move.

White's passed d-pawn and vastly superior King give him a winning advantage. What's the best way to proceed?

Problem 103

(130)

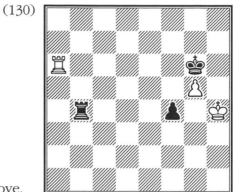

Black to move.

Black's King is in check, but does the first player have any real winning chances?

Problem 104

In an endgame, which minor piece dominates if there is a pawn race involving passed pawns on both sides of the board?

Problem 105

In an endgame, what can you do to make a Knight superior to a Bishop?

Problem 106

(131)

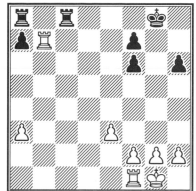

White to move.

White is obviously doing well, but claiming a clear, easy win is quite another matter. Write down your general observations about this position and then, based on the power and logic of these observations, show a concrete way for White to proceed.

Problem 107

(132)

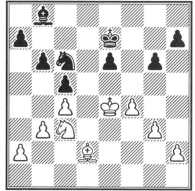

White to move.

White is clearly better here, but a forced win is nowhere in sight. Can you formulate a plan that will give you some chances to score the full point?

Problem 108

(133)

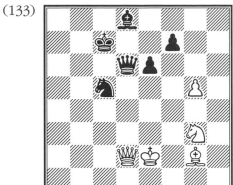

White to move.

White is a pawn down, his remaining pawn on g5 is weak, and his Knight on g3 is hanging. Things look grim for the first player. Is there any hope of holding this position?

Problem 109

(134)

Black to move.

Can Black draw this position?

Problem 110

(135)

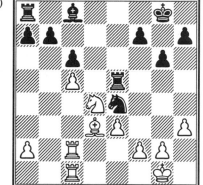

Human versus computer,
1996.
Black to move.

The machine played 1...Bd7. Is this best?

Problem 111

(136)

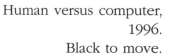

White to play.

How would you play this position? Take a little time and see if you can figure out a winning plan.

Problem 112

(137)

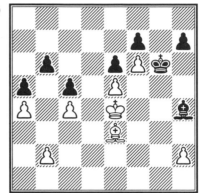

White to move.

Can White win this position? If so, how?

Problem 113

(138)

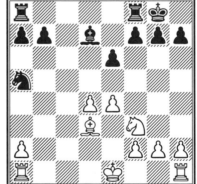

White to play.

How should White proceed in this position?

Problem 114

(139)

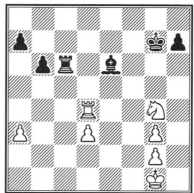

White to move.

This is an extremely interesting endgame. Who do you think stands better? I'm looking for a general feel of the position rather than a specific move.

Problem 115

(140)

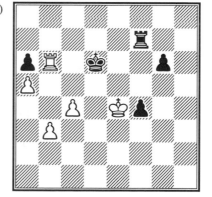

Black to move.

Black is in check and must decide where to move his King. Things look bad no matter what he does. Does the second player have a chance here?

(LEFT TO RIGHT) VLASTIMIL HORT, ANATOLY KARPOV, LJUBOMIR LJUBOJEVIC, AND JUDIT POLGÁR

Players of all strengths constantly ask me how to get better. Seeking some sort of generic cure-all, they expect me to bark out a few words of wisdom and make their lives easier and their ratings fatter.

Like a magic eight ball, all titled players come with juicy platitudes, many of which might be offered up on the altar of profundity:

Profound Platitude 1 — *Good things happen to those that work hard!*

This one always creates a frown. Who in the world wants to work a nine to five job, come home, take out their chessboard, and suddenly realize that the truly exhausting work is only now beginning?

Profound Platitude 2 — *Study endgames first. The middlegame and opening can be contemplated later in your chess development.*

Another winning piece of hot air. After years of study, you come to the board armed with a deep understanding of the true meaning of coordinate squares in King and pawn endgames. Unfortunately, you fall for a basic opening trap and fail to make it past the fifteenth move.

Profound Platitude 3 — *Send me a check and we'll see what can be done.*

A lifetime ago, John Grefe (right after winning the U.S. Closed Championship) gave me a shortened version of this (i.e., "Where's your money?") when I asked him a chess-related question. More recently, a well-known grandmaster responded in this same way when confronted by an earnest teenage chess addict. Needless to say, I've never seen this answer actually improve anyone's game.

Profound Platitude 4 — *It's not the openings themselves that are important, but the ideas behind them.*

Since most opening books only deal in endless masses of moves and little explanation of the ideas behind them, the poor student is forced to go back to Profound Platitude 3 if he wants any real answers in this area.

Profound Platitude 5 — *It's not winning that counts. The joy of playing the game is its own reward.*

Yeah, right. After absorbing this bit of swill from your chess guru, bide your time and watch closely when he actually loses. Note how his fists flail in the air, how his face has turned beet red, how endless excuses seem to be pouring from his gibbering lips.

These platitudes aren't very helpful, are they? The truth is, the best chess advice that I've ever gotten can be summed up in the following way:

Look at lots and lots of annotated master games!

So simple and yet so rewarding. You see openings explained by the master himself, middlegames dissected and discussed in great detail, and endgames lovingly reenacted by the World Champion of your choice. In other words, you get the whole package!

Master games can be gone over in several ways:

✦ Play over dozens, or even hundreds, of them quickly, chess movie style, a couple of minutes per game. Your subconscious will digest different patterns, even as your conscious mind reels from the never-ending flow of mysterious chess moves.

✦ Play through them slowly. Explore every note and comment that the master offers.

✦ Quickly play through the opening phase of the game, cover up your hero's moves and try to figure out what he did. Write your thoughts and guesses down in a notebook, check to see what was really played, and then repeat.

   When the game is finished, look at it again and study the master's notes. See how close his thinking process and move selection came to yours.

✦ Jot down questions whenever you don't understand a specific plan, position, move, or comment. Then share this material with your chess teacher. Hmmmm, we seem to have come back to Profound Platitude 3 again!

In this section, we'll be taking the idea of an annotated game a step further. Here you will be expected to analyze the game, or a cluster of moves, by yourself before looking at my notes. By doing this, the moves and notes will take on a much deeper and more personal meaning for you.

Problem 116

Annotate the following game starting after Black's seventh move:
1.d4 Nf6 2.Nf3 g6 3.Bf4 Bg7 4.Nbd2 c5 5.e3 d6 6.c3 Nc6 7.h3 0-0
8.Bc4 Re8 9.0-0 e5 10.dxe5 Nxe5 11.Bxe5 dxe5 12.Ng5 Be6 13.Bxe6
fxe6 14.Nde4 Nxe4 15.Qxd8 Rexd8 16.Nxe4 b6 17.Rfd1 Kf8 18.Kf1
Ke7 19.c4 h6 20.Ke2 Rxd1 21.Rxd1.

Problem 117

Play through the following game: 1.d4 Nf6 2.Nf3 g6 3.Bg5 Bg7
4.Nbd2 d5 5.e3 Ne4 6.Nxe4 dxe4 7.Nd2 c5 8.c3 cxd4 9.exd4 Qd5
10.Be3 0-0 11.Be2 e5 12.Qb3 Qxb3 13.Nxb3 f5 14.d5 b6 15.Rd1
Bb7 16.Bg5 Bf6 17.Bxf6 Rxf6 18.c4 Nd7 19.0-0.
   Annotate these moves and then assess the final position.

Problem 118

Annotate this whole game: 1.d4 d6 2.c4 e5 3.d5 f5 4.Nc3 Nf6
5.Bg5 Be7 6.Bxf6 Bxf6 7.e4 0-0 8.Nf3 Na6 9.Bd3 f4 10.h3 Nc5
11.0-0 a5 12.Na4 Nxa4 13.Qxa4 Bd7 14.Qc2 Kh8 15.c5 Qe8 16.c6
bxc6 17.dxc6 Bc8 18.Rab1 Qg6 19.Kh1 Qh6 20.Qe2 g5 21.Nh2
Rg8 22.Ng4 Qg6 23.b4 axb4 24.Rxb4 Be7 25.f3 h5 26.Nf2 g4 27.fxg4
hxg4 28.Nxg4 Bxg4 29.Qxg4 Qxg4 30.hxg4 Rxg4 31.Rb7 Bd8
32.Bc4 Kg7 33.Rfb1 Kf8 34.Rb8 Rxb8 35.Rxb8 Ke7 36.a4 Rg3 37.Rb3
Rxb3 38.Bxb3 d5 39.exd5 Kd6 40.a5 Kc5 41.a6 Kb6 42.Bc4 Be7
43.Kg1 Bd6 44.Kf2 Ka7 45.g3 fxg3 46.Kxg3.

Problem 119

Annotate the following game: 1.d4 Nf6 2.Nf3 b6 3.e3 Bb7 4.Bd3
e6 5.Nbd2 c5 6.c3 Nc6 7.0-0 Bd6 8.e4 cxd4 9.cxd4 Be7 10.a3 h5
11.b4 Qc7 12.Bb2 Rg8 13.Rc1 a6 14.Re1 g5 15.g3.

Problem 120

Annotate this whole game. Then see if you can correctly list the strengths and weaknesses of the player (not the position, but the player himself) with the White pieces: 1.e4 c5 2.Nf3 d6 3.Bb5+ Nd7 4.c4 a6 5.Ba4 Qc7 6.Nc3 e6 7.0-0 Ngf6 8.Qe2 Be7 9.d4 cxd4 10.Nxd4 0-0 11.Be3 Nb6 12.Bb3 e5 13.Nf5 Bxf5 14.exf5 Rac8 15.g4 h6 16.h4 Nh7 17.g5 hxg5 18.hxg5 Bxg5 19.Bxg5 Nxg5 20.Qg4 Qe7 21.Kg2 Nh7 22.Rh1 d5 23.cxd5 Qg5 24.Qxg5 Nxg5 25.Rh5 f6 26.d6+ Rf7 27.Rah1, 1-0.

Problem 121

Annotate this whole game: 1.c4 Nf6 2.Nc3 g6 3.e4 d6 4.d4 Bg7 5.Be2 0-0 6.Bg5 Na6 7.Qd2 e5 8.d5 Qe8 9.f3 Nh5 10.Be3 f5 11.0-0-0 Nf4 12.g3 Ng2 13.Bf2 f4 14.Bf1 Ne3 15.Bxe3 fxe3 16.Qxe3 Nc5 17.Bh3 Na4 18.Kb1 Nxc3+ 19.Qxc3 Bh6 20.Bxc8 Rxc8 21.h4 c6 22.Nh3 cxd5 23.exd5 e4 24.f4 b5 25.Qb4 bxc4 26.Qxd6 Qb5 27.Qe6+ Kh8 28.Ng5 Rb8 29.Rd2 Bg7 30.Nf7+ Rxf7 31.Qxf7 Bxb2 32.Rc2 Bc3+, 0-1.

Problem 122

Annotate this game: 1.e4 c5 2.Nf3 Nc6 3.d4 cxd4 4.Nxd4 Nf6 5.Nc3 d6 6.Bg5 a6 7.Qd2 Nd7 8.Be2 g6 9.Nd5 f6 10.Ne6 Qa5 11.Ndc7+ Kf7 12.Nd8+ Kg7 13.Ne8+, 1-0.

Problem 123

(141)

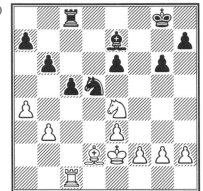

White to move.

The position in the diagram came about after Black's 22nd move (22...Be7). Black's game appears to be slightly inferior but solid; true, the pawn on e6 is isolated, but nothing can attack it.

Annotate the following moves and try and explain what White is up to: 23.b4 c4 24.b5 Kf7 25.Bc3 Ba3 26.Rc2 Nxc3+27.Rxc3 Bb4 28.Rc2 Ke7 29.Nd2 c3 30.Ne4 Ba5 31.Kd3 Rd8+ 32.Kc4 Rd1 33.Nxc3 Rh1 34.Ne4 Rxh2 35.Kd4 Kd7 36.g3 Bb4 37.Ke5 Rh5+ 38.Kf6 Be7+ 39.Kg7 e5 40.Rc6 Rh1 41.Kf7 Ra1 42.Re6 Bd8 43.Rd6+ Kc8 44.Ke8 Bc7 35.Rc6 Rd1 36.Ng5 Rd8+ 47.Kf7 Rd7+ 48.Kg8, 1-0.

Problem 124

1.c4 e6 2.d4 d5 3.Nf3 Be7 4.Nc3 Nf6 5.Bg5 0-0 6.e3 h6 7.Bxf6 Bxf6 8.Qd2 b6 9.cxd5 exd5 10.b4 Bb7 11.Rb1 c6 12.Bd3 Nd7 13.0-0 Re8 14.Rfc1 a515.bxa5 Rxa5 16.Bf5 Ra6 17.Rb3 g6 18.Bd3 Ra7 19.Rcb1 Bg7 20.a4 Qe7 21.Bf1 Ba6 22.h4 Bxf1 23.Rxf1 h5 24.Re1 Raa8 25.g3 Qd6 26.Kg2 Kf8 27.Reb1 Kg8 28.Qd1 Bf8 29.R3b2 Bg7 30.Rc2 Ra7 31.Rbc1 Nb8 32.Ne2 Rc7 33.Qd3 Ra7 34.Qb3 Ra6 35.Nf4 Rd8 36.Nd3 Bf8 37.Nfe5 Rc8 38.Rc3 Be7 39.Nf4 Bf6 40.Ned3 Ra5 41.Qxb6 Rxa4 42.Rc5 Ra6 43.Rxd5 Qxf4 44.Qxa6 Qe4+ 45.f3 Qe6 46.Qc4 Qxe3 47.Ne5 Rf8 48.Rc5 Be7 49.Rb1 Bxc5 50.Rxb8, 1-0.

This is a long, hard game. Can you figure out what was going on?

Problem 125

In this game, both players were ten-year-old girls with ratings in the 1400 range. Do their moves make sense and, when a mistake is played, can you recognize it?

1.e4 e5 2.Nf3 Nc6 3.Bc4 Nf6 4.d3 Be7 5.0-0 0-0 6.c3 d6 7.Re1 Bg4 8.h3 Bh5 9.Nbd2 Re8 10.Nf1 a6 11.Ng3 Bxf3 12.Qxf3 Na5 13.Bg5 Nxc4 14.dxc4 Qd7 15.Nf5 Qe6 16.b3 Bd8 17.Bh6 gxh6 18.Qg3+ Ng4 19.Qxg4+ Qg6 20.Nxh6+ Kf8 21.Nf5 Qxg4 22.hxg4 Bg5 23.Rad1 Rad8 24.g3 Rd7 25.Kg2 Red8 26.Rh1 Kg8 27.Rh5 f6 28.Rhh1 c6 29.Rhf1 and White won a piece and the game.

Problem 126

The following game is given without notes. Try to list the names of the main themes. For example, if one side tries for a smothered mate, say so. If we see one side making use of an unprotected piece, list that.

1.e4 c5 2.Nf3 Nc6 3.d4 cxd4 4.Nxd4 g6 5.Nc3 Bg7 6.Be3 Nf6 7.Be2 0-0 8.Qd2 d5 9.Nxc6 bxc6 10.e5 Ng4 11.Bxg4 Bxg4 12.h3 Bf5 13.g4 Be6 14.Qd4 f6 15.f4 Qc7 16.exf6 Bxf6 17.Qc5 Bh4+ 18.Ke2 Bc8 19.Nxd5 Ba6+ 20.c4 Qb7 21.Nb4 e5 22.Nxa6 exf4 23.Bd4 Rae8+ 24.Kf3 Re3+ 25.Kg2 f3+ 26.Kf1 Rfe8 27.Kg1 Bg3 28.Rf1 Re1 29.Bc3 Qxb2, 0-1.

Problem 127

Take a look at this bare game score.

1.e4 Nc6 2.d4 e5 3.d5 Nce7 4.c4 Ng6 5.Bd3 Bb4+ 6.Nc3 Nf6 7.Bd2 0-0 8.Nf3 Bxc3 9.Bxc3 Nf4 10.0-0 Nxd3 11.Qxd3 d6 12.h3.

Play through all twelve moves, then go back and annotate all of them to the best of your abilities. Also take a guess as to the strength of both players.

Problem 128

Annotate the following game. Don't forget to add an assessment of the final position: 1.e4 e6 2.d4 d5 3.e5 c5 4.c3 Nc6 5.Nf3 cxd4

6.cxd4 Qb6 7.Nc3 Nge7 8.Na4 Qd8 9.g4 Ng6 10.Bd2 f6 11.h4 fxe5 12.h5 Nge7 13.dxe5 Bd7 14.Nc5 Qc7 15.Ng5 Nd4 16.Rc1 Qxe5+ 17.Be3 Nec6 18.Nd3 Qf6 19.f4 Bd6 20.Nf3 Nxf3+ 21.Qxf3 0-0-0 22.Bxa7 Bc7.

Problem 129

Annotate the following game. Aside from noting the tactics, try to figure out why Black got into trouble. What important rule did he violate that ultimately led to his demise?

1.e4 e5 2.Nf3 d6 3.d4 Bg4? 4.dxe5! Bxf3 5.Qxf3 dxe5 6.Bc4 Nf6 7.Qb3! Qe7 8.Nc3 c6 9.Bg5 b5? 10.Nxb5! cxb5 11.Bxb5+ Nbd7 12.0-0-0 Rd8 13.Rxd7! Rxd7 14.Rd1 Qe6 15.Bxd7+! Nxd7 16.Qb8+!! Nxb8 17.Rd8 mate.

Problem 130

Annotate this game, starting after Black's 8th move: 1.g3 g6 2.Bg2 Bg7 3.e4 c5 4.Nf3 Nc6 5.0-0 Nf6 6.d3 0-0 7.Re1 d6 8.Nbd2 Rb8 9.a4 b6 10.Nc4 Bb7 11.h4!? Qc7 12.Bd2 Rbd8 13.Qc1 d5 14.Bf4 Qc8 15.exd5 Nxd5 16.Bh6 Rfe8 17.Bxg7 Kxg7 18.h5 Nf6 19.h6+ Kg8 20.Qf4 Nh5 21.Qd2 f6 22.a5! b5 23.a6! Ba8 24.Na5 e5 25.Qc3 Nd4 26.Nb7! Bxb7 27.axb7 Qxb7 28.Nxd4 cxd4 29.Bxb7 dxc3 30.bxc3 Re7 31.Rxa7 Kf8 32.Rb1.

Problem 131

Annotate this game. White missed a wonderful opportunity, see if you can spot that moment.

1.e4 e5 2.f4 exf4 3.Nf3 Be7 4.Bc4 Nh6 5.d4 c6 6.Bxf4 d5 7.exd5 cxd5 8.Bb5+ Nc6 9.0-0 Nf5 10.Nc3 0-0 11.Qd2 Bf6 12.Ne2 Nd6 13.Bd3 Ne4 14.Qe1 Re8 15.c3 a6 16.Qb1 Na5 17.Ng3 Nxg3 18.Bxg3 h6 19.Be5 Be6 20.Qc2 Rc8 21.Qf2 Nc4 22.Bxc4 Rxc4 23.Nd2 Bxe5 24.Nxc4 Bxh2+ 25.Kxh2 dxc4 26.Rae1 Qd7 27.Re3 Bd5 28.Rxe8+ Qxe8 29.Re1 Qd7 30.Qe3 Kf8 31.Qe5 f6 32.Qg3 Kf7 33.Qh3 Qxh3+ 34.Kxh3 Be6+ 35.Kg3 Bd5 36.Kf2 Be6 37.g3 Bd5 38.Ke3 Ke6 39.Rb1 Kd6 40.b3 b5 41.bxc4 Bxc4 42.a4 Kd5 43.axb5 Bxb5 44.Rf1 Bxf1, 0-1.

LARRY CHRISTIANSEN

SOLUTIONS

ANATOLY KARPOV AND JUDIT POLGÁR

JACK PETERS

Problem 1

(142)

Black to move.

Black, whose ...f7-f5 was answered by exf5, has to recapture his pawn on f5. What's the best way to do this?

Solution 1

1...Rxf5 doesn't make any sense for a number of reasons: It places the Rook on a vulnerable square, gives White control over e4, and doesn't make any particular gains. But 1...Bxf5 would probably prove very tempting to most players. In fact, how can a move that recaptures a pawn, develops a piece, and threatens the enemy Queen be bad?

The problem with 1...Bxf5 is that White gains control over the e4-square after 2.Nde4. Then 2...Nf6 3.Bxc5 dxc5 4.Bd3 favors White since the pawn structure is in his favor and e4 will remain in his hands. Also good for the first player is 1...Bxf5 2.Nde4 Nxe4 3.Nxe4 Bxe4 4.Qxe4 Nf6 5.Qc2. In this case, White owns the two Bishops and will generate queenside play with an eventual c4-c5.

So it turns out that 1...Bxf5, for all its glitter and bluster, really doesn't do much for the Black position because it doesn't give Black anything new to work with other than regaining the pawn.

Black's best move is **1...gxf5**, a move that horrifies many players because they think they are opening up their kingside. Putting this misconception aside for a moment, let's list the move's good points:

✦ It keeps the White pieces off of e4.

✦ Black's central pawns are now mobile and both sides will always have to weigh the pros and cons of moves like ...f5-f4 and ...e5-e4. Moving the f-pawn to f4 hands over the e4-square. Pushing the e-pawn to e4 gives up the f4-square, though in some lines he might be willing to do this since it ensures that his g7-Bishop will have an active future. Compare this with 1...Bxf5 2.Nde4 when the g7-Bishop is doomed to play a passive role.

✦ It opens the g-file. Here we finally square off with the view that Black's King is open. Who has more space on the kingside? Black, of course. This means that he will seek his chances on that side of the board since you usually play where your spatial plus exists. So the open g-file fits right into Black's plans, and he will try and make use of it by playing ...Kh8 and ...Rg8 at the right time.

Once again, it's important that the student looks at both 1...Bxf5 and 1...gxf5 with fresh eyes. One move (1...Bxf5) doesn't do anything to help Black's kingside hopes and gives White the use of a great square, while the other offers the second player several positional plusses.

Summary of Imbalances and Ideas
[diagram (142)]

➤ White owns more queenside space thanks to his pawns on c4 and d5.

➤ White would like to add to his queenside gains by an eventual a2-a3 followed by b3-b4, chasing the Black Knight away from its excellent perch and preparing to rip open lines in that area. Plus, this will open files for the Rooks, which would like to penetrate into the enemy position after c4-c5.

➤ Black's c7-d6-e5 pawn chain gives him more kingside space. He would like to translate this into an eventual kingside attack.

➤ Black is a pawn down and must decide how to get his pawn back. If possible, the recapture of the pawn should aid in his kingside dreams!

➤ At the moment, White's Knights and Queen are eyeing the e4-square. If possible, Black should avoid letting this important central square fall into enemy hands.

Problem 2

(143)

Bondarevsky-Smyslov,
Moscow Championship 1946.
White to move.

This position arose after 1.e4 e5 2.Nf3 Nc6 3.Bb5 a6 4.Ba4 Nf6 5.0-0 Be7 6.Bxc6 dxc6 7.Re1 Nd7 8.d4 exd4 9.Qxd4 0-0 10.Bf4 Nc5 11.Qxd8 Bxd8 12.Nc3 f5. How should White react to this advance of Black's f-pawn?

Solution 2

Before judging the diagrammed position, let's first take a look at the following, once popular, opening variation: 1.e4 e5 2.Nf3 Nc6 3.Bb5 a6 4.Ba4 Nf6 5.d4 exd4 6.0-0 Be7 7.e5 Ne4 8.Nxd4 0-0 9.Re1 Nc5 10.Bxc6 dxc6 11.Nc3.

Here White was considered to be better for quite a while thanks to his active kingside majority—the threat of f2-f4-f5 is quite annoying. However, 11...f5! ended the variation's popularity since the resulting White passed pawn will be firmly blocked by ...Ne6. For example, the position after 12.f4? Ne6 13.Nxe6 Bxe6 favors Black because there is no longer any play on the kingside or in the center, while all the queenside chances reside with Black because his Bishops aim in that direction and he also enjoys a pawn majority there.

Once we understand that a passed pawn is useless if firmly blockaded (in fact, it can actually turn into a disadvantage!), we can see that White's best move from the diagram is certainly not 13.e5 since 13...Ne6 14.Bd2 g5, stopping White from challenging the blockade by Ne2-f4, can only be good for the second player. In passed pawn situations the game often hinges on the square in front of the pawn. If the owner of the passer can control that square, then the pawn is usually a big plus. However, if the defender gains complete control over the square in front of the pawn, then the passed pawn turns into a dud. Thus, once you bite into the blockading square, it's very important not to allow the opponent to make a successful challenge to your dominance of it.

With all this in mind, it should now be clear that a skilled player only accepts a passed pawn if he feels he has play elsewhere (and thus its advance isn't of any great importance), or if he can prevent the defender from setting up a successful blockade.

Since 13.e5 isn't good, and since the position is about to open up, it is wise for White to strive for equality by ridding Black of his two Bishops. This can be done by **13.Bg5!** when the chances will be more or less even.

Summary of Imbalances and Ideas
[diagram (143)]

➤ Black has just played ...f7-f5 and threatens to win a piece by ...fxe4, with a double attack on f4 and f3. White needs to deal with this threat.

➤ Black has two Bishops versus White's Bishop and Knight.

➤ Black's queenside pawn structure has been compromised. However, the doubled pawns are proving rather useful at the moment: the c7-pawn stops White from leaping into d6, while the c6-pawn kills the Knight on c3 by keeping it off of d5.

➤ White doesn't want to open the position if Black retains his two Bishops.

➤ White can create a passed pawn via e4-e5. However, if he does so, who will control the e6-square in front of the passer?

➤ Since Black owns two Bishops, is there any way for White to swap one off?

Problem 3

After 1.e4 e5 2.Nf3 Nc6 3.Bb5 a6 4.Ba4 Nf6 5.0-0 Be7 6.Qe2 b5 7.Bb3 0-0 8.c3 d6 9.d4 Bg4 10.Rd1 exd4 11.cxd4 d5 12.e5 Ne4 13.a4 bxa4 14.Bxa4 Nb4 15.h3 Bh5 16.Nc3 Bg6 17.Be3 Rb8, we reach a position that was once thought to be all right for Black. However, a new move was unveiled that cut to the heart of the position and showed that White is actually clearly better. How would you play the White position?

(144)

Short-Karpov, Linares Match 1992
White to move.

Solution 3

Short played the surprising and strong **18.Na2!!**. This idea of Anand's, who helped Short in his pre-match preparations for the Karpov match, shows that White considers the b4-Knight to be much more important than its brother on e4. The reason is simple: the b4-Knight is the main guardian of Black's weak points on a6, c6 and d5. By trading it off, all these sore spots become accentuated and Black is suddenly placed on the defensive.

As you can see, it's important to list all the negatives in the enemy camp. Once you're aware of them, you should look for a way to make them as vulnerable as possible. On occasion, a particular piece is the glue that holds things together. A simple exchange can sometimes send your opponent's house of cards crashing to the ground.

The game continued **18...c5 19.dxc5**. Fritz claims that 19.Nxb4 wins a clear pawn: 19...Rxb4 20.Bc6 cxd4 21.Bxd4 a5 22.Bc3. **19...Nxc5 20.Nxb4 Rxb4 21.Bc6 Qb6 22.Bxd5 Rxb2 23.Qc4 Rc2 24.Qg4 Qc7 25.Nd4 Rc3 26.Nc6 Re8 27.Bd4 Rc2 28.Nb4** and Black lost the Exchange and the game.

Summary of Imbalances and Ideas
[diagram (144)]

➤ Black has an isolated pawn on a6 (on a half-open file) and a backward pawn on c7 (also on a half-open file). Black's pawn on d5 is also in need of careful support.

➤ The c5 and c6 squares might be vulnerable to an eventual White invasion.

➤ The b4-Knight is the glue that holds the Black position together because it defends the weak points on a6, c6, and d5.

➤ If White can get rid of the b4-Knight, all of Black's weaknesses should become an overwhelming burden.

➤ White's only real weakness is the pawn on b2, but Black's army, bound to his own weak-points, isn't coordinated enough to mount an attack against it without allowing his own position to suffer in some way.

Problem 4

What do the following two fairly well-known opening systems have in common? The answer lies in the meaning of Black's ...g7-g5 advance.

1.e4 c5 2.Nf3 Nc6 3.d4 cxd4 4.Nxd4 g6 5.c4 Bg7 6.Be3 Nf6 7.Nc3 Ng4 8.Qxg4 Nxd4 9.Qd1 Ne6 10.Rc1 Qa5 11.Bd3 b6 12.0-0 g5.

(145)

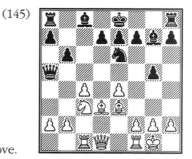

White to move.

1.e4 c5 2.Nf3 d6 3.d4 cxd4 4.Nxd4 Nf6 5.Nc3 a6 6.Bg5 e6 7.f4 Be7 8.Qf3 Qc7 9.0-0-0 Nbd7 10.Bd3 h6 11.Bh4 g5.

(146)

White to move.

Solution 4

In both cases Black is fighting to gain control of the e5-square and turn it into a permanent home for his pieces.

Allow me to explain in more detail: During a lecture in Los Angeles where I would look at people's games and comment on them, I noted that many members of the audience were able to recognize weak squares, but only if these weaknesses already existed. However, the idea of creating a weakness was alien to them.

To illustrate the concept of creating such weaknesses, even in the opening, I offered the following example:

1.e4 c5 2.Nf3 Nc6 3.d4 cxd4 4.Nxd4 g6 5.c4 Bg7 6.Be3 Nf6 7.Nc3 Ng4 8.Qxg4 Nxd4 9.Qd1 Ne6 10.Rc1 Qa5 11.Bd3 b6 12.0-0

I would prefer 12.f4, stopping the following maneuver.

12...g5

Most of the sixty or so players watching my lecture thought this was horrible, though a few liked the idea of starting an immediate attack against the White King. My first order of business was to explain that 12...g5 had nothing to do with attacking the White King. Instead, Black is fighting to gain absolute control over the e5-square.

How does ...g6-g5 affect the e5-square? By stopping f2-f4, White won't be able to use a pawn to chase away a Black piece that decides to reside on e5. Thus, e5 becomes an important support point. Actually, it's known as an artificial support point—a manufactured weak square!

13.Qd2 Bb7 14.Rfd1 d6 15.a3 h5 16.Rc2 Bd4!

Also good is 16...Qe5, but it makes sense for Black to exchange dark-squared Bishops because White's Bishop is one of the only pieces that can eventually attack e5.

17.b4 Qe5 and Black's control over the dark-squares, particularly e5, gave him a good game in Ljubojevic-Korchnoi, Tilburg 1987.

The crowd didn't seem particularly convinced, so I threw yet another opening at them where playing for the e5-square was everything:

1.e4 c5 2.Nf3 d6 3.d4 cxd4 4.Nxd4 Nf6 5.Nc3 a6 6.Bg5 e6 7.f4 Be7 8.Qf3 Qc7 9.0-0-0 Nbd7 10.Bd3 h6 11.Bh4 g5

Black goes all out to remove White's f4-pawn from the board, even if it means losing a pawn, so that the e5-square will fall into his hands.

12.fxg5

At times 12.e5!? is played in order to start a tactical battle where Black won't have access to that juicy central post on e5.

12...Ne5

The eagle has landed!

13.Qe2 Nfg4 14.Nf3 hxg5 when the e5-square, plus the fact that White's pieces on c3 and d3 are rather inactive, ensures Black adequate play. **15.Bxg5 Bxg5+ 16.Nxg5 Qc5** leaves Black with a very active position.

Summary of Imbalances and Ideas
[diagrams (145) and (146)]

➤ Playing to create a weak square in the enemy camp that will eventually become a home for one of your own pieces—preferably a Knight—is a mainstay of advanced chess strategy.

➤ At times a square isn't weak in the normal sense, but you can make it so by ensuring that the enemy pawns can't ever chase your pieces from the square you are after. The game used in our first example highlights ...g7-g5 as doing this: White wants to chase the Black pieces from the e5-square, but his inability to play f2-f4 makes this a vain hope.

➤ In both examples, Black creates an imbalance—a weakness on e5—by the unorthodox ...g7-g5. The price? Black can't castle kingside (leaving your King in the center isn't a joy). This support point, and the weaknesses in Black's kingside that came about by creating the support point with ...g7-g5, all become the focus of the ensuing play.

Problem 5

After 1.d4 Nf6 2.Bg5 Ne4 3.Bh4 c5 4.Qd3, (from Winterton-Rajlich, North Bay 1997) we arrive at an interesting position.

(147)

Black to move.

Black's Knight is attacked and he has to decide how this threat should be dealt with. What is the correct decision here?

Solution 5

Believe it or not, we have already come to the key moment in this game! White is attacking the enemy Knight and hopes to wrest control of the e4-square from his opponent. Black's choices appear to be fairly clear: he can run with his Knight, he can defend it with 4...d5 (4...f5 is too weakening), or he can throw in 4...Qa5+, though it's not clear what Black has accomplished after 5.c3.

But why let White force you into a certain direction? He has played this strange new move (4.Qd3) and dares to tell you what to do! Are you going to put up with this? Before reacting, first try and detect the flaws in White's position.

Did you find some? Here is the list:

✦ Moving that dark-squared Bishop to g5 left the b2-pawn unprotected.

✦ The Bishop on h4 is not guarded. Remember, all unprotected pieces should be noted since this state of affairs allows tactical operations against them.

✦ The d4-pawn is under pressure.

✦ The c1-square doesn't have a defender.

✦ The a1-Rook is unprotected.

Can Black make use of these facts? During an actual game try to spot all positional and tactical possibilities and then try as hard as you can to make something of them. Never tell yourself that you *must* do this or *must* do that. The word "must" should be taken out of your chess vocabulary!

4...Qb6!

Instead of bowing to White's wishes, Black shocks his opponent by ignoring the illusory enemy threat. The very fine 4...Qb6 threatens to pick up the b-pawn and the Rook. It may be hard to accept, but this move actually wins by force!

5.b3

Of course, 5.Qxe4 Qxb2 followed by 6...Qxa1 would win for Black. Now White has renewed the threat against e4 and has kept the Black Queen out of b2 (or has he?).

5...Qh6!

Suddenly the h4-Bishop's lack of a defender becomes important and the weakness of c1 combines to create an almost comic situation.

Note how, once again, Black ignores White's "threat." How many players would bow to the fact that the e4-Knight is under attack?

6.Nf3

Develops and defends h4. Slightly worse is 6.Qxe4?? Qc1 mate.

6...Qc1+ 7.Qd1

It's become painfully clear that White's 4.Qd3 was a complete failure.

7...Qb2 8.Nbd2 Nxd2 9.Nxd2 Qxd4 and Black had a solid extra pawn and confidently scored the full point.

Summary of Imbalances and Ideas
[diagram (147)]

➤ Lots of "little" things combine to create the tactical operations that highlight this position: Black's Knight on e4 is undefended and is directly attacked; White's Bishop on h4 is undefended, his pawn on b2 is undefended, his Rook on a1 is undefended, and the c1-square is undefended.

➤ All tactical operations are based, in some part, on undefended pieces, inadequately guarded pieces, or an insecure King.

➤ A large part of chess strength is based on willpower. After 4.Qd3 White is trying to tell his opponent what to do. It's Black's job to see if he must succumb to this dictate or rise above it and inject the position with the stamp of his own vision.

Problem 6

After 1.e4 d5 2.exd5 Nf6 3.c4, is 3...c6 a good idea?

(148)

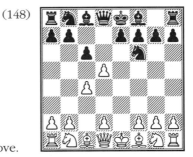

White to move.

Solution 6

Yes, it's an excellent offer. In fact, White does best to refuse it by 4.d4, transposing into the Panov-Botvinnik Variation against the Caro-Kann (1.e4 c6 2.d4 d5 3.exd5 cxd5 4.c4).

If White does take on c6 by 4.dxc6, Black replies with 4...Nxc6 and gets tremendous positional compensation for his sacrificed pawn. White's pawn on d2 is backward and weak, the d4-square is owned by Black, and all the Black pieces will be very active.

In general, a pure sacrifice for development or attack entails a leap of faith. You have to prove compensation by dynamic means. But a pawn sacrifice that gives you activity, quick development—two dynamic advantages—*and* the wonderful positional/static plusses mentioned in the previous paragraph simply has to be good!

One example of what can happen from this position is the following contest between two players in the 2000-2100 range:

3...c6 4.dxc6 Nxc6 5.Nf3 e5 6.d3 e4

Black is trying to mash his opponent because he has more fighting units in play.

7.Qe2 Bg4

Black continues to develop. He is not worried about the loss of another pawn because its capture signifies a further loss of time by White.

8.dxe4 Nd4 9.Qd3 Nxf3+ 10.gxf3 Qxd3 11.Bxd3 Bxf3 12.0-0 0-0-0

Yet another gain of time. The pawn on e4 isn't going away.

13.Bc2 Nxe4 14.Bxe4 Bxe4

Black's advantages are obvious: he has the superior pawn structure, a safe King and the two Bishops. His attack worked because he had several elements that allowed him to pursue an initiative—development, central control, and active pieces residing in the embattled area.

The finish is worth seeing:

15.Nc3 Bf3 Of course, 15...Bd3 was also possible, winning a pawn for nothing. **16.Be3 Rd6 17.Rfc1 Rg6+ 18.Kf1 Rg2 19.Bxa7 Rxh2 20.Ke1 Bb4 21.a3? Rd8!, 0-1.**

Summary of Imbalances and Ideas
[diagram (148)]

➤ Sacrificing a pawn for a cheap trap should be avoided, but all sacrifices that offer both dynamic and static plusses have to be examined very seriously.

➤ In the position after 3...c6 4.dxc6 Nxc6, Black is a pawn down, giving White one static plus—material. But Black would enjoy a variety of compensating factors: active pieces (dynamic), a lead in development (dynamic), more central space (static), and control over the hole on d4 (static).

Problem 7

After 1.d4 f5 2.Nf3 Nf6 3.Bf4 e6 4.e3 b6 5.Bd3 Bb7 6.Nbd2 Be7 7.0-0, how should Black play this position?

(149)

Black to move.

Solution 7

Black should take a moment away from normal development and grab the imbalance of the two Bishops by **7...Nh5!** since 8.Be5 d6 9.Ne1 dxe5 10.Qxh5+ g6 favors the second player. The game Stuart-Suveg, corr. 1999 continued **8.Re1 0-0 9.Ne5 Nxf4 10.exf4** and now, since he owns the two Bishops, Black played **10...c5** in an effort to open up some lines and make his Bishops superior to the White Knights.

This is what the opening is all about. You create an imbalance and then develop your pieces and pawns to squares that will help highlight this difference.

Summary of Imbalances and Ideas
[diagram (149)]

➤ At the moment, there aren't any significant imbalances.

➤ White has a bit more central space, while Black has more kingside space.

➤ You should always be on the lookout for ways to create new imbalances. In the present position,

Black's 7...Nh5! grabs the two Bishops, giving him something tangible to work with.

➤ Once you get the two Bishops, do your best to open up the position so the Bishops can show their strength.

Problem 8

Take a look at the position that arises after 1.d4 Nf6 2.c4 c5 3.d5 e5 4.Nc3 d6 5.e4 Be7 6.Bd3 0-0 7.Nge2.

(150)

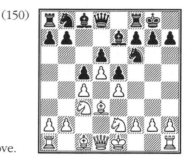

Black to move.

If you had to choose between 7...Bg4, 7...Nbd7, 7...Na6, 7...Ne8, 7...g6, and 7...h6, which would you play?

Solution 8

Quick development is a good idea, but only if you are placing your pieces on squares where they can work with the other pieces toward a common goal! In other words, don't just move them for the sake of saying they are developed! Find their optimum homes and go out of your way to get them there.

In the position under discussion after White's 7.Nge2, the moves 7...Bg4 and 7...Nbd7 mindlessly develop a piece without any thought to the pawn structure or an actual plan. Tossing the Knight to the side with 7...Na6 is more sensible, because Black is at least showing some interest in playing for a ...b7-b5 advance via 8...Nc7 followed by 9...a6 and 10...Rb8—in other words, Black has a clear reason for his move; it doesn't matter if it's actually any good or not. The two kingside pawn moves are not particularly attractive: 7...g6 allows 8.Bh6 when the Rook must move to the inferior e8-square (it wants to stay on f8 so it can help with an eventual ...f7-f5 advance). Even worse is 7...h6, a move that doesn't do anything at all. White wasn't threatening Bg5, so why spend a valuable move on nothing?

Though 7...Na6, intending queenside expansion, is playable, much stronger is **7...Ne8!**. This odd-looking move not only ignores development, but it actually breaks two other "laws" at the same time:

+ Never bring a Knight to the first rank.

+ Never move the same piece twice in the opening.

What could be the reason for such madness? Take a few moments and try to figure it out for yourself. Black didn't bring his other Knight out, or move his Bishop to g4, because those moves didn't help him pursue the most effective plan. This plan centers around the pawn advance ...f7-f5. In a closed position, you must play for pawn advances on the wings. This kind of pawn advance gives you more space to maneuver in, and also opens up lines for your Rooks.

The nifty Knight retreat 7...Ne8 prepares ...Bg5, exchanging a poor piece for a good one, and also intends to continue with ...g6 (more preparation for ...f7-f5), when Bh6 can be comfortably met by ...Ng7 which defends the Rook and aims another piece at f5. Of course, 7...Ne8 also gets out of the way of the f-pawn; something that has to be done if the ...f7-f5 advance is ever going to be possible.

Summary of Imbalances and Ideas
[diagram (150)]

➤ The center is closed so play on the wings is indicated.

➤ Both sides need to play on the wings with pawns. Thus White will examine b2-b4 with play on the queenside and f2-f4 with play on the kingside. Black will look at ...b7-b5 and ...f7-f5.

➤ Black has a very poor Bishop on e7. How can he trade it off for White's superior c1-Bishop?

➤ Black's correct 7...Ne8! kills a few birds with one stone: it prepares the ...f7-f5 advance, it prepares

...g7-g6 since the Knight can jump to g7 in the case of Bh6, it allows Black to go for queenside play with ...Ne8-c7 aiming at a ...b7-b5 advance, and it prepares to activate the passive e7-Bishop by ...Bg5.

Problem 9

(151)

Black to move.

This popular main line position of the King's Indian Defense, reached after 1.d4 Nf6 2.c4 g6 3.Nc3 Bg7 4.e4 d6 5.Be2 0-0 6.Nf3 e5 7.0-0 Nc6 8.d5 Ne7 9.Ne1, is a good test to see if you understand what's expected when a closed position is reached in the opening. Black has only two logical moves here. Can you list them? To find the answer, you will have to understand the nature of the position as a whole.

Solution 9

When the center is closed, play must be sought on the wings. However, instead of aiming for piece play as you would in an open position, you should instead lead with your pawns so that territory is gained and half-open or open files for the Rooks are created.

How can you determine which side of the board to play on? Just look at where your pawns point and play in that direction because that's where your maximum space lies. In the present position, Black's pawn chain points to the kingside (c7-d6-e5). Thus, he needs to push the pawn that stands next to the top of his chain (e5 is the top of the pawn chain). This means that ...f7-f5 is his plan when Black's space advantage on the kingside would then be clear.

White's chain at e4-d5 aims at the queenside, so an eventual space-gaining c4-c5 advance is called for. If Black had a pawn on c5 instead of e5, then White would play for e4-e5.

With these facts in mind, the only moves that make sense for Black are 9...Nd7 or 9...Ne8. If you tried 9...Bd7, you are caught up in the trap of "development at all costs." Don't develop if it has nothing to do with the needs of the position! By moving the Knight back to d7 or e8, Black gets out of the way of the f-pawn and prepares his thematic ...f7-f5 advance.

Summary of Imbalances and Ideas
[diagram (151)]

➤ When the center is closed, you must aim for play on the wings.

➤ Black's pawns point towards the kingside. Thus, that's where he'll seek his chances.

➤ Black must play for the ...f7-f5 advance. This means that the f6-Knight has to move out of the pawn's way.

Problem 10

In a skittles game, after 1.e4 g6 2.d4 Bg7 3.Nf3 d6, White played 4.h3 and said, "Strengthening d4 and e5." Does this make sense, or did he have too much to drink before the game?

(152)

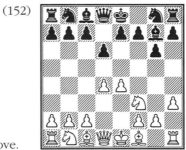

Black to move.

Solution 10

Though it's not clear if White did or didn't have too much to drink, his comment makes perfect sense—though why he would announce this is another matter! White's f3-Knight is a key piece in the fight for the d4 and e5 squares. By playing h3—not the best move, but sensible nonetheless—White prevents ...Bg4 followed by ...Bxf3, getting rid of this Knight and weakening the first player's control over these two points.

Summary of Imbalances and Ideas
[diagram (152)]

➤ Black's Bishop and d6-pawn combine to fight for the e5-square.

➤ Black's Bishop is aiming at White's d4-pawn.

➤ When you own a big center, it's your responsibility to make it indestructible.

➤ Playing h2-h3 ensures that Black can't trade his c8-Bishop, which isn't doing anything in the battle for e5 and d4, for the f3-Knight, which is a major player in the dark-square battle.

Problem 11

After 1.e4 g6 2.d4 Bg7 3.Nf3 d6 4.h3 Nf6 5.Nc3 c6 White often plays 6.a4, stopping Black from gaining queenside space with ...b7-b5 and, in many lines, threatening to play a4-a5 with a clear spatial plus in that sector. Black can now reply with 6...a5. What are the pros and cons of this move?

(153)

Black has just played 6...a5.

Solution 11

On the plus side, 6...a5 stops White's a-pawn in its tracks and lays claim to the b4-square, which he can occupy with ...Nb8-a6-b4. The one negative aspect of 6...a5 is that it weakens the b6-

square. Though this weakness seems inconsequential at the moment, it could turn out to be a real problem.

To properly explore the question of b6 becoming a weakness, let's carry out the sequence in the following manner: **7.Be3 0-0 8.Qd2 Na6 9.Be2 Qc7**, At times Black can consider a ...d6-d5 thrust. However, then the drawbacks of his earlier ...a7-a5 would show themselves: 9...d5 10.exd5 cxd5 and a gaping hole has appeared on b5. If the a-pawn were still on a7, then ...a7-a6 would cover this point. Note the similarity between Black's hole on b5 and White's on b4. After 9...d5 10.exd5 cxd5 Black can't defend b5. White, though, can always chase Black invaders out of b4 with a timely c2-c3. **10.0-0 e5 11.dxe5 dxe5 12.Rad1**. This position, a logical consequence of 6...a5, is very nice for White because he can now show us why the ...a7-a5 advance was not covered with gold. A close look will convince any player that the b6-square has been seriously compromised. White will play directly for the occupation of either b6 or d6 with **13.Qc1!, 14.Nd2** and **15.Nc4** when the b6 and d6 squares can now be called holes. Of course, Black might be able to chop this Knight off with ...Bc8-e6xc4, but then White would enjoy two Bishops in an open position.

Summary of Imbalances and Ideas
[diagram (153)]

➤ White has a nice center, and Black will eventually try and chip away at it by ...d6-d5 or ...e7-e5. Now that Black has played ...a7-a5, he won't consider ...c6-c5 because that would leave a gaping wound on b5.

➤ A potential weakness has appeared on b6. White can try and make use of it by Be3. If Black plays ...e7-e5, White can take on e5, freeing the e3-b6 diagonal for his Bishop, and then bring a new piece to bear on both b6 and d6 by Nf3-d2-c4.

➤ A Black Knight can settle into b4 by ...Nb8-a6-b4, but this isn't permanent because White can always move his c3-Knight and chase the enemy horse away by c2-c3.

Problem 12

After 1.c4 e5 2.Nc3 Nc6 3.Nf3 g6 4.g3 Bg7 5.d3 d6 6.Bg2 f5 7.0-0 Nf6, White usually plays for a b2-b4 advance. Why is this advance important, and should he prepare it with 8.Rb1 or 8.a3?

(154)

White to move.

Solution 12

White's pawns are pointing towards the queenside so that is where he should seek his play (always play where your territory lies). Since closed or semi-closed centers dictate that you use pawns to add to your spatial plus and to open up files for your Rooks, White needs to advance his b-pawn to b5 which also loosens up the g2-a8 diagonal for the g2-Bishop.

This leads us to the big question: why not prepare b2-b4 with a2-a3 instead of Rb1? First, b2-b4 creates a loosening of the a1-h8 diagonal. Getting the a1-Rook off that diagonal makes good tactical sense! Second, b2-b4-b5 might eventually lead to the opening of the b-file if Black were to play ...c7-c6 at some point. If that happens, you want your Rook on b1 controlling that file! Finally, **8.Rb1** actually saves time! Let's take a look at the following possible moves: 8.a3 0-0 9.b4 a6. Now White would like to advance to b5 and, if Black chopped that pawn off, he would prefer to capture towards the center. Obviously, this would not be possible as things stand. Thus, 10.Rb1 followed by 11.a4 and then 12.b5 is called for. If White plays correctly, though, with 8.Rb1, then the same moves won't prove bothersome at all: 8...0-0 9.b4 a6 10.a4 followed by 11.b5 when White has gained a full move over the previous variation.

Summary of Imbalances and Ideas
[diagram (154)]

➤ White's pawns point towards the queenside. This means that he would like to increase his control of space in that area. The best way to do this is b2-b4-b5.

➤ 8.Rb1 is far superior to 8.a3 because pushing b2-b4 weakens the a1-h8 diagonal. Getting the Rook off this dangerous line is a wise thing to do.

Problem 13

Analyze these moves: 1.d4 d6 2.c4 e5 3.d5 Nf6 4.Bg5 Be7 5.Nc3 0-0 6.e4 Nbd7 7.Nge2 Qe8 8.Ng3. Do they make sense? Who stands better? Did either player make any major mistakes?

Solution 13

Did you do your best? Okay, let's see if your view of what was happening conforms to reality. This game was played by two B-players: **1.d4 d6 2.c4 e5 3.d5**

The Queen exchange by 3.dxe5 dxe5 4.Qxd8+ Kxd8 offers White very little since Black's King will find a safe home with ...c6 followed by ...Kc7. Remember that a centralized King is only a problem if it doesn't have a safe place to live and if the enemy forces can reach it. In this case, White can't put any heat on the Black King at all.

3...Nf6 4.Bg5?!

This move is poor because White has no intention of capturing on f6. Since Black can end the pin with ...Be7, why is the Bishop going to g5? Only stick your Bishops on g5 or b5 if you intend to capture the enemy Knight, if you think the pin will prove bothersome to your opponent, or if your Bishop is happy to back up after it gets hit with ...h6 or ...a6.

4...Be7

This position seems innocent enough and neither side sensed that something important was in the air. What might tell them that a tactic was waiting to be unleashed? Go to the head of the class if you noticed the undefended state of the Bishop on g5.

5.Nc3??

Such a natural move can't be bad, can it? Here it actually loses the game!

(155)

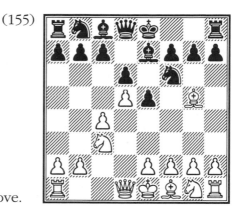

Black to move.

5...0-0??

Black fails to take advantage of the unprotected White Bishop on g5. This could have been done with the common but instructive 5...Nxd5! when a capture on d5 allows 6...Bxg5 while 6.Bxe7 is calmly met by 6...Nxe7 with a sound extra pawn.

6.e4??

White was feeling pretty good about his position here but this still loses the game. Putting that Bishop on g5 didn't turn out to be a very good idea for White, did it?

6...Nbd7??

Once again 6...Nxd5!, seemingly hanging the Knight to White's whole army, steals a pawn since 7.Qxd5, 7.Nxd5, 7.cxd5, and 7.exd5 all fail to 7...Bxg5, while 7.Bxe7 allows the Knight to retreat to safety by 7...Nxe7.

By not being on the lookout for undefended pieces, both sides are oblivious to the tactical possibilities in the position.

7.Nge2??

Sigh...ignorance really can be bliss, can't it?

7...Qe8??

A horrible move. Black makes two huge mental mistakes here. First he misses the winning 7...Nxd5. All right, we have all missed tactical shots at one time or another. Worse is the fact that Black wants to play a trick based on a ...Nxe4 tactic, contorting himself to set it up—by getting into that frame of mind, he ceases to worry about solid positional concepts like development or control over the center. Never play for tricks; you have to believe that your opponent will always play the best move.

8.Ng3

White takes aim at the juicy square on f5 and ignores Black's tactical attempt. Suddenly Black realized that his intended 8...Nxe4?? would fail to 9.Ngxe4 when g5 is protected. It is also important to mention that 8...Nxd5?? now loses to 9.Nxd5 Bxg5 10.Nxc7—courtesy of the Queen move to e8!

After 8.Ng3 White had a clear advantage but Black somehow went on to win the game anyway.

This game shows us that the most natural moves in the world become blunders if you overlook elementary tactics.

Summary of Imbalances and Ideas

➤ When White played 4.Bg5, neither side realized how important this decision really was. Natural moves and deep strategy mean nothing if pieces are not properly defended! As it turned out, the undefended state of the g5-Bishop colored every move that was subsequently seen.

➤ Don't pin a Knight via Bg5 or Bb5 or, if you're Black, by ...Bb4 or ...Bg4, unless you've decided to capture the horse, or have seen that the pin can't easily be broken.

Problem 14

(156)

White to play.

This position, reached from a once-popular Nimzo-Indian line after 1.d4 Nf6 2.c4 e6 3.Nc3 Bb4 4.e3 c5 5.Nf3 d5 6.Bd3 0-0 7.0-0 Nc6 8.a3 Bxc3 9.bxc3 dxc4 10.Bxc4 Qc7 11.Be2 e5 12.Bb2 Rd8 13.Qc2 Bg4 14.dxe5 Nxe5 15.c4 Nxf3+ 16.gxf3 Bh3 17.Rfd1 Rxd1+ 18.Rxd1 Rd8, is very interesting from the point of view of opening imbalances. List the imbalances and, from that, deduce White's correct plan and his best move.

Solution 14

The main imbalance in this position centers around the powerful b2-Bishop vs. the far less active Black Knight. Everything White does should be aimed at enhancing this particular advantage.

Many players, of course, would get bent out of shape over the fact that White's King is open and that his pawns are doubled. However, these things are actually a plus: the doubled pawn on f3 keeps the Black Knight off of e4 and g4—following Steinitz's rule that the way to beat Knights is to take away all their advanced posts— while the open g-file can be used by White after Kh1 and Rg1.

This idea of playing on the g-file fits in nicely with the b2-Bishop's presence, since both take aim at the g7-point. You wouldn't play on the g-file if it had nothing to do with your other imbalances.

With these facts in mind, White would be badly mistaken if he tried 19.Bxf6 because he would be giving up his super Bishop for an inferior minor piece. It would also be incorrect to trade Rooks or allow a trade of Rooks since that would limit your attacking potential and end any ideas you might have had of playing down the half-open g-file.

This leaves us wondering where to move our Rook. Evidently, the best choice is **19.Rb1**, placing it on a half open file and intending Kh1 followed by Rg1. In that case, most of White's pieces would be working together. White's Queen is aimed at the kingside, as are the Rook and Bishop.

In the game Taimanov-Sliwa, Moscow 1956, Black wasn't able to successfully deal with these ideas: **19...Qd7 20.Kh1 Bf5** Trying to place the Bishop on g6 and close down the g-file. **21.e4 Bg6 22.Qc3 Ne8?** Too passive. Better was 22...Qh3 followed by 23...Nh5!. **23.Qe5! Qd2?** A tactical oversight. **24.Rd1!** and Black realized that 24...Qxe2 would fail to 25.Qxg7+!. The game ended in a few moves: **24...Qa5 25.Rd7 Ra8 26.Kg2 b6??** This loses. Black would still be alive after 26...Qb6. **27.Qd5 Qa4 28.Bd1**, 1-0.

Summary of Imbalances and Ideas
[diagram (156)]

➤ White has two Bishops versus Black's Bishop and Knight.

➤ White's King is a bit open but if he can play Kh1 followed by Rg1, the Rook on the open g-file will work nicely with White's pressure down the a1-h8 diagonal.

➤ White's pawns on c4 and f3 take the d5, e4 and g4 squares away from the enemy Knight.

Problem 15

After 1.e4 c5 2.Nf3 Nc6 3.d4 cxd4 4.Nxd4 Nf6 5.Nc3 d6 6.Be2, is 6...e5 a reasonable move for Black? Whether it is or isn't, what are its ramifications?

(157)

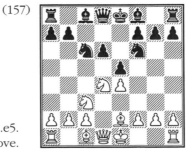

Black just played 6...e5.
White to move.

Solution 15

This move has become a common answer to 6.Be2 and is known as the Boleslavsky Variation. Though moves such as **6...e5** have to be played with great care due to the subsequent weakness of the d5-square, in the present case it's acceptable to allow the creation of this hole. Of course, Black will have to make sure he retains pieces that can guard it. Thus, after **7.Nf3** Black would play **7...h6!**, stopping 8.Bg5 followed by Bxf6, when a key defender of d5 has been removed. After **8.0-0 Be7 9.Re1 0-0 10.h3 a6 11.Bf1 b5**, Black would have an active position with chances for both sides.

Many years ago, the Czech Grandmaster Pachman mentioned this position and listed the ideas behind 6...e5 in the following way:

✦ Control of d4 and f4, preventing White from occupying d4.

✦ Preventing the dangerous e4-e5.

✦ Preparing a speedy development with ...Be7 and ...Be6, when he has control of d5.

✦ Often Black succeeds in playing ...d6-d5. If White seeks to prevent this, he must generally occupy the d5-square with a Knight and, after Black exchanges the piece, retake with his e-pawn. The result is then a superiority on the kingside for Black.

✦ It is interesting to note that Black's operations on the c-file are mostly more effective than White's on the d-file, for the pawn on d6, protected by the Bishop, is a great barrier for White.

Summary of Imbalances and Ideas
[diagram (157)]

➤ White has to move his Knight, and the available squares aren't particularly appealing: 7.Nf5 allows 7...Bxf5 followed by ...d6-d5; 7.Ndb5 gets hit by 7...a6; 7.Nb3 places the Knight on a square where it has little future; and 7.Nf3 blocks the f-pawn.

➤ By playing ...e7-e5, Black has left himself with a backward pawn on d6 and a hole on d5. The battle will revolve around whether White can make use of these factors.

Problem 16

(158)

White to move.

This common type of position and the plans that come out of it was first brought to world attention in the game Botvinnik-Capablanca, AVRO 1938 which White won brilliantly. Though this position isn't quite the same as the Botvinnik-Capablanca game, the ideas are identical and have been used in many guises.

See if you can spot White's most effective plan, and Black's best counter to it.

Solution 16

White has two Bishops and a central majority of pawns. If he wants to make use of both these factors, he should play **1.f3!,** taking the e4 and g4-squares away from the Black Knight and preparing for an eventual central expansion by e3-e4. Of course, this might take a while to actualize, and moves like Qe1-f2—giving more support to e3 and d4—Bd2, Rae1, and Ng3 will most likely be played at some time or other. However, when White finally manages to successfully play e3-e4, the center pawns can easily become very strong.

Black's answer to this idea is to play in a prophylactic manner by ...c7-c5, putting pressure on d4, ...b6 and ...Bb7, increasing the pressure against e4, ...Qc7, and ...Rad8, placing more heat on d4. In this way Black not only makes e3-e4 difficult to achieve, he also makes a statement to the effect that the center pawns will become targets if White succeeds in their advance.

All professional players are well acquainted with these structures and the ideas associated with them. After many years, it's become accepted that this kind of position tends to be favorable for White and few grandmaster games now feature it.

Summary of Imbalances and Ideas
[diagram (158)]

➤ If you look at the central advances that are available to both sides, you will see that Black has ...c5-c4, a move that doesn't do anything positive because the d3-Bishop calmly moves back to c2 while all the pressure has come off the d4-pawn. White's central push is e3-e4, a move that gains central space and prepares to move the e-pawn on to e5 where it pushes the enemy pieces back in panic.

➤ White needs to play for c3-c4 by f2-f3. Then a slow buildup designed to strengthen White's control over d4 and e4 is called for, i.e., Qe1-f2 guards d4, Ne2-g3 puts more pressure on e4.

➤ White has two Bishops, and succeeding with e3-e4 opens things up, making the Bishops more useful.

Problem 17

(159)

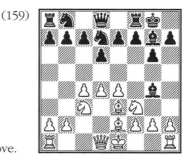

White to move.

After 1.d4 Nf6 2.c4 g6 3.Nc3 Bg7 4.e4 d6 5.Nf3 0-0 6.Be2 Bg4 7.Be3 Nfd7, figure out Black's plan (you can't play properly in the opening if you don't know what your opponent is trying to do) and then pick which of the following White moves appear to be most threatening to the second player: 8.h3, 8.d5, 8.Qc2, 8.Qb3, 8.Ng1, 8.Nd2.

Solution 17

White has several good moves in this position: 8.Qd2, 8.0-0, 8.Rc1 and even the ugly 8.h4 are all common. But only one of the listed choices confronts Black with any real problems. To make a proper decision, you will first have to understand Black's idea behind ...Bg4 followed by ...Nfd7. He actually has two ideas in mind, both centering around the d4-square:

✦ Black might play ...c7-c5, hitting d4, when d5 can be answered by ...Bxc3+, ruining White's queenside pawn structure.

✦ Black also intends to play ...Nc6, hitting d4, followed by chopping off the f3-Knight, one of the main defenders of d4, and ...e7-e5. Then d4-d5 can be answered by ...Nd4 when this important central square falls into Black's hands.

Clearly, anything White does should address these two Black plans. White has an advantage in central space, so if he can successfully nullify Black's threats, he'll be able to come out of the opening with a promising position. Let's go down the list of moves:

8.h3 doesn't make any sense since it virtually forces Black to continue with his planned conquest of d4: 8...Bxf3 9.Bxf3 Nc6 when the threat of 10...e5 ensures Black good play.

8.d5 doesn't seem logical. Why open the a1-h8 diagonal for Black's Bishop and give Black's Knight access to the c5 and e5 squares?

8.Qc2? moves the Queen to a useless square where it no longer protects the besieged d4 pawn. Black gets a fine position with 8...Bxf3 9.Bxf3 Nc6.

8.Qb3 is simply answered by 8...Qc8 when White's Queen isn't well placed on b3 because it has nothing to do with the d4-square.

8.Nd2? cuts off the White Queen's view of d4. After 8...Bxe2 9.Qxe2 Nc6, Black's threats against d4 are beginning to come to fruition.

8.Ng1! is the only one of the listed moves that actually makes sense. Though it might look a bit odd, a serious study of its virtues will quickly convince the student that it smacks of logic. The first point is that Black's g4-Bishop has nowhere to run. Thus, 8...Bxe2 is forced, when 9.Ngxe2 allows White to maintain his grip on d4. Compare this with the original position in which ...Bxf3, taking a defender away from d4, was threatened.

Another, somewhat more esoteric, point is that Black's normal plan of 9...e5 10.d5 f5 isn't as effective as it usually is in the King's Indian because his light-squared Bishop plays a major role in the ensuing kingside attack. Exchanging these Bishops is usually favorable to White, since he's trading off Black's good Bishop for White's bad one.

The most important thing to realize, though, is that all the listed moves, with the exception of 8.Ng1, failed to deal with the threats against d4.

Summary of Imbalances and Ideas
[diagram (159)]

➤ You can't find a proper move unless you know what your opponent's up to and what your best plan is.

➤ Black's Bishop is striking at d4, while his other Bishop is striking at one of the main defenders of that same square. It's clear that Black intends to hit d4 in some way, i.e., ...Nc6, ...c5, ...e5, or a combination of these ideas.

➤ Now that you know what Black is up to, find a move that strengthens your grip on d4.

Problem 18

(160)

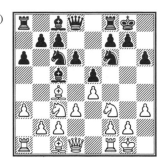

White to move.

If you had to choose between 1.Be3, 1.Bd2, or 1.Na4, which would you play?

Solution 18

The answer should be very clear. Playing 1.Bd2 develops the Bishop, but why would it want to be on such a passive square? Don't develop just for the sake of development!

Even worse is 1.Na4?, since 1...Ba7 leaves the Knight looking very silly on a4. In fact, Black threatens to win a piece by 2...b5.

Correct is **1.Be3**, since **1...Bxe3** (If I was Black, I would avoid this capture; indeed, I'd let White take on c5 since, after ...dxc5, the half-open d-file and the grip on d4 would ensure Black a happy future.) **2.fxe3** leads to a tremendous improvement in White's position. Why? There are several reasons: 1) The squares on d4 and f4 were vulnerable. Now, after 2.fxe3, neither can be touched by a Black piece. 2) Black's c5-Bishop is clearly superior to White's undeveloped piece on c1. Thus, trading an inactive unit for an active enemy piece makes good sense. 3) White's pawn on f2 isn't doing anything. In fact, it's not playing any real role in the battle. Also, White's f1-Rook is just a bystander. After 2.fxe3, the f2-pawn suddenly becomes a key player, and the f1-Rook sits on a nice half-open file.

It should be clear that, at times, courting a doubled pawn in the opening can be a very sensible thing to do. Yes, doubled pawns can be weaknesses, but they can also give you a grip on several important squares and create open files that catapult your Rooks into the fight.

Summary of Imbalances and Ideas
[diagram (160)]

➤ At the moment White's c1-Bishop is less active than Black's on c5 even though Black's c5-Bishop is thought to be a "bad" Bishop while White's c1-Bishop is thought to be "good."

➤ Always try and trade your less active pieces for the opponent's active ones.

➤ White's Rook on f1 has no open files to use.

➤ Black has solid control over both d4 and f4.

➤ It's clear that 1.Be3 addresses the points just listed. White offers a swap and actually hopes for 1...Bxe3 since 2.fxe3 not only deprives Black use of d4 and f4, but it also opens up the f-file for White's Rook.

Problem 19

True or false: In the Silman thinking system, the idea of the opening is to develop your pieces as quickly as possible.

Solution 19

False! It's been said that no development is better than a bad development. Rushing to get your pieces out without knowing what's going on is a sure recipe for disaster. The real idea behind the opening is to create an imbalance (Bishop versus Knight, giving your opponent a weak pawn, gaining space, etc.) and then to develop your forces around this difference.

For example, as Black you can often create a Knight versus Bishop situation by playing ...Bg4xf3 or ...Bb4xc3. But will your Knight prove better than his Bishop? Who knows! Instead of asking this question and hoping for a positive answer, it's your responsibility to *create* the answer by setting your pawns and pieces up in such a way that the whole position highlights the advantages of a Knight over a Bishop.

Problem 20

After 1.d4 Nf6 2.c4 e6 3.Nc3 Bb4 (the Nimzo-Indian Defense), 4.e3 c5 5.Nf3 Nc6 6.Bd3 Bxc3+ 7.bxc3 d6 8.e4, Black plays 8...e5. What is his strategic justification for playing in this way?

(161)

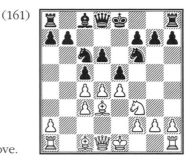

White to move.

Solution 20

Black's whole opening concept revolves around the battle between White's two Bishops and Black's Bishop and Knight. By playing ...e5, Black stops White from ripping the center open with an eventual e4-e5 because an open center would favor White's Bishops. He also freezes the White e-pawn and thus makes the d3-Bishop inactive, opens up the c8-h3 diagonal for the c8-Bishop, and welcomes 9.d5 Ne7 when the closed center should prove favorable to Black's Knights.

Note how Black doubled White's pawns by 6...Bxc3+, giving White the two Bishops but destroying the flexibility of White's pawn formation, and immediately set about creating a closed, Knight-friendly environment by ...d6 and ...e5. When you create an imbalance, make sure you do everything possible to steer it in a direction that will prove comfortable for your side.

Summary of Imbalances and Ideas
[diagram (161)]

➤ There are two major imbalances in this position: White has two Bishops and White's pawn structure has been compromised due to the doubling of his pawns.

➤ Black's ...e6-e5 destroys the flexibility of White's center and also tries to get White to lock up the middle of the board with d4-d5. In that case, the Black Knights might prove more useful than White's Bishops.

➤ Set up the pawns so that the resulting structure favors the minor piece you own.

Problem 21

After 1.d4 f5 2.Nc3 d5 3.Bf4 Nf6 4.e3 e6 5.Nf3 Bb4 6.Bd3 c5, how should White handle this position?

(162)

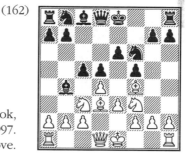

Suveg-Cook,
Golden Knights (corr.) 1997.
White to move.

Solution 21

White has a lead in development and control over the e5-square. The action is too sharp for White to make effective use of e5 right away, so that leaves him trying to get some mileage from his lead in development.

Though White would like to castle here, Black could then play 7...c4 8.Be2 Bxc3 9.bxc3 Ne4 when the c3-pawn is very weak. Anyway, why let the opponent close up the position if you have a lead in development? With this in mind, White played **7.dxc5**, opening up attacking lines. **7...Nbd7 8.0-0** The game then became very sharp: **8...Bxc3 9.bxc3 Nxc5 10.Nd4 Qe7 11.Be5 Ng4 12.Bg3 0-0 13.c4 Nxd3 14.cxd3 e5 15.Nf3**. A hard-fought draw was the eventual result.

Summary of Imbalances and Ideas
[diagram (162)]

➤ White has firm control over the e5-square but Black is threatening to disrupt White's pawn structure on the queenside.

➤ White has a lead in development. In general, you would like to open up the position if you intend to make use of this temporary—temporary because, if you don't make something of it, the opponent will make it vanish by simply developing his pieces—but significant advantage.

Problem 22

After 1.e4 e5 2.Nf3 Nc6 3.Bb5 (the Ruy Lopez) 3...a6 4.Ba4 Nf6 5.0-0 Be7 6.Re1 b5 7.Bb3 d6 8.c3, Black usually castles when White can, and almost always does, play 9.h3, stopping ...Bg4 and preparing for central gains by d2-d4. Why shouldn't Black anticipate this and toss in 8...Bg4 while he has the chance?

(163)

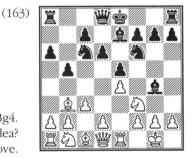

Black just played 8...Bg4.
Is this a good idea?
White to move.

Solution 22

When you study an opening, you can't just memorize the moves and expect to play it properly. It's far more important to master the plans, ideas, and key positions. Then, even if your opponent plays a non-book move (and they always play a non-book move!), you'll still be able to find the correct reply, based on your understanding of the position as a whole.

In the Ruy Lopez, White's most basic ideas center around expansion in the middle via d2-d4, a queenside strike with a2-a4, and the repositioning of the b1-Knight via d2-f1-g3 where it defends e4, is out of the way of the rest of the army, and prepares to leap onto the tasty f5-square.

Once you're aware of this Knight maneuver, the answer becomes rather obvious: White just delays the d4 advance with d2-d3 and goes about his usual business in bringing the horse to g3: **9.d3 0-0 10.Nbd2 Na5 11.Bc2 c5 12.Nf1 Qc7 13.Ng3 Nc6 14.h3**. Since Black doesn't want to play ...Bxf3 and hand White the two Bishops on a platter, the retreat of the Bishop to e6 or d7 is called for when the pin has been broken with gain of time.

Summary of Imbalances and Ideas
[diagram (163)]

➤ It's clear that White is preparing for d2-d4, but Black's last move makes this difficult to achieve in safety.

➤ If White plays h2-h3, Black will go backwards via ...Bh5. Else why bother with ...Bg4 in the first place? How can White gain control of the h5-square?

➤ White doesn't want to play h2-h3 followed by g2-g4 because that would weaken his kingside. But the annoying Bishop must be dealt with in some manner.

➤ Bringing the b1-Knight to g3 via d2-d3 followed by Nb1-d2-f1-g3, refutes Black's Bishop sortie. Then h2-h3 forces the Bishop to take on f3 or retreat and break the pin. After the Bishop retreats, d3-d4 can be safely played.

Problem 23

After 1.e4 e5 2.f4 (the King's Gambit) 2...Bc5 3.Nf3 d6 4.c3 a6?! 5.d4 exd4 6.cxd4 Ba7, (1700 vs. 1900), both sides should instantly see the strategy they are going to pursue and develop accordingly. What is White's correct strategy? What is Black's?

(164)

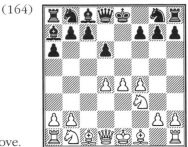

White to move.

Solution 23

White has been allowed to build up a big center, and it's his responsibility to defend it with everything he's got. Remember that the player with a huge pawn center can often win the game simply by making the center invulnerable. Thus, moves like **7.Nc3** defending e4, followed by Be3 defending d4, Bd3 defending e4, and h3 strengthening d4 by stopping ...Bg4, immediately suggest themselves.

Of course, it's Black's responsibility to attack the White center before it smothers him. Black will do this by ...Nf6, ...0-0, and ...Re8. For example: **7.Nc3 Nf6 8.Be3 0-0 9.Bd3 Re8 10.h3 Bf5!** forces White to push the e-pawn and create a weak square on d5. The tempting 10...Nxe4? fails to 11.Bxe4 d5 12.Ng5 dxe4 13.Qh5. **11.e5 Bxd3 12.Qxd3 Nc6 13.Qd2 Nb4 14.0-0 Nfd5** and Black has an excellent position.

Summary of Imbalances and Ideas
[diagram (164)]

➤ White has a big center and should follow the rule that states: "The owner of a large pawn center should do everything possible to make his central position impossible to attack." In other words, when you own a big center, turn it into a rock!

➤ This means that every move White plays should, in some way, strengthen the pawns on d4, e4 and f4.

➤ Black must prove that the White center is an object of attack. Every move he plays will target it for destruction.

Problem 24

After 1.c4 g6 2.g3 f5 3.d4 Bg7 4.Bg2 d6 5.d5 c5 would White do better to develop the g1-Knight to the center by 6.Nf3 or should he place it on the rim via 6.Nh3?

(165)

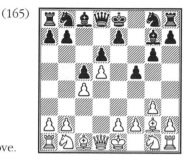

White to move.

Solution 24

This position, from the game Taimanov-Tal, Moscow 1970, features one glaring weakness: the hole on e6. Black might try and mend this problem by ...e5 but by capturing en passant by dxe6, the d5-square would be permanently weak, and the d6-pawn would be permanently backward. In view of this, Taimanov correctly tossed out the basic rule that states, "Never place a Knight on the rim." and instead played **6.Nh3**. Now the Knight is heading for f4 where it not only eyes e6 but it also could leap into d5 in case of dxe6 en passant after Black's ...e5.

Once again we can see that you should develop around the imbalances. Developing for the sake of development, especially if you haven't bothered figuring out the imbalances in that particular position, isn't acceptable.

Summary of Imbalances and Ideas
[diagram (165)]

➤ Black has a glaring hole on e6. White should try to do something that will highlight this weakness.

➤ The only way Black can rid himself of this hole is to play ...e7-e5. However, White can then capture en passant. This would activate the g2-Bishop and also create a new hole on d5.

➤ Playing the Knight to h3 and then to f4 not only eyes e6, it also gets ready to leap into d5 if White gets to capture en-passant (dxe6 in reply to an advance of Black's e-pawn).

➤ Don't just develop. Develop in ways that allow you to address the weaknesses in the enemy camp.

Problem 25

After 1.e4 c6 (the Caro-Kann) 2.d4 d5 3.exd5 cxd5, commonly seen moves at the amateur level are 4.Nc3, 4.c4, and 4.Bd3. What one of these is simply incorrect?

(166)

White to move.

Solution 25

The second choice, 4.c4, is known as the Panov-Botvinnik Attack, and it's one of White's best lines against the Caro-Kann because it puts pressure on Black's center by attacking d5. Note how White's Knight will fit quite nicely behind this pawn when both pawn and Knight join forces to hit d5.

A line favored by amateurs everywhere is 4.Bd3. White places his Bishop on an active square, follows up with c2-c3 defending d4 and stopping a later ...Nb4, and aims for eventual kingside pressure.

The final choice, 4.Nc3, is often seen in amateur chess but it's simply bad. Though White thinks he is developing, you should already know that development without a plan is often worse than no development at all. In the present case, White blocks his c-pawn and places his Knight on a road to nowhere. Think about this. Just where is that Knight headed? The d5-pawn is as solid as a rock, especially after Black tosses in ...e7-e6. The e4-square is also off-limits. Jumping to a4 is moronic and Nb5 is nothing more than a hope and a prayer—Black can always kick it back with ...a7-a6.

When you develop, make sure the move works towards a particular goal with the rest of your forces. Just tossing it out there with no rhyme or reason will get you nothing but trouble.

Summary of Imbalances and Ideas
[diagram (166)]

➤ Unless White hits Black's d-pawn with c2-c4, it will turn into a rock after Black plays ...e7-e6. The mix of the c4-pawn and the Knight on c3 puts real pressure on d5. The Knight itself accomplishes nothing.

➤ At the moment, no important imbalances exist. The sharp c2-c4 usually leads to an isolated White d-pawn, while other moves lead to quieter play.

➤ If White chooses to play quietly and just develop, he must do it in a way that allows all his pieces to work together towards a common goal. Something like Bd3, c2-c3, Bf4, and Nf3 aims all the pieces at Black's kingside. However, playing Nc3 doesn't do anything since d5 is solid and hopping to e4 isn't a very good idea.

Problem 26

After 1.e4 c5 2.c3, the popular Alapin Variation against the Sicilian Defense where White hopes to play d2-d4 with a full pawn center, 2...d5, White almost never plays 3.d3, a move once recommended by Grandmasters Hort and Lombardy. Why has 3.d3 been tossed into the rubbish bin?

(167)

Black to move.

Solution 26

As you might have guessed, the most obvious solution isn't correct. I suspect that the vast majority of amateurs would play 3...dxe4 4.dxe4 Qxd1+ here, not realizing that the position after 5.Kxd1 is extremely pleasant for White. Why? It turns out that the pawn structure gives White all the chances. Moves like a2-a4 followed by Nb1-d2-c4 leave White with a beautifully placed Knight. Then Be3, attacking c5, will leave Black in a bit of a quandary: defending c5 with ...b7-b6 allows a well-timed a4-a5 hit, while ...e7-e6 creates a weakness on d6. The fact that Black has potential weaknesses on c5, d5 and d6, while White doesn't have a weak spot in sight, gives the first player a nice edge that allows him to play for a win with virtually no chance for defeat.

The reason 3.d3 isn't played is that Black can just develop normally with **3...Nc6** when White's rather passive opening can't be considered a success.

Summary of Imbalances and Ideas
[diagram (167)]

➤ Black has more central space and doesn't have to do anything extreme.

➤ Taking on e4 (3...dxe4 4.dxe4) leaves White with more central space. So this will prove a bad idea if White's King turns out to be safe in the middle.

➤ Since Black has a spatial plus, he should continue to annex territory in that sector. Basic moves like 3...e5 or 3...Nc6 have to be good.

Problem 27

After 1.d4 Nf6 2.c4 e6 3.Nf3, Black often plays 3...b6 (the Queen's Indian Defense). What's the logic behind this move?

(168)

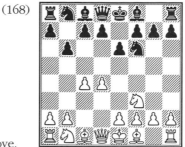

White to move.

Solution 27

White's 3.Nf3 didn't do anything to increase his control over the important e4-square. In fact, it actually blocked the possibility of a f2-f3 advance. Due to this, Black is playing logically by hastening to aim more firepower at e4 with 3...b6. By placing his Bishop on b7, this piece suddenly becomes very active and, together with the f6-Knight, Black is able to lay claim to e4.

It's clear that Black isn't just developing. He's getting his Bishop to an active post where it performs a particular function in unison with other members of its army.

Summary of Imbalances and Ideas
[diagram (168)]

➤ Black's Bishop on c8 isn't performing a useful function. After ...b7-b6, the Bishop can leap to life on a6 or b7.

➤ White's Nf3 actually weakened his control over e4 since f2-f3 could be played if the Knight didn't stand on that square. Black wants to make a claim against e4 as fast as he can.

Problem 28

After 1.d4 d5 2.Nf3 Nf6 3.e3 e6 4.Nbd2 c5 5.c3 Nc6 6.Bd3 Be7 7.0-0, we reach a common position in the ever-popular (on the amateur level) Colle Opening. At this point, two moves that might be considered are 7...c4 and 7...cxd4. What do you think of these two possibilities?

(169)

Black to move.

Solution 28

Both are rather poor, though they're constantly seen in amateur events. Best is 7...0-0, getting the King to safety and keeping all options open. Compare the obviously useful 7...0-0 with 7...c4, a move that takes the pressure off of d4 so Black can make a useless attack against the d3-Bishop. After the Bishop comfortably drops back to c2, White is ready to play e3-e4 when all of his forces will soon aim at Black's kingside. If the pawn still stood on c5, Black might have managed some central counterplay—remember that the best reaction to an attack on the wing is a counter attack in the center—but now White is very solid in the middle and can look forward to making real threats on the King's wing. Lesson: Don't make a one-move threat if it lessens your control over the center.

Also dubious is 7...cxd4 because White is the one who makes gains after 8.exd4. Suddenly White's c1-Bishop has a free c1-h6 diagonal, while the f1-Rook has been handed the half-open e-file on a platter. Your moves are supposed to do nice things for *your* side. Don't make moves that give your opponent all sorts of positive things that he didn't previously possess.

Summary of Imbalances and Ideas
[diagram (169)]

➤ White's army is primed for an eventual e3-e4 advance which opens up central files and frees the c1-Bishop.

➤ Black's pawn on c5 is putting pressure on White's d-pawn. This makes it harder for White to successfully play e3-e4.

➤ If Black takes on d4 (...cxd4) he helps White free his c1-Bishop after exd4.

➤ If Black pushes his pawn to c4, all the pressure against White's d-pawn suddenly vanishes.

Problem 29

(170)

Black to move.

If you had 1...e6, 1...Bf5, and 1...Bg4 to choose from, what would you play?

Solution 29

Your developing move should have something to do with the position's needs. Here we can see that d4 is the base of the pawn chain in White's camp and that Black's Knight is already hitting it. Thus, the move you choose should have something to do with increasing the pressure against d4.

When you look at the problem in this manner, the correct answer should leap at you. It's clear that 1...e6, locking in the c8-Bishop, and 1...Bf5 have nothing to do with the fight for d4. However, **1...Bg4** pins the main defender of d4, so 1...Bg4 attacks d4 and fits in nicely with Black's overall plan. If allowed, he will follow up with ...e6, ...Qb6 putting more pressure on d4, and ...Ng8-e7-f5 (even more pressure on d4!), when the team effort against the d4-pawn is obvious, appealing, and strong.

Summary of Imbalances and Ideas
[diagram (170)]

➤ White has a central advantage in space.

➤ The weakest point in White's camp is his pawn on d4, the base of the pawn chain.

➤ All of Black's moves should focus on this one potentially weak point (d4).

➤ Only 1...Bg4 deals with these facts. By placing pressure on f3, Black takes away a key defender of d4 and sets the tone for his future development. Everything will join in on the fight against White's poor d-pawn.

Problem 30

After 1.c4 c5 2.b3 Nf6 3.Bb2 g6, should White be tempted by 4.Bxf6?

(171)

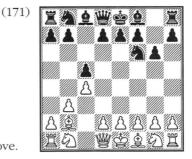

White to move.

Solution 30

In the game Karpov-Browne, San Antonio 1972, White surprised his opponent with the excellent **4.Bxf6!**. Why would such a strong player as Karpov be so willing to give up his fine Bishop for an ordinary Knight? No, he's not doing it just to double Black's pawns—in fact, if Black's c-pawn still stood on c7, where it could defend d5 via ...c7-c6, White wouldn't even have considered 4.Bxf6.

The real point behind Bxf6 lies in the weakness of d5. By chopping off the Knight and pulling the e7-pawn to f6 (the doubled pawns aren't weak, but they are inflexible), White leaves Black in a position where he can't defend the d5-square with a pawn. This fits in perfectly with the opening view that I'm trying to teach: create an imbalance—in this case, Knight vs. Bishop, a more flexible pawn structure and a hole on d5—and then develop your pieces around these facts.

Let's follow the game and see how White honed in on d5: **4...exf6 5.Nc3** Else Black would have played ...d7-d5. **5...Bg7 6.g3 Nc6 7.Bg2** And another piece takes aim at d5. So far White's c4-pawn, c3-Knight and Bishop have joined forces to conquer that tasty square. **7...f5 8.e3** White avoids Nf3 because it wouldn't have anything to do with the game theme. **8...0-0 9.Nge2** and White's grip on d5 couldn't be broken. Note that, if necessary, the e2-Knight can join in on the d5-bashing with Nf4.

Summary of Imbalances and Ideas
[diagram (171)]

➤ No imbalances exist in the diagramed position.

➤ It's up to White to find a way to create an imbalance that, ultimately, will turn the game in his favor. Just waiting for one to appear is a sure-fire way to lose.

➤ Taking the Knight on f6 creates a Bishop versus Knight imbalance and, more importantly, a gaping wound on d5.

➤ Once the hole on d5 is created, all subsequent developing moves will center around further domination of that square, i.e., Nc3, g3 and Bg2, e3 and Ng1-e2-f4.

Problem 31

(172)

White to move.

White's system has left him with a hole on d4. How serious is this? Also, would you label the White position flexible or inflexible?

Solution 31

The hole on d4 isn't serious at all, as long as White makes sure that a Black Knight can't take up permanent residence there. At the moment, ...Nd4 can always be met by Nxd4 when Black will have a doubled pawn on d4 and the hole will be filled.

It's important to understand that a hole is only a serious problem if an enemy piece can make use of it.

The question pertaining to the flexibility of White's position is also rather easy to answer: White's game is very flexible! He can play for queenside expansion via b2-b4-b5, for a central break by d3-d4, or for a kingside attack by f2-f4-f5.

Stepping beyond the parameters given in the problem, let's take this opportunity to address the often-discussed subject of memorization of variations versus understanding the ideas in your system. Some openings, of course, demand a lot of memorization due to their sharp, tactical nature. Most, however, are fairly easy to master by making a study of the system's ideas, structure, and tactical anomalies.

The position in the diagram (a main line of Botvinnik's System in the English, usually reached by: 1.c4 e5 2.g3 Nc6 3.Bg2 g6 4.Nc3 Bg7 5.e4 d6 6.Nge2 Nge7 7.d3 0-0 8.0-0 Be6) is a case in point. Here are some observations that would serve any player in good stead:

✦ White's Nd5 gains in power when Black has a
Bishop on e6 because ...Nxd5 would then be impos-

sible due to cxd5, forking Black's c6-Knight and
e6-Bishop.

✦ Conversely, White might wish to avoid a quick Be3
because then Black's ...Nd4 becomes more of an
issue since Nxd4 hangs a piece to ...exd4, forking
the White pieces on c3 and e3. However, Be3 is
fine if White plays Nd5 first, because then ...Nd4 can
once again be safely met by Nxd4 since the
c3-Knight has moved and can no longer be forked.

✦ If Black plays ...f7-f5, White will often prevent
...f5-f4 by Be3 followed by Qd2. The mixture of the
Queen and Bishop hitting f4, plus the g3-pawn and
the e2-Knight, make Black's hoped-for advance very
difficult to achieve.

✦ White would love to meet ...f7-f5 with exf5.
However, he will only play this move if Black
isn't able to recapture with a Knight because a
Knight on f5 attacks the e3-Bishop and brings
another piece to bear on d4. Thus, the pawn
tension will often remain intact until the e7-Knight
moves away from e7. When that happens, White
will play exf5 followed, if possible, by a central
counter with d3-d4.

I could go on and on, but this information, combined with
the White plans listed earlier, is quite easy to learn and will arm
any White player with enough ammo to make life difficult for his
opponent. No matter what opening systems you play, make a
concerted effort to garner this kind of information about them.
Your results will improve dramatically if you do!

Summary of Imbalances and Ideas
[diagram (172)]

➤ A hole exists on d4. The question centering around
any hole is this: can the enemy turn the hole into a
permanent home for one of his pieces? In this case,
White has it covered and the answer is "no."

➤ The pawn breaks for both sides are clear: White can play for queenside expansion by Rb1 and b2-b4, he can prepare a central strike with Be3 followed by d3-d4, or he can go for a kingside attack by f2-f4.

➤ Any move that White makes must prevent Black from taking up permanent residence on d4, or it should prepare one of the advances just mentioned.

Problem 32

(173)

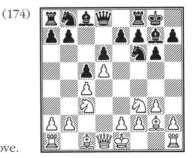

Black to move.

In this first diagram, the bare bones structure should tell you what Black is aiming for.

(174)

Black to move.

Moving on to the second diagram, we can't help but notice that we have the same basic structure as in the previous position, except now we have to determine where to place our pieces. How would you develop your forces if you had the Black position?

Solution 32

Black's pawn chain of e7-d6-c5 points to the queenside, so he naturally wishes to increase his control of space in that sector. Since closed centers demand wing play with pawns, the correct idea is **...a7-a6** followed by ...b7-b5. The only other plan for Black involves ...e7-e6 followed by ...exd5, opening up the e-file.

Though the plan of advancing via ...b7-b5 holds true in both diagrams, the addition of pieces (the second diagram) makes the actualization of your idea harder to achieve. This means that you must use your army in such a way as to make your dreamed of pawn break a reality. Every developing move you make now takes on great importance because if you move it to a square where it has nothing to do with your proper plan, you're taking the first step towards defeat.

In the second diagram, the first move that comes to mind is 1...a6, but, aside from the fact that he doesn't even threaten ...b7-b5 since White has two pieces hitting b5 to Black's one, White can further dampen Black's hopes with a2-a4.

Most amateurs would put off their decision and simply develop with ...Nbd7. However, this doesn't have anything to do with Black's plan. Why not develop the Black pieces to squares where they can help make the ...b7-b5 advance a reality? A series of moves that nicely fits the bill is **1...Na6 2.0-0 Nc7** followed by ...a7-a6, ...Rb8 and, if necessary, ...Bd7. Notice the huge difference between placing the Knight on d7 where it doesn't aid in the planned ...b7-b5 and on c7 where it plays a key role.

Summary of Imbalances and Ideas
[diagrams (173) and (174)]

➤ In general, the pawn structure will tell you what plan to adopt. Learn to hear the message your pawn structure is telling you!

➤ In both diagrams, Black's pawns point towards the queenside. He also has chances to initiate a central break via ...e7-e6. Thus, the second player must try to create successful ...b7-b5 advance, or play for ...e7-e6.

➤ White has a central space advantage, so he will try and prevent Black's queenside expansion (a2-a4 will be played at some point) and strive to create a central strike by 0-0 and, after much preparation, e2-e4-e5.

Problem 33

(175)

Beliavsky-Anand, Munich 1991.
White to play.

Black has just played ...Bb7. Break this position down and explain the respective plans for both sides. An exact move or series of moves isn't important.

Solution 33

Anand, after playing ...Bb7: "I knew the theory, but at this point I decided to ignore it and just look at the position. It seemed to me that Black could play very natural moves. The point of this one is to play ...e6 and completely destroy White's center. After the resulting exchanges, Black may be left with a weak pawn (for example, on e6) but it doesn't matter because Black has generated so much active play for his pieces."

White has claimed quite of bit of central space but he paid a price for this: he's behind in development and his King is still in the center. To take advantage of these facts, Black needs to blast open the center and try to scare up some threats against White's centralized King. By playing dynamically and tossing in ...e7-e6 as quickly as possible, Black intends to activate his pieces and get something going before White can get his King to safety and defend his center.

After **1.Qd2 Nf5 2.Bh2 dxe5 3.fxe5 e6! 4.0-0-0** (4.d6 Nd7 leaves e5 in a state of collapse) **4...exd5 5.Nxd5 Nc6** (with the threat of ...Ncd4), Black achieved an excellent position.

The lesson here is simple: When you own a big center, make it indestructible. If you're opponent has a large center, do everything you can to chop it down.

Summary of Imbalances and Ideas
[diagram (175)]

➤ Black has a lead in development.

➤ Black's King is castled while White's monarch is still stranded in the center.

➤ White has a large pawn center. This means that if White succeeds in finishing his development and defending his center, he will have a significant plus.

➤ When your opponent has a big pawn center, you must do everything you can to destroy it and show that it's a weakness instead of a strength.

➤ When your opponent's King is stuck in the center, you must try to open things up and create roads that will allow your pieces to reach it.

Problem 34

After 1.Nf3 d5 2.d4 Nf6 3.c4 c6 4.Nc3 e6 5.e3 Nbd7 6.Qc2 Bd6 7.Bd3 0-0 8.0-0 Qe7, we have a common position in the Semi-Slav Defense. White has tried many moves here: 9.e4, gaining central space, and 9.b3, preparing to fianchetto the c1-Bishop and also giving White the chance to meet ...dxc4 with bxc4, both make sense. How would you judge the aggressive 9.c5?

(176)

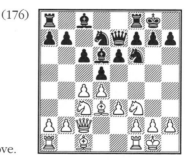

White to move.

Solution 34

At one time this move would have been the object of derision; White makes a one-move threat that's easily dealt with and, by doing so, takes all the pressure off the Black d5-pawn. Today, it's a respected alternative to the more pedestrian 9.e4 and 9.b3.

Of course, White knows that Black will safely pull his Bishop back to c7. The real reasons for c5 will be clear after another couple of moves: **9...Bc7 10.e4** White is the first to grab the center. Passive development by 10.Bd2 e5 would have been a pleasure for Black. **10...dxe4 11.Nxe4** and now we've reached a formation that appears to be good for Black, since the d5-square is firmly in his hands. The reason White went into this via 9.c5 is that he feels his control over e5 and d6 outweigh the weakness of d5. Also note that 9.c5 stopped Black's normal freeing maneuver ...b7-b6 followed by ...c6-c5.

One more point: though the d4-pawn is backward, a pawn is only weak if the enemy is able to attack it. Black's lack of space and passive pieces can't prove the weakness of d4. Indeed, the d4-pawn is a tower of strength since it defends c5 and clamps down on the critically important e5-square!

Summary of Imbalances and Ideas
[diagram (176)]

➤ White has a bit more queenside space (his c-pawn is on c4 while Black's is on c6), but both sides have various plans to expand in the center.

➤ Black is playing for an ...e6-e5 advance though he might toss in ...dxc4 first. Playing ...e6-e5 will give him lots of central space and will also free the c8-Bishop.

➤ Occasionally Black will choose to free himself with a well-timed ...c6-c5 advance.

➤ White can either anticipate Black's central advance and simply develop with b2-b3 followed by Bb2, or he can strike in the middle first with e3-e4.

➤ The c4-c5 advance grabs a bit of queenside space and stifles ...c6-c5 counters before advancing in the center with e3-e4.

Problem 35

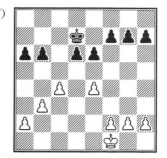

(177)

Black to move.

This bare bones illustration of a Hedgehog structure, typically found in the English Opening and the Sicilian, allows us to illustrate Black's two main plans. Do you know them?

Solution 35

Black can make use of the possible pawn breaks ...b5 and ...d5. If Black plays 1...b5, he has suddenly equalized the space in that sector. 2.cxb5 axb5 would give Black a queenside space edge. If White didn't take on b5, Black would then grab more territory by 2...b4. Or, if he wanted to give White a pawn weakness, he could play the simple 2...bxc4 and after 3.bxc4 the White c-pawn is isolated.

Black can also challenge White's supremacy in the center with ...d6-d5 (of course, this will be backed up by a myriad of pieces) when Black's forces usually burst out of their confinement and become very active.

Summary of Imbalances and Ideas
[diagram (177)]

➤ Black's d-pawn is backward and is vulnerable to attack by White's Rooks and White's dark-squared Bishop. When White achieves this structure, he would love to tie Black down to the defense of this pawn. Easier said than done!

➤ Usually the d-pawn is well defended by Black's dark-squared Bishop and a host of other pieces (Queen, Rook, and even Knight).

> ➤ Black's position is very solid. He will strive to put pressure on White's e4-pawn, and he will constantly annoy White with threats of ...b6-b5 and/or ...d6-d5.

> ➤ All Black's moves will act as preparation for his two big breaks (...b6-b5 and ...d6-d5).

> ➤ White will try to contain those two breaks and, thanks to his space advantage, squeeze Black to death.

> ➤ This is another example where familiarity with a specific pawn structure allows you to place your pieces on logical and efficient squares.

Problem 36

After 1.d4 Nf6 2.c4 e6 3.Nf3 b6 4.a3 (the Petrosian System in the Queen's Indian Defense) 4...Ba6 5.Qc2 Bb7 6.Nc3 c5 7.e4 cxd4 8.Nxd4 Nc6 9.Nxc6 Bxc6 10.Bf4 Nh5 11.Be3, take a look at 11...Bd6 and then describe its good and bad points.

(178)

White to move.

Solution 36

In L.Christiansen-Karpov, Wijk aan Zee 1993, Karpov indeed played 11...Bd6. This move was intended to be the start of major offensive against White's dark-squares on e5 and f4, thereby justifying the offside position of the Knight on h5. You didn't think Black played 10...Nh5 just to make a one-move attack against White's Bishop, did you? This kind of plan is commonly seen in modern openings. In fact, in his zeal to control f4, Black might even toss in ...Qf6, ...Be5, and ...g7-g5.

Unfortunately for Karpov, even the deepest positional ideas need to be supported by tactical realities. In this case, the Bishop on d6 and the Knight are both unprotected. Christiansen took advantage of this by moving his Queen back to d1, winning a piece, whereupon Karpov promptly resigned!

I found it interesting to see a well-known chess curmudgeon (probably in the 2100 range, though he considers himself a grandmaster!) write that 11...Bd6 was imbecilic because it blocked the d-pawn. Most players are so stuck in convention that they can't stand seeing a move that steps away from well-trodden paths. Even after I wrote to him and pointed out all the good that ...Bd6 was intended to do, he still held on to his opinion and wrote back, "It blocks the d-pawn, therefore it can't be good!"

Remember that a mastery of typical patterns is highly recommended—in fact, it's crucial! It's a tool that will help you recognize previously seen situations and recall what other players did to solve the position's problems. However, don't do what this gentleman did and allow pattern recognition to turn into a prison that will blind you to a rainbow of chess possibilities.

Summary of Imbalances and Ideas
[diagram (178)]

➤ White has an advantage in central space.

➤ White's e-pawn is being eyed by Black's c6-Bishop, and the first player has to make sure it's adequately defended.

➤ Black is eyeing the dark-squares on e5 and f4. He also intends to increase the pressure against e4 by ...Be5, with the threat of ...Bxc3+.

➤ Black's pieces on d6 and h5 are undefended. If your pieces are "loose," make sure you're aware of this fact. In other words: learn to be paranoid when your pieces aren't well protected.

Problem 37

(179)

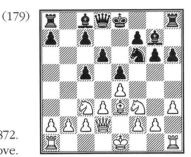

Zukertort-Steinitz, London 1872.
Black to move.

What would you do in this position?

Solution 37

The center is fairly closed so both sides will pursue pawn breaks on the wings. White will try for b2-b4 and/or f2-f4 while Black will eventually play for a ...f7-f5 advance. However, keeping an eye on the key central squares d5 and d4 will also be a priority. At the moment, Black has two Bishops, but the Bishop on g7 is blocked and bad. Black would also like to castle but he can't do this due to Bxh6. How will he finish his development? The answer is surprising: he doesn't bother!

1...Ng8!

Instead of developing a piece, Black actually undevelops his Knight! How can such a move be explained? Quite simply! The idea is that the Knight was not really doing much on f6. The d5 and g4 squares were not available to it, d7 is a road to nowhere and h5 sticks it on the side of the board. Since Black was not happy with his Knight's placement, he decides to swing it around to c6 via e7 where it eyes both b4 and d4, frees the f7-pawn, and plays a much more important role in the center.

Some of you may be asking, "How can Black afford this obvious waste of time?" The answer should be easy to understand: If the position were open, this maneuver by the Knight would not be a good idea because time becomes very important in wide-open positions. However, in this case the center is semi-closed, making quick development less important, so a bit of lengthy maneuvering is acceptable if it increases the flexibility of the position as a whole.

After **2.Nh2 Ne7 3.f4 exf4 4.Bxf4 g5 5.Be3 f5 6.0-0 f4 7.Bf2 Nc6**, Black achieved a strategically winning position thanks to his two active Bishops, advantage in kingside space and control over the b4 and d4 squares. Note that White's Knight can jump into d5, but Black can eventually chase it away by ...c7-c6.

Remember: it's not development that's important in the opening, but what your pieces accomplish once you get them out.

Summary of Imbalances and Ideas
[diagram (179)]

➤ Black's King is in the center but White won't be able to take advantage of this fact if he can't open up the position.

➤ Black can't castle due to Bxh6.

➤ White is playing for b2-b4. He could also move the Knight and play for f2-f4, though this would activate the g7-Bishop after ...exf4.

➤ Black's doubled pawns are very good: the c5-pawn gives him a firm grip on d4, while the c7-pawn can be used to kick away any piece by ...c7-c6 that dares leap into d5.

➤ Black would love to play ...f7-f5-f4, with an enormous amount of kingside space.

➤ Black's ...Ng8! prepares to swing the Knight, which wasn't doing anything on f6, around to d4 via e7 and c6. It also unblocks the f-pawn and prepares ...f7-f5.

(LEFT TO RIGHT) ANATOLY KARPOV, JEROEN PIKET,
VLADIMIR KRAMNIK, VISWANATHAN ANAND,
VASSILY IVANCHUK, AND GATA KAMSKY

Problem 38

Answer the following questions. No moves are necessary:

Solutions 38

38.1 What is an imbalance?

Any difference in the two respective positions. Try and create as many imbalances as possible if you think you can ultimately make them serve your cause. Don't allow an imbalance to be created if you think it will be to your opponent's advantage.

38.2 Name the seven main imbalances.

Superior minor piece; pawn structure; space; material; control of a key file or square; lead in development; initiative. Note that a lead in development and the initiative are temporary imbalances while the others tend to be permanent features of the position.

38.3 What are the main components of the "Silman Thinking Technique?"

Figure out the positive and negative imbalances; figure out the side of the board you wish to play on; don't calculate! Instead, dream up various fantasy positions, i.e., positions that you would LOVE to achieve! Once you find a fantasy position that appeals to you, you must decide if you can reach it. Look at the moves you wish to calculate—called candidate moves. These moves are the moves that lead to your fantasy position. Note that calculation is the *last* thing you do.

38.4 What is a plan?

Making positive use of the existing characteristics of a position. Note: you don't do what you want to do, you do what the position needs. There is often a big difference between these two things.

38.5 What is the difference between a static and dynamic advantage or imbalance?

A static imbalance is a long-term plus, usually highly positional in nature. A dynamic imbalance is short-term and often tactical in nature.

38.6 What is the difference between a good and bad Bishop?

A good Bishop isn't blocked by its own pawns. A bad Bishop is blocked by center pawns standing on its own color.

38.7 Can an active Bishop also be bad?

Yes, an active Bishop can also be a bad Bishop. In general, toss terms like "good" and "bad" out the window. The only thing that should concern you is the following question: "Is your Bishop doing a useful job?" If not, find a way to get it into the game!

38.8 What are the three cures for a bad Bishop?

Trade it off for a piece of equal (or superior!) value; get your pawns off of the color of the Bishop; get your Bishop outside the pawn chain.

38.9 What do Knights need to reach their full power?

They need advanced, permanent support points. A Knight is as good as a Bishop on the fourth rank, superior to a Bishop on the fifth, and often as good as a Rook on the sixth.

38.10 Explain Steinitz's rule on how to beat Knights.

Take away all their advanced support points.

38.11   If your opponent has two Bishops, what should you do?

Close the position and turn the two Bishops into a liability; trade one off and leave him with only one Bishop.

38.12   Why are two Bishops usually superior to two Knights?

A Bishop's weakness is its inability to control squares of both colors. A Knight doesn't have the mobility of a Bishop, but it can ultimately land on every square on the board. Two Bishops complement each other by covering both white and black squares. Two Knights can get in each others' way. Such Knights often don't work well together.

38.13   Why is extra territory a good thing?

The side with less space often has trouble finding active squares for his pieces. Top players covet spatial gains because they hope to squeeze their opponent to death within the confines of his cramped position.

38.14   What should the side with less space do to make the situation more acceptable?

Trade off as many pieces as possible. This will give your remaining pieces more room to move about in.

38.15   Why is a full pawn center a good thing to have?

It gives its owner more space, and it restricts the movement of the enemy pieces.

38.16   How can a player make use of a full pawn center?

If you can make it indestructible, the opponent won't be able to create any counterplay and will likely perish due to his lack of space.

38.17   What must you do if your opponent creates a full pawn center?

You must prove that it's a weakness. Attack it for all your worth!

38.18 Are doubled pawns always bad? If not, what are their good points?

Doubled pawns are often good because they give their owners use of a half-open or open file and also can offer extra control over important squares.

38.19 How does one make use of an isolated d-pawn and how does one play against it?

The isolated d-pawn (from White's perspective) gives its owner use of the e5-square, which can be used as a fine home for a Knight, and a central space advantage. White will use these things to create threats against the enemy King.

Black will fight to control the square in front of the d-pawn on d5. Then he will strive to trade all the minor pieces, effectively ending White's attack. Once this is done, Black can place a Rook on d5 and another heavy piece on d7 or d8, doubling against the d4-pawn. A timely ...c6-c5 or ...e6-e5 makes use of a probable pin along the d-file to force the win of the besieged pawn.

In general, White will want to retain Queens early in the game, highlighting his attacking chances. However, if too many minor pieces get exchanged, White will want to trade off the Queens. This allows his King to safely come to the center and defend d4. He might also want to trade off the Rooks (if his attacking chances vanish) because without the Rooks, Black won't be able to put an optimal amount of pressure on d4.

38.20 Do Rooks always stand well on open files?

No. The open file is unimportant if you can't use it to penetrate into the enemy position. Place your Rooks on an open file if penetration points exist on it, or if you stop your opponent from taking control of it and ultimately penetrating into your position.

38.21 When you triple on an open file with two Rooks and a Queen which takes up the rear, what is this called?

Alekhine's Gun.

38.22 A static plus usually calls for slow play while a dynamic plus usually calls for fast play (often fast play leads to the creation of a static, long-lasting advantage). With this in mind, tell me if you must play fast or slow when you possess:
a. A lead in development.
b. An isolated d-pawn.
c. Play against your opponent's backward pawn.
d. The initiative.
e. A material advantage.
f. A superior minor piece.
g. Play against a weak square in the enemy camp.
h. An advantage in space.

a. FAST. If you don't use it quickly, it will fade away.

b. FAST. The iso gives you dynamic compensation for its potential weakness. If you don't make fast use of that dynamism, the pawn's intrinsic weak points will begin to torment you.

c. SLOW. This is a static advantage. Take your time and build up your forces against it.

d. FAST. Having the initiative means having control of the game. You must make use of this before it fades away.

e. SLOW. Material is forever. If everything else is equal, you should win the game. Thus take your time and neutralize your opponent's compensation for his material deficit.

f. SLOW. This is a positional feature that can be used throughout the game.

g. SLOW. Take your time and make sure that your opponent can't wrest the square away from you. Eventually use it as a home for one of your pieces.

h. SLOW. Space lets you play for a slow, painful squeeze. The longer you take, the more your opponent suffers.

38.23   True or false:
   a. It's better to be behind in material than to have a position that's devoid of activity.
   b. A Bishop should usually be considered as slightly better than a Knight.
   c. Bishops enjoy open positions.
   d. A Rook reaches the zenith of its power on the eighth rank.
   e. A Rook on the seventh rank is often worth a pawn.
   f. Two Rooks on the seventh are known as "roving eaters."
   g. An attack against the enemy King is the most effective plan in chess.
   h. Knights are most effective on the eighth rank.
   i. A protected passed pawn is always a good thing to have.

a.   TRUE. Material often takes a back seat to the possession of active pieces or an active plan.

b.   FALSE. A Bishop and a Knight should be considered as equal. Every particular position holds its own answer.

c.   TRUE. Bishops are usually better than Knights in open positions.

d.   FALSE. The seventh rank is the Rook's promised land.

e.   TRUE.

f.   FALSE. They are known as pigs or hogs on the seventh because they tend to eat everything in their path.

g.   FALSE. Central play is the most effective plan in chess.

h.   FALSE. A Knight is most effective on the sixth rank. It doesn't control as many squares on the seventh and eighth ranks.

i.   FALSE. A protected passed pawn can actually be a disadvantage if the opponent manages to blockade it with a Knight before it gets further than the fifth rank.

Problem 39

A systematic pawn advance designed to knock aside the opponent's pawn fortifications is known as a pawn break. Name some advantages that this kind of pawn advance might bring.

Solution 39

Pawn breaks serve the following purposes:

+ An advance of pawns gains space.
+ A pawn advance can open files for your Rooks.
+ A pawn advance can open diagonals for your Bishops.
+ A pawn advance can create weak squares in the opponent's camp.
+ A pawn advance can also lead to pawn weaknesses in the enemy camp.

Problem 40

In positions with locked centers, should you attack on the wings with pieces or pawns?

Solution 40

The center pawns in a closed position limit the activity of both side's armies. The Rooks in particular have trouble finding a way to join in the battle. Due to this, it's important to attack on the wings with pawns first, usually in the direction that your pawns point because that is the area where you own more space.

(180)

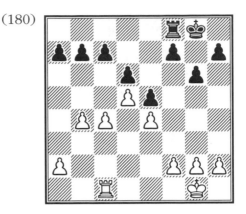

In this bare bones diagram, Black's pawn chain on c7-d6-e5 aims at the kingside, so Black is more or less obliged to play on that side of the board with 1...f5. By bringing a pawn up to join with his lead e-pawn, Black creates some influence on d4, e4, f4 and g4. Now he obviously owns more territory on the kingside than his opponent does. His pieces (in a normal situation, both sides would own a whole armada of men) suddenly have more room to maneuver in that sector of the board, and the Rook on f8—dead to the world when the pawn stood on f7—experiences feelings of empowerment now that the pawn has expanded its horizons to f5.

Using this same logic, White seeks a c4-c5 advance, when his command of queenside space would demand respect, and the c1-Rook is suddenly in possession of an open file because White can open up that file with cxd6 whenever he wishes.

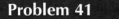

Problem 41

(181)

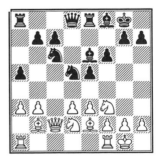

White to move.

In the game Fischer-U.Andersson, Siegen 1970, White played 1.Kh1 Qd7 2.Rg1 Rad8 3.Ne4 Qf7 4.g4. Odd-looking moves to be sure, but in our next game, something similar seems to occur over a hundred years earlier!

(182)

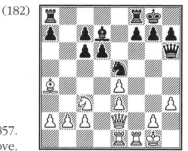

L.Paulsen-Morphy, New York 1857.
Black to move.

Here the legendary Paul Morphy played 1...Kh8 2.Nd1 g5 3.Nf2 Rg8.

What is the point of the plans chosen by both great players, and was Fischer emulating Morphy?

Solution 41

In the Fischer game, Black appears to have a nice position with more space and active, centrally placed pieces. But Fischer uses a maneuver that might strike the amateur as very odd, and is far from obvious even to seasoned masters.

1.Kh1 Qd7 2.Rg1 Rad8 3.Ne4 Qf7 4.g4

White has created an artificial support point on e4. In this contest, Fischer managed to grab the initiative on both sides of the board.

4...g6 5.Rg3 Bg7 6.Rag1

The only way Black can make a challenge for the e4-square is to play an eventual ...f6-f5. However, this would open up the g-file and allow the White Rooks to come crashing in. In other words, Fischer's doubling of Rooks is a prophylactic maneuver designed to prevent Black from ever playing ...f6-f5.

6...Nb6 7.Nc5 Bc8 8.Nh4

With a solid center (you can't successfully attack on the wing unless you have firm control over the center) and an imposing buildup of forces on the kingside, Fischer decides to go after the Black monarch. But don't let this distract you from the point of this example: g2-g4 is designed to give White permanent control over the nice e4-square; if an attack eventually also comes to pass, then so much the better.

8...Nd7 9.Ne4

White has no intention of trading his fine Knight for the pathetic thing on d7! Never trade your good pieces for the opponent's bad ones. After 9.Ne4, Black's game was passive and he soon had a completely lost position.

9...Nf8 10.Nf5 Be6 11.Nc5 Ne7 12.Nxg7 Kxg7 13.g5

Loosening up the a1-h8 diagonal!

13...Nf5 14.Rf3 b6 15.gxf6+. White easily scored the full point.

The Morphy game also saw a strong kingside attack come to pass with similar moves:

1...Kh8 2.Nd1 g5! 3.Nf2 Rg8 4.Nd3 g4 5.Nxe5 dxe5 6.hxg4 Bxg4 7.Qf2 Rg6 8.Qxf7 Be6 9.Qxc7 Rxg2+ 10.Kxg2 Qh3+ 11.Kf2 Qh2+ 12.Kf3 Rf8+ 14.Qf7 Rxf7 mate.

Very impressive play from Morphy, and the similarity of the Fischer and Morphy games is clear when you consider Fischer's Kh1/ g4 and Morphy's ...Kh8/...g5. However, though the examples are visually the same, the real point behind the plans chosen by Fischer and Morphy are actually quite different! In the Fischer game, he played the g4 advance in an effort to create an artificial support point on e4 for his Knight. In the Morphy game, the e5-support point already existed, and ...g7-g5 was played solely with mate in mind.

Three things I'd like you to keep in mind from this problem:

- ✦ The ability to create an artificial support point should be a basic part of everyone's game.

- ✦ A kingside pawn advance doesn't necessarily mean that you are playing for mate. Indeed, sometimes a massive buildup of kingside pieces is more prophylactic than aggressive.

Summary of Imbalances and Ideas
[diagram (181)]

➤ White possesses an extra center pawn. This gives him a solid grip over the key central squares on c4, d4, e4, and f4.

➤ Black possesses more central space.

➤ White usually strives to free himself with a d3-d4 advance, challenging Black's central advantage in space and giving more scope to the White forces.

➤ White can move a Knight to e4, but Black has the ability to chase it away at the right time by ...f6-f5.

➤ By playing Kh1, Rg1, and g2-g4, White permanently prevents ...f6-f5 and, as a result, turns the e4-square into an artificial support point.

Summary of Imbalances and Ideas
[diagram (182)]

➤ White's pawns on e4 and e3 are doubled and isolated. Black can put pressure on them by placing his Rook(s) on the e-file.

➤ Black's doubled c-pawns are quite useful: the c7-pawn turns d6 into a rock, while the c6-pawn takes the b5 and d5 squares away from White's Knight. On the other hand, the Black Knight has taken up permanent residence on the superb e5-post.

➤ White's minor pieces are stuck on the queenside and can't leap to the kingside without a great deal of difficulty. Black's minor pieces are already aimed at White's King.

➤ Black's plan of ...Kh8, ...Rg8, and ...g7-g5 is directed at the White King. By advancing the g-pawn to g4, Black will rip apart White's kingside defenses and also bring the Rooks into the attack.

Problem 42

(183)

Chikovani-Geller, Gori 1968.
Black to play.

Name the tactical theme that Black employs in this game.

Solution 42

Theme: Overloaded White Queen, which is defending both the g5-Bishop and the d4-Knight. **1...Nfxe4 2.Nxe4 Nxe4 3.fxe4 Bxd4+** when **4.Qxd4 Qxg5 5.Qxd6** is equal as far as material is concerned, but leaves White with an inferior pawn structure and a clear disadvantage.

Summary of Imbalances and Ideas
[diagram (183)]

➤ White's d4-Knight is only defended by its Queen.

➤ White's g5-Bishop is only defended by its Queen.

➤ If Black can pull the Queen away from the defense of one of these pieces, it may be hanging.

➤ White has more central space and might eventually develop pressure against Black's backward pawn on d6. If given time, he will play moves like Rad1, Nc2 opening up the d-file, and, if necessary, Bf4, when d6 is a very sick pawn indeed.

➤ Black would normally play for a freeing ...d6-d5 advance, or he might seek to play for maximum piece activity by ...a7-a5-a4 (turning c5 into an artificial support point), ...Qa5, ...Re8, etc.

> Though there are many positional imbalances to consider, all these things become unimportant when a tactical feature rears its spiny head and detonates the position.

Problem 43

(184)

G.Kamsky-M.Adams, London 1989.
Black to play.

Black can make use of a thematic idea. It won't sit around forever, so you better take notice and make a grab for the brass ring.

Solution 43

In this kind of position, Black's play comes on the queenside while White's is clearly on the kingside. In general, you want to play where your space lies, and you shouldn't allow yourself to get distracted and lose sight of your correct plan.

However, sometimes opportunity knocks and allows you to stop your opponent's play before it gets started. Care must be taken, though, to avoid falling into the trap of reacting to the other guy's plans and, as a result, failing to further your own. In the present case, Black is able to end White's kingside ideas permanently, so the time taken to do so is very well spent.

1...h5

Black realizes that if he can close up the kingside, he will have a free hand on the other side of the board. The point of ...h5 is that 2.h3 isn't possible due to 2...hxg4, when the pin on the h-file leads to material gain for Black. This means that White is left with either 2.gxh5, when 2...Rxh5 leaves White with many weaknesses on the kingside, or 2.g5, as seen in the actual game.

2.g5 g6

Making sure the kingside stays completely clogged up. Now Black's King has a safe haven on g7 and White's aspirations for a kingside attack are already a thing of the past. Black had an excellent game after **3.c3 a6 4.Be3 Bxe3 5.Qxe3 0-0**.

Yes, you should usually play on the side where your strength lies. But if you can take a few moves off and permanently stop your opponent's plans, then don't hesitate to do so.

Summary of Imbalances and Ideas
[diagram (184)]

➤ White has more space on the kingside and would eventually like to open lines on that side of the board by f4-f5.

➤ Because of the early advance of his kingside pawns, the White King doesn't have any safe place to run to.

➤ If Black can force White to advance his g-pawn, a subsequent ...g7-g6 would permanently lock up the kingside and end White's hopes in that area.

Problem 44

(185)

M.Adams-D.Bronstein, London 1989.
White to play.

White appears to stand better due to his pressure against d5, the possibility of a central advance by c2-c4, and the hole on e6. What's the best way to make use of these plusses? Does White actually have the better game?

Solution 44

This position is easy to assess incorrectly. Yes, White does indeed have pressure against d5 and e6—though saying a square is weakened and finding a way to actually take advantage of it are often two different things—and also retains possibilities of playing c2-c4. These things are so "obvious" that no less a player than Bronstein completely mishandled the Black side while Adams felt he had good chances for a slight plus here.

It's interesting to note that IM John Watson, who is very familiar with this type of French Defense pawn structure, took one glance and claimed an edge for Black! His opinion forces us to look at the good things in Black's camp (tactically and strategically). Then a different picture begins to emerge: the second player has pressure against d4, c2, and d3. In some lines, h2 can also come under fire. These facts allow Black to generate considerable counterplay. That game continued:

1.Nh5

This prepares to swing the Knight to f4 where it hits the targets on e6 and d5. 1...Bxh5 2.Bxh5 gives White the two Bishops and leaves Black weak on the light-squares. You see, White isn't trying for a knockout. He is quite happy to quietly add new advantages to his list. Since 1...Qd7 18.N5f4 Bf7 19.Bg4 f5 20.Bf3 leaves a new hole on e5 that a White Knight would love to dive into via Ne5, one could easily be led to believe that White is developing a nice initiative.

Though Adams wasn't completely sure that he had a real advantage here, he was quite high on this move, giving it an exclamation point. However, deeper invesitgation leaves me thinking that 1.Nh5 is actually an error, and that White should have played 1.c4!, making the "target" on c2 into a dynamic unit, when 1...Rc8 2.c5! bxc5 3.dxc5 might be a bit better for the first player since the b2-Bishop has suddenly sprung to life.

1...Nb4

Adams points out that 1...Bf7 2.N5f4 Re8 might have been best, though this seems a bit passive to me. Actually, it's not clear if

1...Nb4 is really so bad. Nevertheless, worth serious consideration is the active 1...Qc7 when White would have to think about equalizing: 2.g3 (2.h3!?) 2...Bxd3 3.Qxd3 g6 (3...Nb4!?) looks good for Black.

2.Nxb4 axb4

On 2...Bxb4, White retains a slight edge with 3.c3 Bd6 20.Ba3 Re8 21.g3 thanks to the weakness of d5.

3.Rxa8 Qxa8 4.Bc1

This logical move brings the Bishop back into play and hits the important f4-square. However, White would have done better with 4.g3! when lines like 4...Qa2 5.Re6! are quite reasonable for the first player.

In the actual game, Black now played 4...Qb8? and found himself in a bad situation after 5.Nf4 Bf7 (preferable was 5...Bxf4 6.Bxf4 Qxf4 7.Rxe7 when White is better, but not as much as in the actual game) 6.g3 Qb7 7.Ng2 Bg6 8.Bf4. White went on to win smoothly: 8...Qd7 9.Qe2 Re8 10.Bxd6 Qxd6 11.Qb5 Rc8 12.Nf4 Bf7 13.Bg4 Rxc2 14.Re6 Qd8 (14...Bxe6 15.Qe8 mate is hardly an improvement) 15.Rxb6 f5 16.Bd1 Rc1 17.Rb8 Nc8 (or 17...Rxd1+ 18.Kg2 Nc8 19.Qc6 winning—Adams) 18.Kg2 Be8 19.Qb7 Bf7 20.Bf3 Rc7 21.Qxb4, 1-0.

Much stronger, though, was **4...Qc6!** Not 4...Rc8? 5.Bf4 Bxc2 6.Qe2! when Black is in real trouble. After 4...Qc6, which hits c2 and defends d6, Black seems to be a bit better: **5.Bf4! Bxh5 6.Bxh5 Bxf4 7.Rxe7 Bxh2+ 8.Kh1 Bd6 9.Re6 g6 10.Bf3 Kg7 11.Qe1 Rc8** when White's pressure and the opposite colored Bishops give the first player good drawing chances.

Summary of Imbalances and Ideas
[diagram (185)]

➤ Black's d-pawn is an object of attack.

➤ The e6-square is a prime target for occupation, preferably by a White Knight.

➤ Black must constantly worry about the c2-c4 advance.

➤ White's g3-Knight isn't well placed and is not contributing anything towards the fight against d5 and e6. How can this problem be addressed?

➤ Don't forget Black's trumps! Pressure against d4, c2, d3, and h2 gives him excellent counterplay.

➤ Everything looks rosy when you only take one side's plusses into consideration. That's why it's so important to look at what's happening from both sides of the board.

Problem 45

(186)

Black to move.

Would 1...a5 be a reasonable choice for Black?

Solution 45

Normally Black would not play a move like ...a7-a5 because it leaves him with a backward pawn on b6. However, once we give in to reality—which is that Black will end up with a weak pawn anyway due to White's plan of a4-a5xb6—we find that Black's 1...a5 is actually quite logical since now White will be left with a weakness on a4.

For those that still have doubts about 1...a5, just do the math: If White gets to play a4-a5 followed by axb6, Black will have a weakness on b6 while White's potentially weak a-pawn will be gone. However, after 1...a5, White will have to nurse the weak a4-pawn for the rest of the game.

Summary of Imbalances and Ideas
[diagram (186)]

➤ White has a passed d-pawn, but it's not going anywhere at the moment.

➤ White's weak pawn on e3 is in constant need of supervision.

➤ White intends to play a4-a5 followed by axb6 when Black, after recapturing on b6 with his pawn, will be left with a backward b-pawn.

➤ White's a-pawn is isolated and potentially weak.

➤ White's passed pawn will prove worthless if he can't break the blockade on d6.

Problem 46

(187)

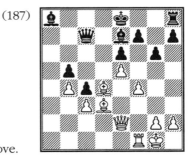

White to move.

White's Bishop is threatened and he only has three squares to choose from. What is his proper move and, more importantly, what's the proper evaluation?

Solution 46

This position, a possible variation from the game Anand-Bareev, Linares 1993, is strategically winning for White since **1.Be4 0-0 2.Ra1** leaves Black in a hopeless situation: his e7-Bishop, though technically good, is inactive. White's "bad" Bishop is very active, and allows White's Rook to penetrate to a7. White controls the only open file and, in time, will scoop up the Black pawn on b5.

Remember: when relating to Bishops, the terms "good" and "bad" don't really mean much. It's far more important to label them "active" or "inactive."

Summary of Imbalances and Ideas
[diagram (187)]

➤ White's Bishop is attacked and must move to safety.

➤ White enjoys more central space thanks to his e5-pawn which restricts the e7-Bishop.

➤ White has complete control over the highly important a-file. This allows him to penetrate to a7 with his Rook, or play Ra5, putting immediate pressure against b5.

➤ Black has no targets to aim at while White can entertain various nasty ideas down the open a-file.

Problem 47

(188)

Frasco-Goldberg, Santa Monica 1997.
White to move.

White obviously has a significant advantage due to Black's backward pawn on c7. What's the best way to proceed?

Solution 47

White's pressure down the c-file gives him a clear advantage, but that doesn't mean you can expect the game to win itself. In the actual contest, White played the most natural move on the board: 1.Rfc1, but after 1...Qd8! 2.Nc4 b6 Black was back in the game.

Correct would have been **1.b6!** when **1...Nxb6 2.Bxd6 Rd8 3.Bxc7** is very strong for White. The most interesting lines occur after **1.b6! c5**. Now **2.dxc6!** leads to fascinating complications, though also strong is the more restrained 2.Nc4 Qb8 3.Bb2 followed by Ra1. After **2.dxc6! Bxb3 3.cxb7 Qxb7! 4.Bxb7 Rxa3** we arrive at a position that, at first glance, seems rather dull. White would not dream of ending up in a position like this for the sake of a tactical lark. However, there is more here than immediately meets the eye since **5.Nxb3 Nxb6 6.Nd2! Na4 7.Nc4 Ra2 8.Bd5+!** (and not 8.Nxe5 Kh7!) **8...Kh7 9.Rfc1** leaves Black in serious difficulties.

Summary of Imbalances and Ideas
[diagram (188)]

➤ Black's c-pawn is sitting on a half-open file and is begging to be attacked.

➤ The c5-square is a nice home for the Black Knight. If he can play ...b7-b6 followed by ...Nc5, he can close off the c-file and get back in the game.

➤ The only thing defending d6 is the base of the pawn chain on c7. A well-timed b5-b6 blows up that base.

Problem 48

(189)

Larsen-Gligoric, Moscow 1956.
White to play.

Annotate the following moves:

1.a5 dxc4 2.Qxc4 Rf8 3.axb6 Qxb6 4.Nd6 Bb5 5.Nxb5 axb5 6.Qd5 Rxa1 7.Rxa1.

Solution 48

Black is regaining his piece and seems to be doing all right. However, Larsen finds a nice way to turn the tables in his favor. The refusal to give in to the opponent's ideas and the endless search for the initiative are key components in a great player's makeup.

1.a5!

This creates a nasty threat on b6. Since 1...b5 2.Nb6 and 1...bxa5 2.Nxa5 dxe4 3.Nxc6 Qxc6 4.Bd5 are both hopeless for the second player, Black is forced into a position where White enjoys a superior pawn structure and a more active minor piece.

1...dxc4 2.Qxc4

Attacking the f7-pawn.

2...Rf8?!

Avoiding 2...Bxe4 3.Qxe4 b5 4.Qf5 when the dual threat of Qxf7+ and Rd7 is scary, but perhaps not as bad as it seems: 4...Bd6 5.Bd5 Rab8 6.Qxf7+ Qxf7 7.Bxf7+ Kxf7 8.Rxd6 Rxc2 9.Rxa6 Rxb2 10.Rb6 Rc8 11.a6 Rcc2 12.a7 Ra2 with a draw. Of course, White's Bishop was better than Black's, and he shouldn't have been in such a hurry to cash in.

3.axb6 Qxb6 4.Nd6

Continuing to force Black's hand by swinging at f7.

4...Bb5 5.Nxb5 axb5 6.Qd5 Rxa1 7.Rxa1 and the pressure against f7, combined with the weakness of both b5 and e5, eventually led to a White victory.

Summary of Imbalances and Ideas
[diagram (189)]

➤ White is up a piece for a pawn, but Black has forked White's Knights and should be able to regain the lost material.

➤ If White can't retain the extra piece, he should look for a way to make positional gains, or to grab the initiative and place his opponent on the defensive. This is possible because Black is busy trying to get that piece back!

➤ Tender points in Black's camp are b6 and f7. White's efforts should address these two areas.

Problem 49

(190)

M.Adams-W.Watson,
British Championship 1990.
Black to move.

Let's consider three moves for Black: 1...Qc7, 1...0-0, and 1...a6. Two of these moves are perfectly reasonable, while one is a major error. Which one of these moves would you label with a question mark?

Solution 49

1...a6? is very poor, though it was played in the actual game, due to 2.Na4 since 2...b5 3.Bb6 picks up the Black Queen. In the game, Black answered 2.Na4 with 2...Qc7 when 3.Nb6 Rb8 4.Rac1 0-0 5.Rfd1 left White with a nice bind that he eventually turned into a win.

You have to be aware that every pawn move potentially weakens a square! So be careful and don't let your opponent's pieces leap into self-inflicted holes.

Summary of Imbalances and Ideas
[diagram (190)]

➤ White is a pawn up.

➤ White has a lead in development and two nice open /half-open files for his Rooks (the c-file and d-file).

➤ Black's position is very solid, though the d6-square is a bit loose. If he can trade some pieces and prevent White's forces from taking control of d6, then things should turn out well for the second player.

➤ Black should avoid ...a7-a6 because it creates a hole on b6 that White can immediately use.

Problem 50

(191)

White to move.

Black threatens to chop off White's Bishop on e5. How would you deal with this obvious but bothersome fact?

Solution 50

Structurally White has a problem on the c-file, since he has a backward pawn there. Black also has a backward pawn on e6, but he is trying to get rid of White's e5-Bishop so a later ...e6-e5 will give him a strong center.

You should also have noticed that Black's King is still in the center, so this, combined with White's long-term problems on c3, forces him to seek dynamic play. In general, you will either have to choose between quick play based on dynamics, or slow play based on statics.

Since 1.f4 is impossible due to the pin along the g1-a7 diagonal, and since a Queen exchange after 1.Qd4 fails to offer White anything because White's pawns on d4 and b4 will come under pressure after 1...Qxd4 2.cxd4 Ne7, the first player is forced to find something with a touch of imagination.

Bishop retreats are all lame: 1.Bf4 and 1.Bg3 are both comfortably met by 1...Ne7, while 1.Bd4 Bxd4 2.Qxd4 Qxd4 3.cxd4 Rc8 4.Na3 Ne7 also gives Black his share of targets to strike at.

At this point some players might throw their hands up in despair, but it turns out that White has two interesting possibilities. The first is **1.Bd3**, freeing the d1-h5 diagonal and indirectly defending the attacked Bishop. Now **1...Bxe5 2.Qh5+ Ke7 3.Qxe5 Nf6** leads to an unexplored position with chances for both sides.

White's other move is even harder to spot: **1.Qe1!?** (first played by D.Otero). After **1...Bxe5 2.Bh5+ Ke7 3.Qxe5 Nf6** White does best to play **4.Qg5** with chances to take advantage of Black's central King.

Summary of Imbalances and Ideas
[diagram (191)]

➤ When faced with difficult problems, you can't afford to play a lazy response. If you want success, you must look deeply into the position's possibilities.

➤ White is structurally worse, but Black's uncastled King gives him good dynamic chances. This means that White is forced to play with imagination and verve.

➤ Always understand whether the plusses in your position are based on static or dynamic considerations. This will give you a solid clue as to what kind of move you're expected to find.

Problem 51

(192)

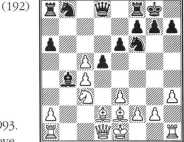

Oll-Anand, Biel Interzonal 1993.
Black to move.

What's happening and how should Black continue?

Solution 51

The weak White c-pawns ensure that Black will, at the very least, regain his lost pawn. However, White's uncastled King is quite another matter. The slightest hesitation will give White time to bring his King to safety, so Black tries to keep his opponent off balance by sharpening the play.

1...d4!

This allows Black's Queen to come strongly into play. Also, castling is still out of the question for White.

2.exd4

Forced. 2.Na4 Qa5 favors Black according to Anand, while 2.Ne4? Nxe4 3.Bxb4 dxe3 is losing for White.

2...Qxd4 3.Qc2

3.Rc1 Rd8 stops White from castling.

3...Nc6

Black gets his final piece into play. True, White is now able to castle, but the active Black pieces are still able to run roughshod over the enemy position.

4.0-0 Qe5

This fine move frees the d4-square for the Knight, and also eyes the Bishop on e2.

5.Qa4

Anand, in his excellent games collection (*My Best Games of Chess*. Published by Gambit), mentions 5.Rfe1 Rad8 6.Bf3 Nd4! 7.Rxe5 Nxc2 8.Rd1 Rxd2 9.Rxd2 Bxc3 and Black wins.

5...Rad8 6.Be1 Nd4 7.Qxb4 Nxe2+ 8.Nxe2 Qxa1 and Black won in a few more moves.

Summary of Imbalances and Ideas
[diagram (192)]

➤ Black is a pawn down but both the White c-pawns are very weak.

➤ White's King is not castled, so Black would like to begin active operations before the White monarch reaches a safe location. In general, an uncastled King sends a flare up that begs the enemy to attack with all the energy he possesses.

Problem 52

(193)

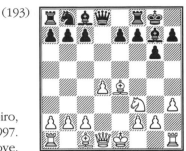

Diana Durham-J.Shapiro,
Los Angeles 1997.
Black to move.

Black played 1...c6. Is this a good move? If not, what would you recommend?

Solution 52

The passive 1...c6? is more or less a useless move (what purpose does it serve?). Black should have taken advantage of the fact that White's King is still in the center with **1...c5!** when 2.dxc5 Qa5+ is fine for Black, and 2.d5 f5 3.Bd3 Qxd5 picks up an important pawn.

By starting a fight and challenging White's spatial plus in the center, Black assures himself of good play. A pointless move like 1...c6, however, gives White a free hand to do anything he wishes, and allows White to retain his advantage in territory.

Summary of Imbalances and Ideas
[diagram (193)]

➤ White has more space in the center.

➤ White's King isn't castled yet, while Black's is tucked safely away.

➤ Since White's isn't castled, Black should begin a fight right away! This fight should revolve around the center, with Black challenging White's domination in that sector.

Problem 53

(194)

Kindermann-M.Adams,
Novi Sad Olympiad 1990.
Black to move.

What do you think of 1...f4 in this position?

Solution 53

Black did indeed play **1...f4**. Adams' comment concerning this move (from *Chess in the Fast Lane* by Bill and Michael Adams. Published by Cadogan) is highly instructive: "By placing all his pawns on dark squares, Black severely restricts White's Bishop. Indeed, it is hard to even develop it. The problem with this is that the Knight settles on e4. It is less useful than it might appear there, partly since too few other pieces co-operate with it and partly because although it is impregnable, it is also short of strong posts to head for."

2.Ne4 Nb3 3.Rb1 Kg7!

The alternatives would allow White to mount an attack by means of h3-h4. Now ...Qg6 is possible, when any attacking attempt by White is easily repelled.

4.h4 Qg6 5.Qe2 Rac8 6.hxg5 hxg5 7.Rd1

This makes things easy for Black. White had to try 7.Qg4.

7...Rcd8!

Now 8.Rxd8 Rxd8 9.Qxc4 Rd1+ is the end of all things for White, so he decides to develop his Bishop. Unfortunately, this allows Black to create an iron vise on the d-file.

8.Bd2 Rd3 9.Be1 Red8 10.f3 g4 11.Kf1

White loses a piece after 11.fxg4 Rxd1 12.Rxd1 Rxd1 13.Qxd1 Qxe4, though he could have still played for a while. Now, after 11.Kf1, things get ugly.

11...g3, 0-1. The threat of ...Qg6-h5-h1 (or h2) is winning for Black.

Summary of Imbalances and Ideas
[diagram (194)]

➤ Black had more space on the kingside, in the center, and on the queenside!

➤ Normally a player would avoid a move like ...f5-f4 since it creates a hole on e4. However, a Knight on e4 can't do much by itself, and the rest of White's pieces are entombed in his own camp.

➤ Once Black locks in the enemy Bishop, he takes a moment out to ensure the safety of his King. This is always a good idea: when winning a game, never forget to make sure that your King is impervious to harm. This avoids unpleasant surprises.

Problem 54

The position we're interested in occurred after:

1.e4 e5 2.Nf3 Nc6 3.Bb5 Nge7 4.c3 a6 5.Ba4 d6 6.d4 Bd7 7.h4!? h6 8.h5 exd4 9.Nxd4 Nxd4 10.cxd4 d5 11.e5 Bxa4 12.Qxa4+ Nc6 13.Be3 Qd7 14.Nc3 Bb4 15.Qc2 0-0 16.0-0-0 Bxc3 17.Qxc3 f6 18.f4. What would you play for Black at this point?

(195)

Quinteros-Larsen, Manila 1973
Black to move.

Solution 54

18...a5!

Now ...Nb4 is in the air and this, mixed with ...Qf5, could prove very bothersome for White. By getting White to react on the queenside, Black doesn't have to worry about White creating threats on the other side of the board.

The ability to dictate the play is known as the "initiative."

19.a3

Keeping the Knight out of b4 but letting Black take control of the light squares on b3 and c4. This ultimately leads to an almost winning minor piece advantage for Black.

19...a4

Now both b3 and c4 can be used as homes for the Black Knight.

20.Kb1 Na5 21.Qd3 Nc4 Jumping to the sixth rank with ...Nb3 looks tempting, but the Knight on c4 hits targets on a3, b2, e5 and e3 and is therefore stronger. Black eventually used this Knight and a queenside pawn advance via ...b7-b5-b4 to create a decisive attack on the White King.

In this game Black forced White to dance to his tune and never had to face counterplay on the opposite wing. It's also important to note that Black wasn't just playing for mate. He mixed queenside attacking ideas with the important positional concept of creating a superior minor piece. Such an advantageous piece can be used as an attacker in the middlegame or as an eater of pawns in the endgame.

Summary of Imbalances and Ideas
[diagram (195)]

➤ White has a spatial plus in the center and on the kingside.

➤ Black needs to get something going in the one area that White doesn't control: the queenside.

➤ Did you notice the Bishop versus Knight imbalance? If you did, you should have tried to figure out a way to make your Knight permanently superior to White's Bishop.

Problem 55

(196)

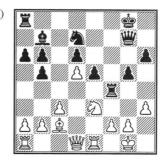

Anand-Kamsky, Las Palmas Match 1995.
White to play.

White played 1.a4. Does this make any sense, and if it doesn't, what would you suggest?

Solution 55

Anand's **1.a4!!** is actually a very deep move. The idea is to force an exchange of one pair of Rooks after 1...bxa4 2.Rxa4. This, in turn, will give White permanent control over the f5-square. The idea of using his a1-Rook in the fight for f5 is striking. By trading the a1-Rook, which isn't doing anything to enhance White's control over f5, for the f4-Rook, which is defending that square, White, in effect, allows the a1-Rook to enter the fight against f5. This shows why the Indian Grandmaster has been the World's number two for several years now.

Anand points out that neither 1.Bf5 Rf8 2.Be6+ Kh8 nor 1.g3 Rf6 2.Bf5 Raf8 gives White much.

After 1.a4, the game continued:

1...Raf8

Avoiding 1...bxa4 (1...b4 2.g3 Rff8 3.cxb4 leaves White with an extra pawn) 2.Rxa4 Rxa4 (or 2...Raf8 3.Rxf4 Rxf4 4.Bf5! and Black has no defense against g2-g3) 3.Bxa4 b5 4.Bc2 Nf6 5.b3 when White has control of f5 and can continue with c3-c4 shoring up the d5-pawn.

2.axb5 a5 3.Rf1 Bc8 4.g3 and though the game remains complicated, White's advantage isn't in doubt. Anand eventually scored the full point.

Summary of Imbalances and Ideas
[diagram (196)]

➤ Black has a little pressure against d5 and is trying to create some sort of kingside attack thanks to his control of the half-open f-file.

➤ White's Rook on a1 isn't an active participant in the game. This needs to be addressed.

➤ White's Bishop is far more active than Black's.

➤ Black has a hole on f5. White's play should revolve around increasing his control over this important square.

Problem 56

(197)

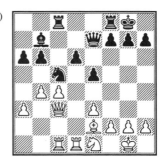

Karpov-Parma, Caracas 1970.
Black to move.

In Problem 85 I discuss the technique of asking, "What wonderful thing does this move do for my position?" before playing any individual move. Annotate the following moves and explain what wonderful things both sides' choices do for their cause. 1...Ne6 2.Qd3 Rfd8 3.Bf3 Bxf3 4.Nxf3 g6 5.Nd2 Nc7 6.Ne4.

Solution 56

1...Ne6?

Returning to our question of "What wonderful thing does this move do for my position?" we can see that Black has failed to live up to expectations. The Knight move is passive, places the horse on a square without a future (it can't jump to d4, f4 or c5) and lets White trade Bishops on the f3-b7 diagonal. Better was the natural 1...Ne4. This move gains time by attacking the White Queen, keeps the Knight active and blocks the b7-f3 diagonal, thus preventing a Bishop exchange and the subsequent weakening of d5.

2.Qd3

In contrast to Black's last retreat, White's move is easy to understand: he gets his Queen off the dangerous c-file, takes aim at d6 and eyes the light squares d5 and e4. That's a lot of good stuff with no negative baggage.

2...Rfd8 3.Bf3

This trades off Black's active Bishop and clamps down on the weakened d5-square by getting rid of one of Black's main d5 defenders.

3...Bxf3 4.Nxf3 g6 5.Nd2

Though White's Knight looked all right on f3, it really wasn't doing anything there. The f3-square was just the first stage of a long journey to nirvana. White now prepares to bring his Knight to d5 via e4-c3 or b1-c3.

5...Nc7

Trying to keep a grip on d5.

6.Ne4

Places the Knight on a strong central post and attacks d6. White sees that 6...d5? loses material after 7.cxd5 Rxd5 (7...Nxd5 8.Rxc8 picks up a piece) 8.Qxd5! Nxd5 9.Rxc8+ Kg7 10.Rxd5 when Black can resign.

Notice how we had something good to say about every White move? Every time he touched a piece his position improved in some way. After 6.Ne4 White's advantage is clear and he went on to win a long game.

Summary of Imbalances and Ideas
[diagram (197)]

➤ Black has a backward pawn on d6.

➤ White's pawn on c4 can easily turn into an object of attack.

➤ Black's Bishop on b7 is superior to its White counterpart.

➤ White enjoys more space on the queenside.

➤ White would love to exchange Bishops for two reasons. First, Black's is the more active piece. Second, the Black Bishop is the d5-square's main defender; once the Bishops are swapped off, the d5-square will most likely turn into a home for a White piece.

Problem 57

(198)

Anand-Inkiov, Calcutta 1986.
White to move.

While there's no doubt that White has the better game, turning this into something concrete is quite another matter. If you had to choose between 1.c3, 1.Nec5, 1.Nbc5, 1.Nxf6+, 1.Bxf6, or 1.c4, what would you pick?

Solution 57

In a way, I think this solution will come easier to a weaker player than to an expert or master. Why? Because, from a purely static viewpoint, the correct idea doesn't make positional sense.

The most important thing to realize is that White has a significant lead in development. If he wants to make use of it, he has to play very actively and bring the battle to his opponent immediately.

1.c3 looks nice, but it doesn't increase the pressure and thus allows Black to complete his development by 1...Bd7. Both 1.Nec5 and 1.Nbc5 get nowhere fast after 1...b6. 1.Nxf6+ Nxf6 2.Rxd8+ Bxd8 3.Rd1 Be7 still favors White—his pieces are far more active than Black's—but not nearly as much as in the actual game. 1.Bxf6 also makes Black happy since exchanges tend to make the side with less space easier to handle.

1.c4!

This move creates a gaping hole on b4, something that stronger players try very hard to avoid. However, in this case White's advantage was based on his lead in development, and the only way to make use of it was to chase the d5-Knight away and open up the d-file.

At times one must give something up (the b4-square) in order to achieve a more important goal.

1...Nc7

Anand points out that 1...Nb4 2.Rxd8+ Bxd8 3.Rd1 Be7 4.Nd6 e5 (4...b6 5.Be3 wins a pawn) 5.Nxc8 Rxc8 6.Nxa5 leads to the win of a pawn.

2.Rxd8+ Bxd8 3.Rd1 Be7 and now, according to Anand, **4.Nd6** would have given White a clear advantage simply because his pieces are far more active than their Black counterparts. One line goes 4...b6 5.Bc6! Rb8 6.Bf4 and it's hard for Black to find a reasonable move.

Summary of Imbalances and Ideas
[diagram (198)]

➤ White has a significant lead in development.

➤ A lead in development calls for fast, forceful play.

➤ White can't get into the Black position if the enemy Knight remains on d5, blocking the d-file.

Problem 58

In the game Kurosaki (2147)-Saidy, California 1999, after 1.c4 e5 2.g3 Nf6 3.Bg2 c6 4.d4 exd4 5.Qxd4 d5 6.cxd5 cxd5 7.Nf3 Nc6 8.Qa4 Bc5 9.0-0 h6 10.Ne5 Qb6 11.Nc3 0-0 12.Nd3 d4 13.Nxc5 Qxc5 14.Qb5 Qe7 15.Nd5 Nxd5 16.Bxd5 a6 17.Qc4 Nb4, we come to an important position.

(199)

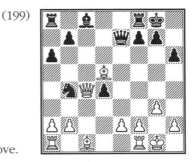

White to move.

Would you choose 18.Bf3, 18.Qxd4, 18.Rd1, 18.Re1, or 18.e3 here?

Solution 58

White has been outplayed and, in the game, he didn't last very long: 18.Re1? Bf5 19.e4 Rac8 20.Qb3 Nc2 21.Bd2 Be6 22.Rac1 Nxe1 and the first player resigned on the 30th move.

Obviously, 18.Qxd4?? fails to the simple 18...Nc2, while 18.e3 gives Black such tasty possibilities as 18...Bf5 and 18...Nxd5 19.Qxd5 Rd8 followed by ...d4-d3.

Finally, 18.Rd1 leaves White weak on the light-squares after 18...Nxd5. Nevertheless, 18.Rd1 is one of White's best tries: 18...Nxd5 19.Qxd5 Qxe2 20.Qxd4 Bh3 21.Qd3 (not 21.Be3?? Rad8 22.Qxd8 Rxd8 23.Rxd8+ Kh7 and White is going to suffer light square death) 21...Qh5 22.Bf4 Rad8 23.Qxd8 Rxd8 24.Rxd8+ Kh7 25.Rd3 Qe2 26.Re3 Qxb2 and Black has all the chances.

Though I wasn't aware of this game, I ended up in the same position (after 17...Nb4) in a blitz game versus the same IM Tony Saidy. I knew I was in trouble when he chuckled after every move, and he became more and more excited as we got closer and closer to the 17...Nb4 situation. "You're lost!" he proclaimed, after slamming down his Knight on the b4-square. Then he added, "We finally have proof that you play just like a 2100 player!"

I had to admit that I wasn't too happy with my game, but as

my remaining minutes ticked away I suddenly saw an interesting way to put up a tough resistance:

18.Bf3!?

Saving the Bishop and giving the e2-pawn some much-needed support. Only give yourself credit for finding this move if you also foresaw the upcoming sacrifice of a Rook.

18...Be6 19.Qxd4 Nc2 20.Qe4!

An important move, pinning Black's Bishop and putting pressure on b7. White will sacrifice the Exchange for a pawn, two Bishops, and a solid position.

20...Nxa1 21.Be3!

In the game I played 21.Bd2, and after 21...Qd7 22.Bc3! Bf5 23.Qe5! f6 24.Qd5+ Qxd5 25.Bxd5+ Kh8 26.Rxa1 I was doing extremely well. Unfortunately, 21...f5! 22.Qb1 Nb3 would have refuted my play.

21...f5 22.Qa4! b5 23.Qd1 Rac8 24.Qxa1 and the White position isn't easy to break down.

In this game White keeps himself in the game by not giving up—it's very easy to shrug your shoulders and admit that your game is bad and you're doomed—and by putting activity ahead of normal material considerations. In the end his active pieces and solid structure, a nice mix of dynamic and static factors, gives him positional compensation for the minor material deficit. Being material down doesn't always mean that you have to attack!

Summary of Imbalances and Ideas
[diagram (199)]

➤ Black threatens to leave White very weak on the light-squares by ...Nxd5

➤ Black's pieces are more active than White's.

➤ White must watch out for forks based on ...Nc2.

➤ White's e2-pawn is under the gun and can easily fall if White allows his Queen to get pulled away from its defense.

➤ White has two Bishops and would like to retain them.

Problem 59

(200)

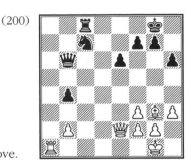

White to move.

This position doesn't appear to be very exciting. Will it be a draw, or does White have a way to generate some play?

Solution 59

GM Larry Christiansen once told me the difference between IMs and GMs wasn't opening knowledge or strategic understanding, it was tactics. He insisted that GMs simply saw more than other players.

Though interesting, this is hardly a revelation. It has always been apparent that masters see more than experts, experts see more than class "A's (1800-1999)," and down the list we go—one fish always being bigger and meaner than the fish below it.

Sadly, it is all too easy to state the importance of tactics, and it is all too difficult to actually improve in this area. Books like *Winning Chess Tactics* by Seirawan, *Chess Tactics For Advanced Players* by Averbach, *The Art of Attack in Chess* by Vukovic and *Think Like a Grandmaster* by Kotov can be very helpful.

As nice as all these products may be, most players simply don't have the time for intense study (what good is a book if you never look at it?). Isn't there a simple rule or point of reference that would allow the amateur to increase his tactical awareness? Actually, there is! Almost all combinations are made possible by an undefended or inadequately guarded piece. This means that whenever you see a piece that is "loose," perk up and look for a trick to take advantage of it.

How can we use this information in regard to the diagramed position? Let's take a look: If Black can get his Knight to the dominating d5-square, he'll stand very well. White can bail out and make a draw with the spineless 1.Bxc7, but the undefended state of the c8-Rook (see how that key tactical device jumps at you!) allows White to virtually force a win with **1.Rc1!**, creating a devastating pin on the c-file. The Knight can't move due to Rxc8 and the Rook can't move since that would hang the Knight. After **1...Qb7** Giving some support to c8 and once again threatening ...Nd5. **2.Qc4** the Knight is threatened a third time and is frozen into place due to the enhanced pressure on the c-file. White wins a piece and the game.

Summary of Imbalances and Ideas
[diagram (200)]

➤ Black would be fine if his Rook were defended.

➤ It's crucial that you recognize the importance of undefended pieces.

➤ White wins a piece by pinning the c7-Knight along the c-file.

Problem 60

(201)

Gligoric-Smyslov,
Yugoslavia vs. USSR 1959.
Black to move.

This position is filled with imbalances. How would you rate Black's chances? What should he do?

Solution 60

If we were to make a traditional judgment based on factors like passed pawns (White has connected passed pawns on d4 and e5) and pawn islands (Black has three islands to White's two), then we would have to say that White stands better. However, the opposite is actually the case. Black is the one who is in charge here!

How did I reach such a conclusion? That's simple: it's not what you have, it's what the things you have are doing.

In the present case, White's connected passed pawns are firmly blocked. In fact, the pawns on d4 and e5 have handed the d5-square to Black's Knight where it attacks the White pawns on c3 and f4, and the Black Bishop on a8 is eating through the wide-open a8-h1 diagonal.

Compare these active Black pieces to White's: The c1-Bishop is blocked by the f4-pawn. The c2-Bishop is blocked by Black's pawn on f5. The White Knight is blocked by its pawns on c3, d4 and f4.

At the moment, Black's pawn on a5 is threatened and there-fore must be defended. He must also find some way to increase the pressure against the targets on c3 and/or f4. In this light, Black's first move makes a good deal of sense:

1...Rb3!

This Exchange sacrifice, a purely positional sacrifice designed to highlight the flaws in White's game, defends a5 with the Queen and creates an immediate attack against c3.

2.Bxb3 cxb3

What has Black gained from his sacrifice? He has strong pres-sure against c3, the scope of his Queen has been enhanced with the opening of the c-file, and his c4-pawn has turned into a pow-erful passed pawn on b3.

3.Ra4 Bf8!?

Seemingly hasty is 3...Nxc3 4.Nxc3 Qxc3 since White can exchange his weak c3-pawn for Black's potentially powerful passed pawn on a5 (it also trades the magnificent Knight on d5 for the dead beast on e2) by 5.Bd2. However, this turns out to be very favorable for Black after 5...Qd3! 6.Bxa5 Rc8 7.Bd2 b2 8.Rb4 Rc2 9.Rb8+ Bf8 10.Rd1 Bf3 11.e6 Kg7.

Of course, White can improve with 4.Ra3! when Black has all the chances, but White might be able to hold the balance. Nevertheless, 3...Nxc3 turns out to be a serious alternative to Black's 3...Bf8.

4.Bb2!?

Defending c3 and stopping Black's b-pawn in its tracks. White would love to successfully play c3-c4, but both players thought that 4.c4 failed to 4...Nb6 5.Rxa5 Nxc4. This is far from clear, though, since 6.Rb5 is not easy to crack. Also note that 4.c4 Nb4 is met by 5.d5! Qxc4 6.d6 with a complete mess.

4...Ne3!

This leads to a rush of tactics after 5.Qxe3 Qc6 6.d5 Qxa4 7.e6 when 7...Bxd5 is met by 8.c4! with chances on the b2-h8 diagonal. One gets the impression that Black must be winning somewhere, but White should probably have gone for the gusto and given this a try.

5.Rfa1 Nc4

The real point of 4...Ne3: Black defends a5 and starts to chip away at the blockade on b2. When you have a passed pawn, do everything you can to destroy the enemy pieces that block it.

6.Ng3 Be7 7.Nf1?

White had to try 7.Qe2 Bd5 8.Nf1, preventing Black from setting up a Queen-first battery on the a8-h1 diagonal with ...Qc6.

7...Qc6 8.Rxc4 Qh1+! 9.Kg3 h5!

Now we see the point of ...Be7. Mate by 10...h4 is threatened, 10.h4 Bxh4 is still mate, and 10.Qh2 is done in by 10...Qf3 mate. White wisely resigned.

Summary of Imbalances and Ideas
[diagram (201)]

➤ White has two connected passed pawns on d4 and e5. However, they are firmly blocked.

> ➤ Black's Knight rules the board from its comfortable perch on d5.

> ➤ Black has a passed a-pawn.

> ➤ The White pawn on c3 is a target.

> ➤ White will constantly have to watch out for mating threats along the a8-h1 diagonal.

Problem 61

(202)

Joseph (1699)-Rice (1946),
Los Angeles 1999.
White to move.

White has just blundered and is now a pawn down with little, if anything, to show for it. Should he just throw his arms in the air and give up, should he slap his opponent's face and demand that a draw be agreed upon, should he kick the pieces across the room to show his displeasure (I've seen grandmasters use this trick on more than one occasion!), or is there a way to put up real (legal) resistance?

Solution 61

Personally I'd do something to scare my opponent (why not make use of my sumo-like size?) and then demand that a draw be agreed upon (after carefully noting that the director was nowhere in sight!); but for those with morals I suppose that an actual move is called for.

We all blunder, and after doing so it's important to get up from the board, time permitting, and clear your head—nothing good can happen if you're still in the midst of an emotional backlash. Forget about the earlier, happier, position and treat this new situation as a challenge. Hunker down, get tough, and insist on finding a way to put up a long, grueling resistance!

In the actual game White decided to retain his two Bishops by 1.Bd2, not appreciating that Black's Knight is stronger than either White Bishop! The finish isn't a happy memory for Mr. Joseph: 1...Bf6 2.Rad1 Rfe8 3.Be3 Bxb2 4.Bxa7 Nc3! 5.Bb6 Nxd1 6.Rxd1 Qxd1+ 7.Bxd1 Re1 mate.

After the game, Mr. Rice recommended 1.Bxe7 Nxe7 2.Qe3, hitting both e7 and a7. Unfortunately, 2...Qd3! leaves White a pawn down for absolutely nothing.

What I found interesting about this position is that neither player paid attention to the possibility of creating a Bishop of opposite color scenario by **1.Bxd5! Bxg5 2.Ba2**. Why is this important? Bishops of opposite colors often give the defending side serious drawing chances because you can defend squares that the enemy Bishop can't attack, and attack squares/pawns that the enemy Bishop can't defend. Suddenly, White isn't necessarily losing in both the middlegame and the endgame. Now he can trade the Queens and Rooks (the more trades the better, since this cuts down on Black's attacking potential) in the hope of reaching various pawn-down drawn positions.

Take the following position as an example:

(203)

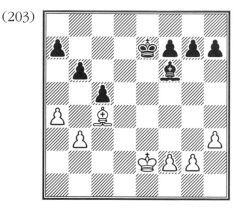

Though White is a solid pawn down, the position is a dead draw. White's Bishop is stopping Black's majority in its tracks, and the White Bishop is also eyeing Black's pawns on the kingside.

From now on, when all seems grim and Ghostbusters won't get the job done, try to create an opposite-colored Bishop situation and then hold on for dear life!

Summary of Imbalances and Ideas
[diagram (202)]

➤ White is a pawn down for nothing.

➤ When things are going against you, don't let depression turn your mind to slush.

➤ Black's Knight on d5 is better than either White Bishop. It really has to be removed from the board!

➤ By Bxd5, White can create a Bishops of opposite color situation. This gives White real chances to hold the position, or, at the very least, of putting up stiff resistance.

Problem 62

(204)

Karpov-Anand, Brussels Candidates
Match 1991.
Black to move.

Black has achieved a comfortable position and now must find a plan. In the actual game, Black played the very odd 1...Rdc8. What is the point of this move and is it any good? If the Rook move isn't correct, what would you prefer?

Solution 62

1...Rdc8!

Yes, this looks strange, but it also makes good sense. Moving the other Rook would allow Bxa7, so Black decided to place the d8-Rook on c8 and make an immediate threat against e4 via ...Bxe4. By pinning the c3-Knight to its Queen, Black forces White to move his Queen back. Then ...Bb4 will hit the c3-Knight directly and once again create a threat against e4. Soon all the

White pieces will be pushed backward to passive squares and Black will generate a nice initiative.

2.Qb1 Bb4

Continuing to weave dark designs against e4.

3.Bd2 Rd8 4.a3 Bc5

White has managed to defend e4, but Black's Bishop has now taken control of the important a7-f2 diagonal while White's dark-squared Bishop has ended up on the poor d2-square.

5.Na4

The Knight isn't happy on a4, but at least he manages to chase the Bishop away from its threatening perch on c5.

5...Bd6 and now after **6.Nc3? Qc7** Black had the more active position and eventually converted this into a win. Note that 6.e5 was White's best chance, though 6...Bxf3 7.exd6 Qxd6 8.gxf3 Nh4 would have given Black excellent compensation for the sacrificed piece.

Summary of Imbalances and Ideas
[diagram (204)]

➤ White's position looks nice at first glance, but a slightly deeper look shows us that he doesn't have an object of attack to train his sights on.

➤ Black is able to create pressure against the White pawn on e4.

➤ Black's pawn on e6 kills the b3-Bishop and stops the c3-Knight in its tracks. This means that the second player has no intention of pushing this pawn to e5!

➤ Black's d6-Bishop and g6-Knight combine to control the e5 and f4-squares.

➤ Black would like to find a continuation that places pressure on the one attackable point in the White camp: e4.

Problem 63

(205)

Goldberg-Royal, Los Angeles 1996.
White to move.

Consider the following possibilities: 1.Nxc6, 1.Nxg4, 1.f4, 1.Bb5, 1.Qa4, 1.h3.

Which one of these moves is best?

Solution 63

The straightforward 1.Bb5 is adequately answered by 1...Rc8, when 2.Qa4 cxd4 3.exd4 Qb6 is okay for Black.

The silly 1.h3 is nothing more than an obvious and useless one-move attack against g4. After 1...Bh5 or 1...Bf5, White has forced the Bishop to move to a safer square.

In the actual game, White played 1.Nxc6?, a bad move that helps Black strengthen his central position by bringing the side pawn on b7 to the more central c6-square (the c-pawns aren't really doubled since Black can play ...cxd4 at the right time and end the illusion).

The two moves that deserve real attention are 1.Nxg4 and 1.Qa4. The calm, positional choice is **1.Nxg4**, which gives White the two Bishops. After **1...Nxg4 2.Be2 Nf6** (2...Nxh2 3.g3 traps the greedy Knight) **3.0-0** White will play to open up the position with a later e3-e4. If he succeeds in this, his Bishops will prove superior to the enemy Knights.

However, White also should be tempted by the tactical **1.Qa4**. Now 1...Bd6 actually loses at once to 2.Nxg4 Nxg4 3.dxc5 with a double attack against g4, via the Queen, and d6.

After 1.Qa4, attempts to get the g4-Bishop to a safer port by 1...Bf5 prove too slow: 2.Bb5 Rc8 3.Qxa7 (a common tactical device) and White has won a pawn.

That leaves 1.Qa4 cxd4. The idea is that 2.exd4 lets Black play 2...Bd6 again, since now there are no discovered attacks via dxc5. If White wants to get something, he's forced to explore the complications that arise after 2.Bb5: 2...dxe3 (White is better after 2...Qxe5 3.Bxc6+) 3.Nxc6 exd2+ 4.Bxd2 and White has a dangerous initiative for the sacrificed pawn: 4...a6 5.Ne5+ Ke7 6.Bf4 Qc5 7.Bd3 Bh5 8.Qb3 Qc8 9.0-0 Bg6 10.Bxg6 hxg6 11.c4, trying to reach that juicy, centralized King by cracking open the center. Black's King would then be in a very uncomfortable position.

Does this mean that 1.Qa4 favors White in all lines? No, Black can squirm out of immediate trouble by **1...cxd4 2.Bb5 Rc8 3.exd4 Qb6** (not 3...Bd6 4.Nxg4 Nxg4 5.h3 Nf6 6.Qxa7) when new problems arise from **4.Nb3** (heading to a5 where the attack against c6 can be intensified). This new try can be met by **4...a6 5.Bxc6+ bxc6 6.Na5 Qb5**.

So what should White play on the first move? 1.Qa4 or 1.Nxg4? Personally, I would prefer the long-lasting positional plusses of 1.Nxg4 *if* I convinced myself that Black could survive, positionally intact, after 1.Qa4.

Summary of Imbalances and Ideas
[diagram (205)]

➤ Black is threatening to chop the Knight on e5.

➤ Black's g4-Bishop can be taken, or it can be used as a tactical weakness via Qa4, pinning the c6-Knight and creating potential discovered attacks against g4 by a well-timed dxc5.

➤ White should create either a long-term positional imbalance (two Bishops by Nxg4), or try and make use of the tactical elements inherent in this position, i.e., the pin along the a4-e8 diagonal by Qa4 or Bb5, and the loose state of the g4-Bishop.

➤ Since Black threatens ...Nxe5, White has to take a stand right now.

Problem 64

(206)

Kasparov-L.Portisch, OHRA 1986.
White to move.

A common position has been reached. White usually tries to place pressure against the "hanging pawns" on c5 and d5. Black relies on his extra space (which those "weak" pawns supply) and his active pieces to turn the game in his favor. Kasparov wanted to make use of the f5-square via 1.Nh4 with the intention of Nf5. Unfortunately, 1...g5 picks up material. Since this doesn't work, White hatches an original idea designed to take away key queenside squares from the Black forces. Do you see what Kasparov found?

Solution 64

1.a4!!

This completely blew Portisch's mind! His comments (made live to an audience during actual play) in the tournament book show how shocked he was: "What move is this? He's just weakening his queenside. Is that really so? Oh no, he's starting to push the pawn to a5 where it will take away the important b6-square from my Knight."

So Black figured out the first point of a2-a4: if the pawn can get to a5 it will severely restrict the movements of the Black Queen and make b6 inaccessible to the d7-Knight.

Naturally, Portisch wanted to stop this from happening. Seeing that 1...a5 would hand the b5-square to White on a platter, he decided to give his Queen the job of pawn-stopper. Unfortunately, he missed the second point of 1.a4: if the Queen moves to a5 it will leave the e7-Bishop unprotected. This little tactical fact turns the previously unplayable Nh4 into a very powerful shot.

1...Qa5 2.Nh4!

Now 2...g5?? 3.Nf5 threatens Nxe7+.

2...Rfd8 3.Nf5 Bf8 4.Nb5

Hammering away at the hole on d6. White isn't giving his opponent a moment's rest.

4...Ne8 5.Bd6

Threatening to win the Exchange with 5.Ne7+ Bxe7 6.Bxe7.

5...Nxd6 6.Nfxd6 Rb8 7.Nxb7

Not only winning a pawn, but also letting Black know that driving the Knight away with ...a7-a6 will leave the a6-pawn in need of a constant defender after the b5-Knight retreats.

7...Rxb7 8.Rxd5 Rdb8 9.Qd2!

Forcing the trade of Queens and leaving Black with a thoroughly miserable endgame to defend.

9...Qxd2 10.Rxd2 and White went on to win.

Summary of Imbalances and Ideas
[diagram (206)]

➤ Black's pawns on c5 and d5 are known as "hanging pawns."

➤ Hanging pawns gain space and possess a lot of dynamic potential. White must constantly be on guard for moves like ...c5-c4 or ...d5-d4.

➤ White's usual recipe in combating hanging pawns is to place the Rooks opposite them on c1 and d1 and then attack them with pieces. For example, Ne5 followed by Bf3, increasing the pressure against d5, is an option.

Problem 65

(207)

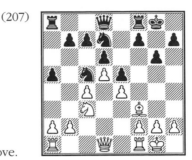

White to move.

Is 1.a3 a good move?

Solution 65

No, 1.a3? a4! stops b2-b4 forever and guarantees that the c5-square will remain in Black's hands. This is a disaster for White since his play should come on the queenside. A successful b2-b4 advance, pushing the Knight back and gaining queenside space, is a virtual must for the first player. Due to this, White's correct first move is **1.b3**, and only then 2.a3 and 3.b4.

Summary of Imbalances and Ideas
[diagram (207)]

➤ White has more central and queenside space.

➤ Black will eventually grab more kingside space with an ...f7-f5 advance.

➤ White's Bishop is a very poor piece.

➤ Black's Knight on c5 is fantastic.

➤ White's play must come on the queenside. To do this, he must successfully get in a b2-b4 advance. This advance gains even more space on the queenside. It also chases the strong c5-Knight from its home.

Problem 66

(208)

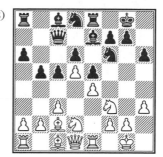

White to move.

What thematic idea should White implement in this position?

Solution 66

1.a4! is a typical device in this kind of position. Now Black can suffer several kinds of positional problems: 1...bxa4 2.Bxa4 leaves the a6-pawn weak and the c4-square in White's hands. 1...b4 hands over c4 immediately. 1...Rb8 lets White take control of the a-file with axb5. Isn't it amazing how this little two square advance of the a-pawn creates such disorder in the Black position?

Summary of Imbalances and Ideas
[diagram(208)]

➤ White's Rook on a1, d2-Knight, and c1-Bishop are inactive. It's clear that something has to be done about this state of affairs.

➤ White usually maneuvers his d2-Knight to g3 by Nd2-f2-g3 where it defends e4 and prepares to leap into f5. After the Knight arrives on g3, White can also consider Nh2 followed by f2-f4, striking in the center and at the kingside.

➤ Another typical idea is g2-g4 followed by Nd2-f1-g3, going all out for a kingside attack.

➤ If White wants to, he can instantly put the a1-Rook to work by a2-a4.

➤ A typical Black plan is to gain queenside space with ...c5-c4. Then ...Nf6-d7-c5 (or ...Nd8-b7-c5) brings the Knight to an active post.

Problem 67

(209)

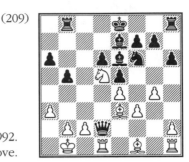

Ivanchuk-Anand, Linares 1992.
White to move.

Discuss this position and then annotate the following moves: 1.Nxf6+ gxf6 2.Rxd2 h5! 3.Rg1 hxg4 4.fxg4 Bc4 5.b3 Bxf1 6.Rxf1.

Solution 67

Black has just captured White's Queen on d2 and expects to achieve a very comfortable position after 1.Rxd2 Nxd5 2.exd5 Bd7. In that case, the d5-hole will be filled by a White pawn and the d6-pawn won't be backward any longer. The resultant position leaves White with no real chances on the queenside. However, Black will be able to generate some play on the kingside with a well-timed ...f7-f5 advance.

To avoid this, White decided to chop on f6, keeping d5 open and the d6-pawn backward.

1.Nxf6+?

A big mistake; Ivanchuk clearly underestimated the reply.

1...gxf6!!

This "ugly" move (Ivanchuk most likely expected something like 1...Bxf6 2.Rxd2 Ke7 3.h4 with a small plus thanks to his play on the kingside) freezes the White kingside pawns and allows Black to turn them into targets with ...h6-h5.

2.Rxd2 h5!

White's problem is that he can't hold his kingside structure together with h2-h3. As a result, his pawns on g4 and h2 will turn out to be long-term weaknesses. Believe it or not, White is now in serious trouble.

3.Rg1

No better was 3.Be2 hxg4 4.fxg4 Rh3.

3...hxg4 4.fxg4 Bc4!!

Another surprising decision. This Bishop was Black's main defender of d5 and f5, yet he rushes to exchange it for an inactive piece that hasn't even moved! Has Black gone mad? No, if we look past its apparent flaws, we will see that this move is, in fact, extremely logical.

It turns out that White threatened to solidify his position with h3 followed by Rg3. Black had to stop this at any cost! By chopping off the f1-Bishop, White won't be able to prevent Black from planting his Rook on h3. Due to this, White's pawns on h2 and g4 will remain targets and Black will achieve the superior position.

True, holes will be created on d5 and f5, but holes don't mean much if no enemy pieces can occupy them!

5.b3

White would have liked to play 5.Bxc4 bxc4 6.Rg3 to keep the enemy Rook off h3, but this is refuted by 6...c3.

5...Bxf1 6.Rxf1. Black stood better since **6...Rh3** left White tied up.

Let's see what Anand had to say about the position after 6...Rh3: "Black appears to have committed a whole list of positional sins: allowing doubled f-pawns, giving White an outside passed h-pawn and exchanging his 'good' Bishop with ...Bc4; yet he is better. Paradoxical? Yes, but this does not mean that the old positional rules have been suspended for the course of this game. Black's play depends on two things. First of all, his long-term aim is to exchange his d-pawn for White's e-pawn by ...d5 and to exchange his f6-pawn for White's g-pawn (either by ...f5 or by forcing White to play g5). Then he will be left with two connected central passed pawns, supported by his King, whereas White will have pawns on c2 and h2 that aren't going anywhere. Secondly, he can only put his plan into action because he has the initiative, and especially as the Rook on h3 disrupts both g- and h-pawns vulnerable to attack. Had Black wasted even one move, White would have fortified his kingside and the old positional values would have reasserted themselves."

This plan came into fruition after **7.Re2 Kd7 8.g5 Ke6 9.gxf6 Bxf6 10.Bd2 Be7 11.Be1 f6 12.Bg3 d5 13.exd5+ Kxd5** when Black's two central passed pawns gave him the advantage. A further error by White allowed Black to glide to a reasonably effortless victory.

Summary of Imbalances and Ideas
[diagram(209)]

➤ White has to decide whether to recapture on d2 or to play the zwischenzug 1.Nxf6+.

➤ Taking on d2 lets Black chop on d5 when White will have to fill in the d5-hole with a pawn.

➤ Taking on f6 lets Black respond with ...gxf6 followed by ...h6-h5, when White's kingside pawns will be objects of attack.

➤ White isn't able to bring another minor piece to bear on d5. This means that the d5 "weakness" isn't as serious as one might think.

➤ Black has a backward d-pawn, but it's firmly protected by the e7-Bishop.

Problem 68

(210)

N.N. (1600)-Silman, lesson 1997.
White to move.

Black has just played ...e5, gaining central space and threatening White's pawn on d4. How should White react to this?

Solution 68

1.Nc4!

In the actual game, White caved in to Black demands and played 1.dxe5 when 1...dxe5 left Black comfortably placed. After the correct 1.Nc4, White creates immediate pressure on e5 and also leaves the d6-pawn in place since he views it as a target. Now 1...exd4 runs into 2.Nxd6 while 1...Re8 2.Re1 followed by 3.Bf1 lets White continue to place pressure against e5 and d6.

It's very important to create your own targets, and to place pressure on your opponent's position at the first opportunity. Just reacting to your opponent's ideas never leads to anything good.

Summary of Imbalances and Ideas
[diagram (210)]

➤ Black is challenging White for control of the center.

➤ If White takes on e5, Black will achieve his goals since dxe5 ...dxe5, would, in effect, trade White's good d-pawn for Black's passive pawn on d6.

➤ Using the h2-Bishop, White should try and find a way to turn d6 into a weakness.

➤ The Knight on d2 isn't doing very much at the moment. Playing the Knight to c4 instantly brings it into contact with its brothers on f3 and h2. All three pieces then join forces to attack e5 and d6.

Problem 69

(211)

Khalifman-M.Adams, Groningen 1990.
Black to play.

Break this position down and assess it. Who, if anyone, is better, and by how much? After figuring this out, show me Black's best move (i.e., the move that highlights the plusses you've found).

Solution 69

Black has a winning advantage. His Knight is enormously superior to White's Bishop, and Black's next move makes sure that it can't be swapped off for White's horse.

Also note the b2-pawn, which will eventually be won by a mixture of a Rook and Knight attack (Rook on a2 and Knight on a4). Once this pawn falls, Black will promote his b3-pawn and the game will end.

1...Bxe4 2.Bxe4 f5 3.Bg2 Qa5 4.h4 Qb5 5.Qc3 Na4 Forcing the exchange of Queens. **6.Qb4 Qxb4 7.Rxb4 Rfb8 8.Rxb8+ Rxb8 9.Rb1 Rc8 10.Bh3 g6 11.e4 Rc2 12.Ra1 Nc5! 13.exf5 Rxb2 14.fxg6 hxg6 15.Be6+ Kf8 16.Ra8+ Ke7**, 0-1.

Summary of Imbalances and Ideas
[diagram (211)]

➤ Black's advanced pawn on b3 freezes the b2-pawn in place and allows Black to treat it as a weakness.

➤ Black's b3-pawn is well protected by the c5-Knight.

➤ Black's first order of business is to ensure the survival of his wonderful Knight. This means getting rid of its one enemy: the White Knight on e4.

Problem 70

(212)

Nimzovich-Tartakower, Carlsbad 1929.
White to move.

White's enormous superiority is obvious. How would you continue if you were blessed with this position?

Solution 70

Black is more or less helpless, so White shouldn't go all out for a "mate or nothing" scenario. Instead he should build up his attack while simultaneously improving the position of all of his pieces.

1.Nh1!

This excellent and very accurate move prepares Qh2 and also intends to improve the position of this Knight by Ng3, heading for both h5 and f5. Though 1.Nd1, intending Ne3, was also good, why not increase your potential by giving your Knight two squares to drool over (f5 and h5) instead of just one (a Knight on e3 only eyes f5). Placing the Knight on g3 instead of e3 also allows White to bring the c3-Knight to e3, when both horses would be poised to leap into f5.

1...f6 2.Qh2 h6 3.Ng3 Kh7 4.Be2

Very tempting was 4.Nd1 followed by 5.Ne3 and 6.Nef5. In that case I can't see how h6 could be held. Nevertheless, you have to admire Nimzovich's patience and calm while playing such an important game—he needed to win to gain outright first place. Nimzovich knows his opponent can't do anything, and he doesn't intend to allow Black even a glimpse of counterplay.

4...Rg8 5.Kf2!

This important move needs to be discussed. Nimzovich was the first player to openly discuss the principle of two weaknesses: that one weakness can often be held, while two stretches the inferior side's defense to the breaking point by keeping him off balance—the attacker can go after two different points at any moment, thus preventing the weaker side from concentrating on one area.

By not castling long, White shows his intention to expand on the queenside by b3, a3, and b4 (why place your King in an area that is about to be ripped open?). This, combined with a powerful kingside attack and Black's overall helplessness, assures White of eventual victory.

After the further **5...Rh8 6.Rh4 Qe8 7.Rg1 Bf8 8.Kg2 Nb7 9.Nh5 Qg6 10.f4** Black was being squeezed from all sides, and this led to a slow, but sure, White win.

Summary of Imbalances and Ideas
[diagram (212)]

➤ The center is closed so both sides need to find their play on the wings.

➤ Black's kingside has been weakened and the h7-pawn is a very obvious target.

➤ White would like to double Rooks on the h-file. Placing his Queen on h2 has the same effect.

➤ Black has a juicy hole on f5 that White would love to occupy. How can a White Knight reach that square?

➤ White has an enormous positional advantage on the kingside and more space in the center and on the queenside. Due to this, Black is helpless, and this allows White to build in a calm manner.

Problem 71

(213)

Garcia Padron-Suba, Las Palmas 1979.
Black to move.

White threatens to win a pawn by Qxd6. How should Black deal with this threat?

Solution 71

Instead of passively bowing to White's will, Black can seize the initiative by creating his own threats.

1...b5!

Doesn't this lose the d-pawn? Well, yes it does, but Black hopes to get something back. The key idea here is: Always follow your own plans. If you can afford to ignore enemy threats to do this, then don't hesitate to do so!

2.cxb5

White gets nothing from 2.Qxd6 bxc4 since 3.bxc4 Bxe4! (and not 3...Qxb2?? 4.Rb1, trapping the Black Queen) 4.Nxe4 Qxb2 gives Black a good game.

2...axb5 3.f3

White does not capture the gift on d6 because he would lose the pawn on e4 after 3.Qxd6 b4!, when a critical defender of e4 will be removed. This is typical of the Hedgehog formation: Black's pieces may sit back on the first rank but that doesn't mean they can't put pressure on the distant White army.

3...b4 4.Na4 d5

Black has a queenside space advantage, thanks to his advanced pawn on b4. It's also important to point out that White's King is less safe than its Black counterpart.

Most importantly, Black never defended his d-pawn and, as a result, has managed to execute both his thematic breaks (...b6-b5 and ...d6-d5). Why waste a move defending when it might turn out to be unnecessary?

5.exd5 Bxd5 6.Nd4 Ra6

This keeps the White Knight out of c6. Black stands better because White's kingside is a bit loose, White's a4-Knight is offside, Black's b4-pawn is holding back two White units, and Black's pieces are more active than their White counterparts.

Summary of Imbalances and Ideas
[diagram (213)]

➤ White has more central space.

➤ White threatens to win the d6-pawn by the simple Qxd6.

➤ Black must guard this pawn, or create threats of his own, thereby fighting for the initiative.

➤ Black's a8-Bishop and f6-Knight are aiming at the e4-pawn. If the White Knight on c3 can be made to move, e4 will fall.

Problem 72

(214)

Black to move.

List the imbalances and form a plan based on them and/or on the creation of new plusses.

Solution 72

This position features a Bishop versus Knight situation that favors the Knight. Why? Because it has a fine support point and is joining with the rest of its army in creating an attack against b3. The doubled a-pawns for Black will act as battering rams that shall toss themselves against the seemingly solid b3-pawn. The backward e-pawn on e7 is adequately defended by its King.

These factors show that the target Black is aiming his guns at is b3. This point can be weakened by:

1...a4

Now Black's Rooks, a-pawns and Knight take aim at b3.

2.Kg1 a5!

This pawn prepares to take its brother's place on a4.

3.Kf2?

White could have stayed in the game with 3.Rbe1.

3...axb3
4.axb3 a4 White loses material and will also lose the game.

Summary of Imbalances and Ideas
[diagram (214)]

➤ Black's Knight is a tower of strength while White's Bishop is a purely defensive piece.

➤ Black's Rooks and Knight all work together in eyeing b3.

➤ An ...a5-a4 advance will allow Black to bring maximum force to bear against b3.

➤ Black's only weakness—the e7-pawn—is solidly defended by the Black King.

➤ Black's doubled a-pawns are not weak since they don't stand on a half-open file. In fact, Black will use both these pawns as battering rams against b3.

Problem 73

(215)

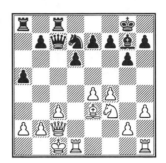

Black to move.

Black's move is so natural that it should be so obvious to all tournament players. What is it?

Solution 73

Black's Bishop on g7 is aiming at the White King, but at the moment it is blocked by the c3-pawn. This bothersome pawn is also defending its monarch from the pressure that Black has built up on the c-file. The second player can solve both these problems by hiring his b-pawn to clear that c3 guy out of the way: **1...b5** followed by 2...b4 would be quite unpleasant for White.

Summary of Imbalances and Ideas
[diagram (215)]

➤ All of Black's forces are aimed at the queenside.

➤ Since White's King resides on the queenside, it's clear that Black should try to open as many lines as possible in that sector. However, Black would still seek his chances on the queenside even if White had castled on the opposite wing!

➤ The c3-pawn is closing off the c-file and also blocking the g7-Bishop's control over the h8-a1 diagonal. This can be torn aside by ...b7-b5-b4.

Problem 74

(216)

Greznikov-Mahfooz Ghafoori,
Continental Open 1996
(two 1900 players).
Black to move.

Black played 1...Nxe2+. Was this a good move? If it is, what is the follow up? If it's poor, please explain why.

Solution 74

It may seem strange to give up such a fine Knight for such a poor Bishop. Nevertheless, this plan of acquiring the two Bishops turns out to be extremely effective against an opponent who doesn't have much play of his own.

Of course, you have to ask if the Bishops will become active in the resulting position before you do this. In the present case, Black obviously feels that they have good chances of eventually sweeping the board.

If you saw that 1...Nxe2+ created an imbalance and understood that you would have to rally all your forces around it, then give yourself a big pat on the back. The capture of White's Bishop doesn't have to be the best move—we are looking for concept here, not accuracy

1...Nxe2+
2.Nxe2

White didn't like the look of 2.Qxe2 d5 when the threat of ...d5-d4, forking White's Knight and Bishop, is annoying.

2...b5

Black mixes his acquisition of the two Bishops with queenside expansion. One nice thing about his idea is that the following moves are easy to play: Black advances on the queenside so his

Rooks can eventually enter the White position. This advance also tries to open the a8-h1 diagonal for his Bishop.

Another solid option was 2...b6 followed by Bb7 and an eventual ...d6-d5.

3.Ng3 Qc7 4.Ng4

White announces that he is playing for mate. This makes sense since that side of the board is where his space advantage lies. However, why should such a one-dimensional idea prove superior to Black's strategy of queenside play (which usually leads to a superior endgame), central play, and minor piece superiority?

4...b4

Excellent! Black ignores White's overtures and continues to expand on "his" side of the board.

5.b3 a5 6.Rb1

The defensive measures that White is taking show that Black owns the initiative. One problem White faces is that any central play that he might initiate via d3-d4 or e4-e5 backfires because such advances would ultimately open diagonals for the Black Bishops.

6...a4

This prepares to open the a-file, something that will eventually lead to a strong Rook penetration into the White camp. White now clicks into overdrive and tries to get something started on the kingside.

7.Nxf6+ Bxf6 8.Nh5 Bc3 9.Qg4

Threatening to close off the c3-Bishops access to g7 by 10.e5 when 11.Qxg7 mate would be staring Black in the face. However, more accurate was 9.e5! when 9...dxe5 (the simple 9...Kh8 10.Qg4 Rg8 keeps Black in control) 10.Qg4 gives White some serious threats.

9...f5!

This refutes White's attack. Now g7 is defended by the c3-Bishop and the Queen. Also note that thoughts of an f4-f5 advance, which would get the e3-Bishop and f1-Rook into the attack, have been stymied.

10.Qf3 Bb7

White is strategically lost. His center is under pressure, Black's Bishops are both very strong and the queenside is completely owned by the Black forces.

White's kingside attack proved to be no match for the slow, but steady, positional pressure that two Bishops and queenside space offered to his opponent.

11.Rf2 axb3 12.axb3 d5

Blasting the center open since 13.e5?? d4 leads to the loss of a piece. Why does Black want to open the center? For two reasons: 1) The best reaction to an attack on the wing is a counterattack in the center. 2) The more open the position becomes, the stronger Black's Bishops will get.

13.Ng3 dxe4 14.dxe4 fxe4. The finish, filled with many tactical errors that I won't address, was: **15.Nxe4 Ra2 16.Re2 c4 17.Bf2 cxb3 18.cxb3 Rxe2 19.Qxe2 Qc6 20.Rd1 Qxe4** and White soon gave up.

Summary of Imbalances and Ideas
[diagram (216)]

➤ Black has control over the d4-square.

➤ Black has a strong central Knight on d4.

➤ Black has more queenside space. This can be heightened by ...b7-b5-b4.

➤ Taking on e2 gives Black the long-term plus of the two Bishops. If he decides to do this, Black must try and open the position. Naturally, he will still seek play on the queenside, because that's where he owns more space.

Problem 75

(217)

I.Sokolov-Shirov, Olympiad 1996.
Black to move.

In the game, Black played the odd looking 1...Bd8. Is this any good? If not, what would you have preferred?

Solution 75

Though a bit out of the ordinary, **1...Bd8** is actually a very important move! The Bishop wasn't doing anything on e7 so Black redirects it to the more important b8-h2 diagonal where it fights for control of the key e5-square.

How can an amateur (or anyone else, for that matter) tell when such a move is called for? In this case, the fact that White seems to control the whole board forces Black to come up with something challenging. This doesn't mean a transparent threat. It means you have to find a plan that prepares to fight for something of your own. If Black were to just sit around and mindlessly develop, he would eventually get pushed off the edge of the planet without really making any obvious mistake. The followup was:

2.Be2 Nxe5 3.Bxe5 Bc7

Black is doing an excellent job of challenging White for control of the key e5-square. It also should be pointed out that exchanges make Black happy since he has less space than his opponent.

4.Na4

Not an impressive move, but where is White's improvement? White gains nothing from 4.Bxc7 Qxc7, so the only real try is the space-gaining, but ugly, 4.f4. True, this creates a big hole on e4 and, as a result, I can't believe that Black is doing too badly here.

Play might continue: 4...Bxe5 5.fxe5 Nd7 (and not 5...Ne4 6.Bf3! when White stands better. Note that 5...Ne4 6.Na4? is worse: 6...Rb8 7.Nb6 Qd8 when the b6-Knight is out of play while the horse on e4 is a tower of strength) and Black, after ...Rb8, ...0-0, and/or ...f6, should get more than enough play.

4...Ba5+

Of course not 4...Bxe5?? 5.Nb6, when White wins the Exchange.

5.Nc3 0-0

Not only getting the King out of the center, but also defending g7 and preparing to continue the fight for e5 by ...Nd7.

6.h4

The tempting 6.Bxf6 gxf6 would not bother Black since he would gain the two Bishops and take control over the important e5-square.

6...h6 7.0-0-0 Nd7 8.Bd6 Re8 9.Rhg1 Bc7 and Black had a comfortable game (key breaks by ...b7-b6, opening up the queenside, and ...e6-e5, blasting open the center, are primed and ready to go) and went on to win a sharp struggle.

Summary of Imbalances and Ideas
[diagram (217)]

➤ White has a considerable advantage in queenside space.

➤ Black would like to challenge White's control over the e5-square. If he can manage this and play ...e6-e5, then his central counterplay should more than make up for White's queenside demonstration.

➤ Black would like to give himself more control over the b6-square, lest a White Knight eventually invade by Nc3-a4-b6.

➤ Black's Bishop on e7 has nothing to do with the two weakest squares in his camp: e5 and b6.

Problem 76

(218)

Anand-Bareev, Dortmund 1992.
White to move.

A glance at the position's main imbalances will make White's first move easy to understand. List the imbalances and your interpretation of White's correct move.

Solution 76

Black has a very bad Bishop on d7. Thanks to the closed nature of the position, White's Knights are the superior minor pieces here.

A glance might tell us that Black will be playing on the queenside while White will be seeking kingside chances, but why should White give Black anything at all? Why not play calmly and try to exploit the Knight versus Bishop advantage?

1.b4!

A great move that freezes Black's b-pawn, forcing it to remain on a light-square where it will forever block the Bishop. 1.b4 also gives the White Knights potential support points on a5 and c5, not to mention the existing support point on d4.

Anand's own words tell the story in a simple yet effective manner: "At first it seems that Black's Knight can reach a good square by ...Na4-c3, but in fact it is not very effective at c3 because it lacks adequate support. By contrast, White's Knights, after Nb3 and Nfd4, have well-supported and useful squares to land on at d4 and c5. Alternatively, White can use the fact that Black has no queenside counterplay to start kingside operations."

1...a5 2.a3 Rfc8 3.Rdc1 axb4 4.axb4 Rxc1+

Black seeks salvation by exchanges, but the static nature of White's advantage can't be dissolved in such a manner. White's plusses will linger on even in a simplified situation.

5.Rxc1 Rc8 6.Rxc8+ Bxc8 7.Qc2 Bd7 8.Kf2 and White enjoyed every advantage the position could give: more central space, good Knight versus bad Bishop, more active King, superior Queen, and chances for expansion on the kingside. All these things led to an eventual White victory.

Summary of Imbalances and Ideas
[diagram (218)]

➤ Black has a bad (and inactive) Bishop on d7.

➤ The center is closed, and that means that, in this case, Knights are superior to Bishops.

➤ White would like to make sure that Black can't free his Bishop. The three things that the owner of a bad Bishop usually tries to do are: trade it off, get it outside the pawn chain, and get his pawns off the color of his Bishop. White would like to stop all these things from happening.

Problem 77

(219)

Black to move.

How would you read this position? Once you list all the imbalances, what move best serves whatever plusses Black may have?

Solution 77

Black should be excited. He has a huge lead in development and White's King is stuck in the center. These factors must kindle the desire to throw some kind of knockout punch. Remember: a development lead is a temporary advantage and must be used before the enemy can catch up. So we've reached a key moment; Black should try hard to punish his opponent!

1...e5!!

Ripping the center open so that the Black army can reach the centrally placed White King. **2.dxe5** Avoiding 2.Nxe5 c5!, which is very strong for Black. **2...Rxe5+ 3.Nxe5** Better was 3.Kd1, though Black would still stand much better thanks to the horrible position of the White King. **3...Qxe5+** gives Black a raging attack since 4.Be2 Re8 picks up material while 4.Kd1 Ne4 creates overwhelming threats against c3 and f2.

It was possible to throw in 1...Rab8 as long as you thought that this move made the following ...e5 advance even stronger (it actually forces the White Queen to run to a better square). However, if you only saw that you could attack White's Queen and went for the free toss, shame on you. One-move attacks should only be played if they have something to do with the position, or if they give you a very specific gain after your opponent has moved his piece to safety.

Summary of Imbalances and Ideas
[diagram (219)]

➤ Black has a significant lead in development.
This calls for a fast-play solution to the position's problems.

➤ White's King is still in the center. This also calls for fast-play from Black else White will tidy things up by Be2 followed by 0-0.

➤ When an enemy King is stuck in the center, do everything possible to rip open central lines. These act as highways for your pieces, and allow them to make quick progress into the opponent's position.

Problem 78

(220)

Vukic-Suba, Vinkovci 1977.
Black to move.

Whose position do you like and why?

Solution 78

Shouldn't White stand better in this type of position? He has more territory in the center and on the queenside, plus the Black pawn on d6 appears to be a target.

This description of the position would be accurate if the Black pawn on d6 had to stay on that square forever. However, Black doesn't have to let White have his way. In fact, Black is dying to throw off his chains and challenge White for territorial rights with an eventual ...d6-d5. This would free both his Rooks, crack open the a8-h1 diagonal for his light-squared Bishop, and get rid of the "weakness" on d6. He also has ...b6-b5 which would activate the c8-Rook and challenge White's queenside spatial dominance.

1...Nh5!

A tricky move that eyes the weakened g3 point and creates a pin on the a1-h8 diagonal.

2.f4

Black threatened to free himself with 2...d5, when his Queen on b8 and the Knight on h5 would combine to attack g3.

2...b5!

White stopped the ...d6-d5 advance but has fallen victim to the sting on the other side of the board. Now 3.cxb5 axb5 4.Qxb5 loses a piece to 4...Bxc3! 5.Qxb8 Nxb8 while the obvious 4...Qxb5 5.Nxb5 Bxb2 is also good enough.

3.cxb5 axb5 4.Bf3

Attacking h5 and trying to force Black to block the long dark-squared diagonal by ...Nf6

4...Ne7

Now the Rook on the c-file, together with the g7-Bishop, threatens to eat the Knight on c3.

5.Nd4 b4!

Defending the b5-pawn and gaining time by attacking the Knight. Now it's Black who can claim an advantage in space on the queenside.

6.Na4 Nf6

Black is ready to make use of his final breaking device—the ...d6-d5 advance, so White decides to strike in the middle first.

7.e5 dxe5 8.fxe5

Black would win a pawn after 8.Bxa8 exd4 9.Bf3 Nf5.

8...Bxf3 9.Nxf3 Nfd5

The resulting position is much better for Black: both of his Rooks stand on open files; his single queenside pawn restrains two White ones; White's pawn on e5 cannot be defended by another pawn; and the Black Knights are making use of the excellent post on d5.

10.Rc1 Bh6 11.Rc4 Ne3 12.Rcc1 N7d5

The Black pieces are slowly finding ways to get into the White position.

13.Rxc8 Rxc8 14.Qf2 Nf5 15.Re2 Be3 16.Qe1 Qb5 17.Nd2 Qd3

Black's pieces sink deeper and deeper into the White camp. Note how the White Knight on a4 is completely shut out of the game.

18.Nf1 Rc2 19.Rg2 Rxg2+ 20.Kxg2 Qe4+, 0-1. White loses his Queen after 21.Kh2 Bg1+.

Summary of Imbalances and Ideas
[diagram (220)]

➤ White has more central space and more queenside space.

➤ Black's d6-pawn is potentially weak.

➤ Black's pieces are all well placed. If he can free them with a thematic ...b6-b5 or ...d6-d5 break, their latent energy can be demonstrated.

➤ The "weak" d6-pawn is dying to advance to d5 and destroy White's spatial plus in the center.

➤ White's kingside has been weakened. The g3-pawn, in particular, might prove vulnerable after Black plays ...d6-d5, opening up the b8-g3 diagonal for Black's Queen.

➤ White will be better if he can permanently contain Black's two pawn breaks (...b6-b5 and ...d6-d5).

Problem 79

(221)

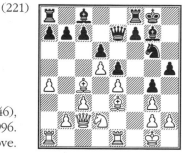

Piacenza (1713)-Lyles (1746),
Continental Open 1996.
White to move.

From the diagram, play continued: 1.b4 h4 2.Be2 hxg3 3.hxg3 Kh7 4.Rf1 Rh8 5.Nb3 Bh6 6.Bxh6 Kxh6. Annotate these moves (maybe they make sense, maybe some of them are bad, maybe all of them are suspect) and then tell me what you think of the final position.

Solution 79

White is playing for queenside gains and for control over the f5-square. Black is trying to somehow get a kingside attack started. The way White ignores Black's illusory kingside threats and quietly builds up his own plusses is impressive.

1.b4

This move gains queenside space and shows complete disdain for anything that Black may conjure up.

1...h4

Black lashes out on the kingside and tries to put a scare into his opponent. This is the point where most amateurs (as White) would start to defend. To his credit, Piacenza doesn't even blink.

It should be noted that 1...f5 would have turned out very nicely for White after 2.exf5 Bxf5 3.Bd3 when White gets to use the e4-square as a home for his Knight.

2.Be2

This move jumps on the fact that g4 is no longer defended by a pawn. White doesn't mind the doubled g-pawns because he sees that the g3-pawn keeps the enemy Knight out of f4 and h4.

I love White's mentality: instead of seeing Black's kingside play as a threat, he is looking at it as a weakness!

2...hxg3 3.hxg3 Kh7 4.Rf1

Clamping down on the f5-square.

4...Rh8 5.Nb3

Laughing in Black's face! I doubt if the Knight is optimally placed here, but White's desire to continue his queenside buildup and ignore his opponent's unsound kingside demonstration is admirable.

Alternatives are 5.a5, 5.Nc4, 5.Qd1, and 5.c4 followed by 6.c5.

5...Bh6

Trading off his bad Bishop for White's good one. There's nothing wrong with this strategy, but the presence of other negative factors will leave Black with a very unsavory position.

6.Bxh6 Kxh6

Black has a very bad game due to his inferiority on the queenside and his weak pawns on g4 and f7. The immediate threat against g4 forces Black to either give up the pawn, play the groveling 7...Qd7, or allow a Queen exchange by 7...Qg5 8.Qc1. This Queen trade would permanently kill Black's attack. In general, the side playing for a queenside attack gets endgame odds since his play is based on the accumulation of small factors. The side playing for a kingside attack is usually in search of a knockout and, as a result, needs to retain the Queens (this acts as his big right hand).

The following moves show just how bad the position is for the second player: **7.Qd1 Kg7 8.Bxg4 Qg5** Black has placed all his hopes in this final attacking gesture. As usual, White just goes about his business and ignores him. **9.Bxc8 Qe3+ 10.Rf2 Raxc8 11.Qf3**. The double threat of 12.Qxe3 and 12.Qxf7+ forced a Queen exchange. White easily scored the full point.

Summary of Imbalances and Ideas
[diagram (221)]

➤ White owns more queenside space and will direct his play in that area. Moves like b2-b4 and a4-a5 will add to his gains in that sector.

➤ Black has a hole on f5.

➤ Black's Knight on g6 is dominated by the pawn on g3.

➤ Black's Bishops are far from active. In contrast, White's Bishops are both fairly active.

Problem 80

(222)

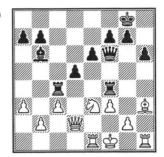

N.Wong-Elizabeth de la Torre,
Knoxville 1997.
Black to move.

Elizabeth, a 10 year-old girl rated 1359, had played a fine game and reached this very interesting position. How would you assess the situation and what do you think Black's best plan is?

Solution 80

Though Black is down a piece for two pawns, she has excellent chances thanks to White's poor King position and the inactivity of White's h1-Rook and h3-Bishop. Being up material doesn't mean much if your pieces can't join in the battle, and White's unfortunate army isn't acting as a team at all. Compare this with Black's forces, which, with the mild exception of the c4-Rook, are all working together in their pursuit of kingside pressure.

1...Rce4!

In the actual game, Black went berserk with the unfathomable 1...Ba5?? and lost. However, 1...Rce4 not only creates a completely original situation where both Black Rooks have somehow jumped over their line of pawns, but it also leaves White in a state of complete paralysis.

I should mention that 1...Rxf3+! is also strong, since after 2.gxf3 Qxf3+ 3.Kg1 Re4 4.Bg2 Bxe3+ 5.Rxe3 Qxe3+ Black gets four connected passed pawns for the piece.

2.Kg1??

Losing. White can avoid material loss with 2.Kf2 or 2.Qf2, though the first player still remains badly tied up.

2...Rxe3 3.Rxe3 Re4!

Starting a nice, forcing sequence that wins material.

4.fxe4 Qf4

This takes away all the free squares from White's King and simultaneously threatens the e3-Rook *and* the White Queen.

5.g3

Trying to mix things up. Normal moves like 5.exd5 Bxe3+ 6.Qxe3 Qxe3+ are also completely hopeless.

5...Bxe3+

Not falling for 5...Qxg3+?? 6.Kf1.

6.Kh2

Of course, 6.Kg2 Qxe4+ wins instantly for Black.

6...Bg1+! 7.Rxg1 Qxd2+, picking up White's Queen and winning the game.

This sharp little contest showed us the importance of bringing every piece into the attack—when you have a goal, make sure your whole army participates.

Summary of Imbalances and Ideas
[diagram (222)]

➤ White has a material advantage: a Knight for two pawns.

➤ White's two minor pieces are not doing much. The h3-Bishop makes a particularly sad impression.

➤ Black's Queen, f4-Rook, and Bishop are all extremely active. The only piece that's not completely involved in the attack is the c4-Rook. Black must try making this piece into a team player.

Problem 81

(223)

Tal-Gligoric,
Candidates' Quarter Final Match 1968.
Black to move.

Things look bad for Black. White has more central space and is preparing a central advance by Nf3 and e4-e5. White also has good chances against the Black King because all of White's pieces are aiming in that direction, while nothing much is happening on the queenside. To say that the queenside is equal and the center and kingside favor White, speaks for itself. What is Black going to do about this state of affairs? His Rook is under attack and a swap would give White control of the open b-file.

Solution 81

1...Qc7!!

This fine move gives up the Exchange for several positional plusses. By making this sacrifice, Black gives himself something to play with. Of course, he could have retained material equality by 1...Rxb1, but then every advantage would have been on the opponent's side. No self-respecting grandmaster would accept such a dismal state of affairs! Never wait around so that you can die without a fight; insist on getting some play. Even if White is still better, at least Black now forces his opponent to play with great skill to prove it.

2.Bxb4 cxb4

In return for his modest material investment, Black has gained a nice majority of pawns on the queenside, fine squares on c5 and c3 for his Knights, increased control over many central dark-squares (thanks to the fact that White has lost his dark-squared Bishop), and pressure on the half open c-file against White's c4-pawn. That's a lot of stuff Black didn't have a moment ago!

3.Rf1

Not falling for 3.Rxb4?? Qc5+, forking the King and Rook. This move threatens to give the Exchange back by Rxf6 when Black's kingside would be shattered.

3...Be7

Giving his f6-Knight more support. If Black could somehow gain permanent control over the e5-square (Knight on d7 and Bishop on f6, for example), he would actually stand better. Unfortunately, it is not so easy for the second player to get his kingside pieces to their best squares and this allows White a chance to make threats in the center.

4.Kh1 a5 5.Qd2!

White is clearly worse on the queenside so he begins to bring all his forces around to the center and the kingside. Note that Tal is not trying to rest on his materialistic laurels. Instead he goes all out to create his own chances elsewhere on the board.

5...Nc5 6.Bc2

White wants to retain this Bishop because it defends e4 and, once the e-pawn advances, will become a strong attacking piece that aims directly at the Black King.

6...Bd8 7.Rbe1 Bc8 8.Nf3 Nfd7

Black is finally ready to claim a great position by 9...Ne5.

9.e5!

A very fine move that gives a pawn away but allows all the White pieces to enter the attack—most notably the e1-Rook and c2-Bishop. It is becoming clear that both sides care about well-placed pieces and clear plans more than simple material gains.

9...Nxe5 10.Qf4

Now White's pieces are all beautifully aimed at the center and the kingside while Black's pieces on c8, d8, c7 and e8 aren't nearly as active as their White counterparts. White went on to win a very long, hard battle.

Summary of Imbalances and Ideas
[diagram (223)]

➤ White has more central space and plans to mash Black there by an eventual e4-e5 advance.

➤ White's pieces are also well placed for an eventual kingside attack.

➤ Black's Rook is under attack and a normal move like 1...Rxb1 leaves White better on the queenside since he would own the open b-file after 2.Rxb1.

➤ Black can't accept a scenario where the queenside, center, and kingside belong to White. Something must be done that allows Black to get some play.

Problem 82

(224)

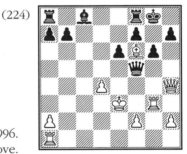

Thomas-Williams, San Francisco 1996.
Black to move.

White appears to have a strong attack. His immediate threat is Rf3 when the Black Queen is attacked, the White Bishop is guarded, and Qh6 will lead to mate. Can Black defend this position?

Solution 82

Black can do more than just defend the position, he can actually take the initiative with **1...e5!!**. Black is two pawns up and doesn't have to worry about giving one back. Thus, for the small price of one tiny pawn, Black opens up the center (White's King is far from happy there!) and frees the Bishop on c8. Now 2.Rf3, as played in the game, loses to 2...exd4+ when Black's pieces will be able to torture White's King on the newly opened e-file. Also in Black's favor is 2.dxe5 Re8 3.Rf3 Rxe5+ 4.Bxe5 Qxe5+ when Black's King is now safe, and he has two pawns for the Exchange and a winning attack.

Summary of Imbalances and Ideas
[diagram (224)]

➤ White's King is very uncomfortable in the center.

➤ When the enemy King is in the middle, you must try your best to open up the center so that your pieces can penetrate into the enemy position.

➤ Black is two pawns up.

➤ One advantage of having extra material is that you can often sacrifice some or all of it back and not have a material deficit.

➤ White threatens Rf3 when the f6-Bishop is defended and Qh6 followed by Qg7 mate is in the air.

Problem 83

(225)

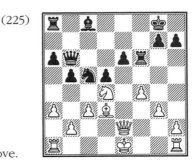

Black to move.

This is a game between two 1600 players. White's position looks pretty good, though his King can't castle. It has already moved to f1 and then back to e1! He has control over the important e5-square, White's Bishop is much better than Black's Bishop, his Knight is very well placed on d4 and the pawn on e6 is backward and weak.

How would you handle the "unfortunate" Black position?

Solution 83

In the actual game, Black became depressed over this sad state of affairs and played 1...Nxd3+?? 2.Qxd3 Bd7 3.Kd2 Rae8 4.Rae1 Re7 5.Re5 with a complete bind that led to a White victory.

Instead of meekly accepting his fate, Black had to address the problems in his position and find a way to cope with them. Taking on d3 and leaving White with a crushing Knight versus a horrible Bishop only made things worse. Instead, Black should have tried:

1...Ne4!

This fine move places the Knight on a strong advanced post, stops the White Queen and Rooks from landing on e5 and takes most of the pressure off of e6.

2.Bxe4?

White gets excited about giving Black doubled pawns, but those doubled guys turn out to be anything but weak. To make matters worse, Black's Bishop now becomes a strong piece and the White Knight is not able to find a road to the e5-square.

Best was 2.Nf3!, keeping an eye on the e5-square, though 2...Bb7 gives Black a dynamic game thanks to the unsafe White King and the super horse on e4.

2...dxe4 3.Kd2 Bb7

This defends e4, threatens to win the Exchange by 4...e3+ followed by 5...Bxh1, and prepares 4...Re8 followed by 5...e5 when Black would stand better due to his powerful passed pawn. He also has play against White's King (plans like ...a5 followed by ...b4 suggest themselves) and an active Bishop which can move to d5 and eye both sides of the board.

How did Black manage to turn a seemingly bad position around? He fought to create some plusses of his own. He took the fight to his opponent and he refused to allow doubt to enter the equation. Simply put, Black had two goals:

✦ To cure the ills of his position, i.e., covering up the hole on e5, making e6 hard to reach, improving the position of his Knight, and playing to activate his Bishop.

✦ To make use of the plusses in his game so that pressure could be placed on White's poorly placed King. Black also has the ability to open the position up by ...a5 followed with ...b4 and/or ...e6-e5.

In the actual game, Black accepted White's verdict that he was worse. In our improved version we saw the second player rebelling at this pessimistic view. Often your position is as good as you think it is. It's far better to be deluded in a positive way by always claiming some sort of advantage than to bemoan your fate and lament the horrors that are in front of you.

Summary of Imbalances and Ideas
[diagram (225)]

➤ White has a good Bishop and a well-placed Knight.

➤ White has a good deal of pressure against the backward pawn on e6.

➤ White would like to make use of the hole on e5.

> ➤ White's King can't castle since it has already moved earlier in the game. This fact leaves White a bit off balance—his King won't be completely safe for quite a while.

> ➤ Black needs to distract White from taking advantage of e6 and e5.

> ➤ Black would like to block off the e-file.

> ➤ If possible, Black would love to rip open the center with a well-timed ...e6-e5 advance, taking advantage of White's central King.

Problem 84

(226)

Grefe-Bellin, World Open 1973.
Black to move.

White, 1973 U.S. Champion John Grefe, seems to be doing very well. He has lots of kingside and central space, he has a firm grip on the important d4-square, pressure against a6 and possibilities of opening the c-file by c2-c3. It's also important to note how bad the b7-Bishop is. International Master Bellin of England was Black. Grefe was clearly the superior player. Will the negative aspects of his position and fear of his powerful opponent make Black crack? What would you do?

Solution 84

1...d4!

Black doesn't care what his opponent's rating is or what championship he's won. The only thing that matters is the present position. Seeing that White is about to take control of the game by Bd4, leaving Black with very little counterplay, Black gives away a pawn so that his b7-Bishop can play a role. In top-flight chess, material considerations often take a back seat to the coordination and activity of one's pieces.

2.Nxd4

Suddenly White is faced with fire down the b7-h1 diagonal! White's reply takes the c6-square away from the Black Queen, but 2.Bxd4!?, meeting 2...Qc6 with 3.Qg3, was also possible.

2...Nc5

First Black activated his b7-Bishop and now the Knight jumps to a great post. After 2...Nc5, Black threatens both 3...Nxa4 and 3...Nxd3 4.cxd3 Qd7 with the threat of 5...Qd5. The rest of the game was a downhill slide for the American player: **3.Be2 Nxa4 4.Rb1 Rac8 5.Bf3? Bxf3 6.Qxf3 Bc5 7.Rf2 Qb6 8.Qe4 Rfd8 9.c3? bxc3 10.bxc3 Nxc3!, 0-1** since 11.Rxb6 Nxe4 would pick up the Exchange.

Summary of Imbalances and Ideas
[diagram (226)]

➤ The kingside is dead to both sides while the center also seems to be closed after White plays Nd4 or Bd4. This means that both sides will be striving to dominate the queenside.

➤ White can open queenside lines at will by c2-c3.

➤ Black's Bishop on b7 is very poor. What can he do to liven it up?

➤ White's pawn on a4 is undefended.

➤ If the d5-pawn were gone, Black might be able to generate threats along the b7-h1 diagonal.

Problem 85

(227)

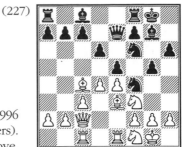

Piacenza-Lyles, Continental Open 1996
(two B players).
White to move.

We all make errors in chess. However, a logical move that turns out to be a tactical mistake or a simple case of flawed judgment are far cries from moves that do more for our opponents than for us. Self-destructive ideas come up in almost every amateur game I have seen and, after lots of thinking, the closest thing to a cure I have found is the following: Whenever you are about to play a move in chess, always ask: "What wonderful thing does this move do for my position?"

As simple as this may sound, I have never had a student who could follow this advice. Why? I honestly don't know. Perhaps the fire of battle blinds us to lessons of the past. Perhaps this verbal inquiry into a move's usefulness leaves a bad taste in one's mouth.

In this game White, who was worried about ...exd4 with threats to his e-pawn, played 1.d5, gaining central space. Was this a wise thing to do? What wonderful thing does this move do for White's position?

Solution 85

White has a nice plus due to his spatial edge in the center, queenside possibilities with a later a2-a4-a5 and b2-b4, and long-term control over the f5-square. Black has just moved his Knight from d7 to f6 and now appears to be putting pressure on e4 with the "threat" of ..exd4. White bought into this lie and, fearing the pawn capture on e4, came up with what he thought was the perfect defense.

1.d5??

First, it must be understood that Black really didn't threaten anything at all. Black's idea of 1...exd4 could have been met with 2.Bxf4 or even 2.cxd4 when 2...Nxe4 3.Bxf4 wins a piece for White and 2...Qxe4 3.Qxe4 Nxe4 4.Bxf4 also leaves Black in a resignable position. So why is White stopping Black from losing the game? Always challenge the opponent's threats, and only react to them if you're 100% sure they deserve respect.

If White really did want to defend his e-pawn, the most logical choice would have been **1.Ng3**. If we ask what wonderful things 1.Ng3 does for our position, we come up with some solid answers: It brings the Knight into a more aggressive position; it takes aim at the f5-square; it firmly defends e4.

Now let's ask the same question about 1.d5. This unfortunate move stops ...exd4, but that capture would have been nice for White since it gives up the center after cxd4. So 1.d5 stops Black from making a mistake. In other areas, 1.d5 sinks even lower down the evolutionary ladder: it closes the center, which makes Black's kingside attack more believable since wing attacks only work if the center is closed or under the attacker's control, and it turns the active Bishop on c4 into a blocked, bad thing. So 1.d5 gives us a bunch of negatives and, obviously, should have been avoided at all costs.

Summary of Imbalances and Ideas
[diagram (227)]

➤ White has more central space.

➤ White can easily gain queenside space by b2-b4 or a2-a4.

➤ Black has a hole on f5 that can easily turn into a wonderful home for a White Knight.

➤ Black appears to be threatening White's e-pawn by ...exd4, uncovering an attack by the Black Queen. If this is true, White should defend e4 with a move that still tries to make use of his other plusses (Ng3, defending e4 and hitting f5 is simple and to the point). If it's an illusion, then White can do anything he wants.

Problem 86

(228)

Black to move.

How would you handle the Black position?

Solution 86

Black's pieces are well placed, but there aren't any targets to strike at. White has doubled pawns and two Bishops. How can this information translate into a plan or move?

The two main considerations are Black's lack of a target and White's doubled pawns. The doubled pawns in this case give the first player added control of the center and are a useful commodity. Thus, Black needs to create a target and chip away at that doubled wall of pawns.

1...b5!

This excellent move does several wonderful things after 2.cxb5 axb5: 1) It suddenly targets the a2-pawn as a potential weakness. 2) The a8-Rook, inactive a moment ago, is now playing an aggressive role on the a-file. 3) With the removal of the c4-pawn, Black's Bishop has gained in scope. 4) With the removal of the c4-pawn, Black has gained control over the d5-square.

A plan like ...Bd5 followed by ...Ra6 and ...Qa8 would bring strong pressure to bear down the a8-h1 diagonal and the a8-a1 file.

Summary of Imbalances and Ideas
[diagram (228)]

➤ Black's Knight on c5 is an excellent piece.

➤ White has the two Bishops, but the d2-Bishop can't claim any particular activity.

➤ White has doubled pawns on c4 and c3, but they are both solid and control key central squares.

➤ Having an attractive position is one thing. Creating targets to attack is quite another. How can Black create targets in this position?

Problem 87

(229)

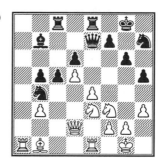

Anand-Kamsky, Las Palmas Match 1995.
White to move.

If you had a choice between 1.Ra7, 1.Nd1, 1.Nc2, 1.g4, or 1.e5, which would you play?

Solution 87

1.Ra7 achieves nothing after 1...Ra8. Don't play a move unless you've seriously considered the ramifications of your opponent's best reply!

1.Nc2 is too passive—White's Knight on e3 is actually destined for great deeds, while Black's b4-Knight will soon find itself in the gutter. Naturally, this can't come to pass if White exchanges Knights with 1.Nc2.

1.g4?? is one of those, "I'm going to mate you at all costs!" kind of moves. Why should White weaken his own kingside in a misguided attempt at mate when solid positional play will leave his opponent completely helpless?

1.e5 goes for the gusto, but you have to understand that you're burning your bridges with moves like this. They either work and prove extremely strong, or fail and lead to a complete disaster. In this case, 1...dxe5 2.d6 Qd7 leaves Black with an extra pawn. Also note that the b7-Bishop has been unleashed and is now very powerful.

The best move is, without a doubt, **1.Nd1!!**.

To understand this move, four things have to be pointed out:

✦ Black threatened to exchange Rooks on the a-file by ...Ra8.

✦ Black threatened to exchange his passive h7-Knight for White's useful f3-Knight by ...Ng5.

✦ White is ultimately aiming for an e4-e5 advance. However, he shouldn't rush into this push until the time is right.

✦ A glaring weakness in the Black camp is the b5-pawn. White would like to attack it and tie Black's pieces down to its defense.

White's Knight retreat, though odd looking, stops Black's ...Ng5 (White's Queen now hits that square) and prepares to swing the Knight around to c3 where it takes aim at Black's loose pawn on b5. Black can save his pawn by moving his b4-Knight and pushing the b-pawn to b4, but that leaves a once-active Knight on a poor square, and also creates a hole on c4.

After **1...Na6 2.Nc3 b4 3.Nb5 Nc7 4.Bd3 Nxb5 5.Bxb5 Red8 6.Bc4!** White has a wonderful position: The Bishop on c4 defends d5 and helps prepare for an eventual e4-e5 advance. White's Queen is ready to infiltrate into the Black kingside with Qh6, and White's Rook is ready to leap to a7. Black, on the other hand, doesn't have any plan at all—he has no weaknesses to attack, no pawn breaks to achieve—just prospects of a dreary defense and lots of pain.

In the end, Black's position fell apart and White scored a nice victory.

Summary of Imbalances and Ideas
[diagram (229)]

➤ Ultimately, White's goal is to blast Black in the center with a well-timed e4-e5 advance. White has a central majority of pawns and would like to use them. However, patience and care are called for.

➤ Black's pawn on b5 is a bit loose, and an attack against it will cause Black considerable unpleasantness.

➤ Black wants to swap his inactive Knight for White's active f3-Knight by ...Ng5. White should try and prevent this.

➤ At the moment, the e3-Knight isn't doing anything to make e4-e5 a reality, nor is it eyeing Black's b5-pawn. White would like to alleviate this situation.

Problem 88

Take a look at the following exciting but error-filled moves from the game Soto (1800)-Cassuto (1640), Los Angeles 1999: 1.e4 e6 2.d4 d5 3.Nc3 Bb4 4.e5 c5 5.a3 Ba5 6.b4 cxb4 7.Nb5 bxa3+ 8.c3 Bc7 9.Bxa3 Ne7 10.Bd6 Ba5 11.Bxe7 Kxe7 12.Qb3 Bc7 13.Qb4+ Ke8 14.Rxa7 Nc6 15.Qc5 Bb6 16.Nd6+ Kd7 17.Qxc6+ Kxc6 18.Bb5+ Kc7 19.Rxa8 Qg5 20.Ne2 Qe7 21.0-0 Rf8 22.Rb1 f6 23.Nf4 fxe5 24.dxe5 g5 25.Nd3 Qg7 26.Ra2.

How would you judge White's 17th move (17.Qxc6+), the position after 19.Rxa8, and White's 26th move (26.Ra2)?

Solution 88

(230)

Position after Black's 16th
move.
White to move.

17.Qxc6+

I've ignored the mistakes (some major!) that have occurred up to this point so we can enjoy the interesting positions that follow. After 16...Kd7 White had to play this Queen sacrifice since his Rook and Queen were forked. Note that 17.Rxa8 Bxc5 18.Rxc8 fails to 18...Qa5 when White's undeveloped kingside will lead to his demise.

At times, necessity forces you to play with verve and imagination!

(231)

Position after 19.Rxa8.
Black to move.

This position came about by force after White sacrificed his Queen on the 17th move. Though down a Queen for a Rook and minor piece, White enjoys a clear advantage. Black's King is in trouble, his pieces are tied up and useless, and the Knight on d6 and Rook on a8 are exceptionally powerful. In fact, together they are much stronger than Black's Queen.

Most amateurs have real trouble coming to terms with the loss of their Queen. Even when they obtain a material plus for the Queen—Rook and two minor pieces or two Rooks—doubt continues to plague them. Instead of being addicted to the Queen, a player must learn to be addicted to what his pieces are doing. Don't get trapped by the name of a piece or their point-count value!

(232)

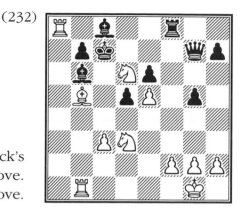

Position after Black's
25th move.
White to move.

26.Ra2?

Moving a dynamically placed piece to a passive square can't be right (in fact, Black eventually won this game). All of White's army is well placed and primed for combat, so the time for decisive action has clearly come.

Extremely tempting is 26.Be8, blocking the f8-Rook's defense of the c8-Bishop. 26...Bd7 27.Nc5!? Pointed out by Chris Brashers during a lecture I gave in Los Angeles. 27...Qxe5 28. Nxd7, but Black has 28...Bxf2+ 29.Kh1 Qxd6 30.Nxf8 Qxf8 31.Rxb7+ Kxb7 33.Bc6+ Kxc6 34.Rxf8 Be1 when the resulting endgame is drawn.

After 26.Be8 Bd7, another possibility is 27.Ra7!? Bxa7 28.Rxb7+ Kd8 29.Rxa7 Rxe8 30.Nc5 Rg8 (not 30...Re7 31.Rxd7+! Rxd7 32.Nxe6+) 31.g4! This is from the fertile mind of Louis Morin. White is trying to place Black is zugzwang, but 31...h5! 32.h3 Qe7! appears to get Black out of trouble.

So far passivity has failed (26.Ra2), and a heavy-handed search for beauty (26.Be8) also didn't quite get the job done, though such measures are often just what the doctor ordered. Instead, it would appear that cold practicality is in order: 26.Ne8+ Rxe8 27.Bxe8. However, Black would get some counterplay with 27...Qf8!.

In the end, let's follow the simple rule that states, "One must open up the position if the King is in the center." Thus, **26.c4!** is White's best plan: **26...Bxf2+** (26...Bd4 loses immediately to 27.Be8!) **27.Kh1! Bd7!** (27...Qg6 loses beautifully: 28.cxd5 Be3 29.Ne8+ Rxe8 30.d6+ Kd8 31.Rba1!! and White mates by force) **28.Rxf8 Qxf8 29.Rf1 Qa8 30.Nxf2** and White has a clear advantage.

Summary of Imbalances and Ideas
[diagram (230)]

➤ Material is even but White's Queen and Rook are forked. In fact, the Rook is attacked twice!

➤ Since quiet moves can't be considered, and normal positional devices have to be temporarily thrown out the window, White is forced to find a shocking and dynamic idea. If one doesn't exist, he'll lose.

➤ White has no choice; he's forced to sacrifice his Queen by Qxc6+.

[diagram (231)]

➤ White has a Rook and a minor piece for a Queen. Normally this wouldn't offer sufficient compensation, however other factors combine to make White's outlook appear to be rosy.

➤ Black's pieces are pathetic: neither Bishop is going anywhere, his King is in constant danger, and his Rook is playing a purely defensive role.

➤ White threatens to chop off the Bishop on c8.

➤ Black must constantly worry about Nxf7.

➤ All these factors must add up to a clear plus for White.

[diagram (232)]

➤ White's pieces are fantastically active. His a8-Rook is so threatening that he has no desire to ever move it away from a8.

➤ Passive moves are not acceptable in such a position. White must choose between a quest for beauty, or the cold, hard logic of practicality.

➤ Chess isn't a gambling game. In the end, White must play the move that he thinks will give him the best (and safest!) chance to win the game.

➤ When the King is in the center, open up the center and good things will happen!

Problem 89

(233)

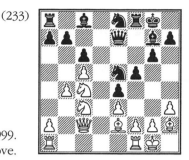

Suveg-Prieto, corr. 1999.
Black to move.

In this seemingly simple position, Black played 1...Nxc4. After 2.Bxc4+, which side would you prefer to play?

Solution 89

Believe it or not, White is struggling to equalize! The problems with White's game revolve around the pinned Knight, potential loss of the d-file, and Black's access to the d3-square. For example, 2...Be6 3.Qb3 Bxc4 4.Qxc4+ Qf7 5.Qxf7+ Rxf7 6.Rac1 Rd7 when Black owns the d-file and has threats like 7...Rad8, 7...Rd3, and 7...Rd2.

In the game, White answered **2...Be6** with **3.Bxe6+ Qxe6 4.Rab1!**, intending to meet **4...Qc4** with **5.Qb3 Qxb3 6.Rxb3 Rd8 7.Rd1**. Eventually he was able to draw. Instead of 4...Qc4, Black could also consider the critical win of a pawn by 4...Bxc3 5.Qxc3 Qxa2 when Black hopes to bring his Queen back to f7 and then rush his Knight to d5 via ...Ne8-f6-d5. Of course, White would prevent the Queen's retreat from a2 to f7 (after 5.Qxc3 Qxa2) by 6.Rb3, with mutual chances.

Summary of Imbalances and Ideas
[diagram (233)]

➤ The pin along the h8-a1 diagonal is annoying.

➤ White must be careful that the d3-square doesn't fall into Black's hands.

➤ Black will want to trade off the light-squared Bishops since White's light-squared Bishop is the guardian of the d3-square.

Problem 90

(234)

Stuart-Suveg, corr. 1999.
Black to move.

White just moved his Queen from c2 to b3. What plan(s) should Black consider in this position, and what was the point of White's last move?

Solution 90

Though it's unusual, Black actually can seek his play on all three parts of the board: he can go for a kingside decision, taking advantage of White's lack of play and the strength of the b7-Bishop, by ...h6 followed by ...g5, when fxg5 ...hxg5 opens up the h-file for Black and also sets up threats like ...Qc6 with ...g5-g4 to come.

In an effort to make use of his central pawn majority and to open up the position for his two Bishops, Black can expand in the center by ...d6 followed by ...e5.

Finally, queenside play can be sought by using the tried and true minority attack, with Black seeking an eventual ...b5-b4 advance.

All these ideas are nice, but you have to always take your opponent's ideas into account before doing anything. White's 1.Qb3 created potential threats of 2.a4 and 2.c4. Since White really doesn't have much else to do, Black played **1...Nb6**, ending White's dreams of activity and intending 2...Bd5. Once this was done, Black was able to go back to the original question of what

side of the board he intends to play on. Eventually he tried the
...d6 followed by ...e5 plan.

Summary of Imbalances and Ideas
[diagram (234)]

➤ Black has two Bishops, a distinct advantage in this
kind of open position.

➤ Black's control over the a8-h1 diagonal leaves
White's King feeling a bit insecure.

➤ Black can create an active central majority by playing an eventual ...d7-d6 followed by ...e6-e5.

➤ Black can play for a kingside attack with a
well-timed ...h7-h6 followed by ...g7-g5 since
fxg5 would open the h-file for Black's Rooks
after ...hxg5.

➤ Black can play for a minority attack on the
queenside with an eventual ...a6-a5 and ...b5-b4.

➤ Before following any of these plans, Black must
figure out White's intention and see if it's worth
stopping. In this case, ...Nb6 followed by ...Bd5
clamps down on the a4 and c4 squares and leaves
White with virtually no active play.

Problem 91

(235)

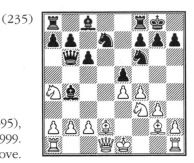

Martin (1360)-Piacenza (1695),
Los Angeles 1999.
Black to move.

In the game, Black played the calm 1...Bxd2+ 2.Qxd2 Qc7. White died a horrible death after 3.Qd3? exf4 4.gxf4 Qxf4 5.Nd2 Ne5 6.Qd4 Bg4 7.h3? Rad8 8.Qc3 Nxd3+! 9.cxd3 Qe3+ and mates.

White was rightfully punished for leaving his King in the center. However, instead of playing 1...Bxd2+, Black could have tried a sharper continuation which he saw and rejected. Was he correct in passing up possible glitter for the more secure and patient course he actually chose?

Solution 91

It's often right to ignore flashy continuations that don't lead to anything but a slight rise in blood pressure. In this case, Black looked at **1...Qe3+** but rejected it due to **2.Qe2**. Unfortunately, a player can't dismiss such variations out of hand; you should go a bit deeper and see if there's anything lurking underneath the position. Indeed, after **2...Bxd2+ 3.Nxd2 exf4!** Black wins a pawn and secures the e5-square for a Knight: **4.Qxe3 fxe3 5.Nf1** Better is 5.Nc4! b5 6.e5 with interesting complications, though Black retains the better game after 6...Nd5 (6...bxc4!?) 7.Na5 bxa4 8.Nxc6 N5b6 9.Ne7+ Kh8 10.Bxa8 Nxa8. **5...Re8 6.Nc3 Nc5**, etc.

Summary of Imbalances and Ideas
[diagram (235)]

➤ White's King is trapped in the center.

➤ A central King usually means that the opponent should play sharply in an attempt to make full use of the situation.

➤ Don't glance a move or two ahead and then reject things if you don't see an obvious followup.

Alekhine used to look one or two moves deep into seemingly placid situations and pretend that the resulting position was actually on the board. He would then scan this new situation for tactical and positional possibilities, often finding surprising tricks and subtle points.

➤ White's e-pawn is on the verge of being eaten.

➤ Black's Queen is under attack, but the White Knight on a4 has left the center, and the e4-pawn, undefended.

Problem 92

This is the game Makarewicz (1800)-Thomson (1900), Pasadena 1999. After 1.d4 Nf6 2.Nf3 g6 3.Bf4 Bg7 4.e3 0-0 5.Be2 d6 6.h3 c5 7.0-0 Qb6 8.Nbd2 cxd4 9.exd4 Nc6 10.c3 Nd5 11.Nc4 Qc7 12.Bg5 f6 13.Ne3 Nxc3, should White play 14.Bc4+ or 14.bxc3?

(236)

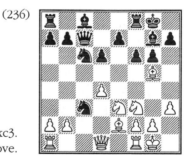

Position after 13...Nxc3.
White to move.

Solution 92

In the actual game White got sucked into a search for a tactical decision and played 14.Bc4+?. However, he hadn't taken a hard look at the resulting position and soon found himself in trouble after 14...d5 15.Nxd5 Nxd5 16.Bxd5+ e6 17.Bxc6 Qxc6 when Black's two Bishops and his control of d5 gave him a clear positional advantage.

Instead of taking this suicidal path, White should have played the calm **14.bxc3 fxg5 15.Nxg5**. Though Black's two Bishops still count for quite a bit after **15...e6**, White retains lots of play with **16.d5!**. Less good is 16.Bc4 d5 or 16.Bg4 Qe7.

Most tactical operations don't lead to a clear material gain or mate. Instead, you must decide what positional factors have been changed in your favor. In the present game White wasn't able to make the transition from tactics to strategy, and ended up paying a heavy price.

Summary of Imbalances and Ideas
[diagram (236)]

➤ Various things are hanging and it's easy to think that tactics will rule here. However, the positional ramifications of a tactical operation must always be kept firmly in mind.

➤ Black is going to get the two Bishops no matter what White does. Since the center is fairly open, which means that the two Bishops will most likely be advantageous, White needs to create some other positional plus for himself before the smoke clears.

Problem 93

(237)

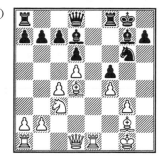

Petrosian-Fischer, Portoroz 1958.
Black to move.

White enjoys the superior position. Do you see why White's game is better? Can Black improve his situation with correct play? How?

Solution 93

Black's lack of space, his inactive pieces and his potentially weak pawns on f5 and h7 all make his life rather difficult. In such situations, all Black can do is to rid himself of his weak points when possible and strive to increase the activity of his pieces.

1...Bxd4+

By pulling the the White Queen away from it's control over h5, Black can safely advance his h-pawn.

In the actual game, Fischer played the poor 1...Rf7? and found himself suffering for the rest of the game after 2.Bf3, stopping the advance of the h-pawn.

2.Qxd4 h5 when Black is able to rid himself of one of his problems by 3...h5-h4. Also note that when the g-pawn is traded for Black's h-pawn, the g6-Knight will have access to h4 and the f4-pawn will suddenly become a bit vulnerable.

Summary of Imbalances and Ideas
[diagram (237)]

➤ Black has potentially weak pawns on f5 and h7.

➤ Black must not let White occupy the e6-square.

➤ Can Black rid himself of one of his weaknesses?

Problem 94

(238)

Makarewicz (1800)-McCrue (1946),
Los Angeles 1999.
White to move.

What would you do if you were White?

Solution 94

White needs to create a weakness in the enemy camp and he needs to grab some space before he's squeezed to death. Black's King is also a bit loose and opening up the position will put a little emphasis on its exposed state. The proper way to accomplish these goals is **1.e4**, taking central space, preparing to open up the e-file so that the Rooks will hit e6 (a quick Rfe1 will follow), and activating the White Queen.

Summary of Imbalances and Ideas
[diagram (238)]

➤ White has less space than his opponent. Are you going to accept this unsatisfactory state of affairs?

➤ Black's King is a bit drafty.

➤ White needs to open lines for his Rooks which, at the moment, are completely inactive.

➤ It would be nice if White had a target to attack in the Black position. Since it's not staring us in the face, you will have to create it.

Problem 95

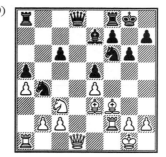

(239)

Karpov-Spassky, Leningrad 1974.
White to play.

How would you play this position? Be ready to discuss its secrets in detail.

Solution 95

White has the two Bishops, though at the moment this doesn't appear to be worth much. White also has potential pressure down the f-file and he would like to eye Black's weak pawns on a5 and c6. Most important is the juicy c4-square, ready and waiting for White to occupy.

The move that addresses most of these points is:

1.Qf1!

Aside from putting pressure on the f-file, White avoids the exchange of Queens because he sees that his Queen will ultimately be stronger than its opposite number. Why? Because the White Queen has a great home waiting on c4 where it eyes c6 and f7. The Black Queen does not have a square of equivalent strength.

In general, trade your weakest pieces but make sure you retain the men that you feel will eventually be better than their enemy counterparts.

It is also important to point out that the obvious and very tempting 1.Rd2 is not so good because at the moment the f-file may be more important than the d-file. Note that there are no penetration points along the d-file: d4, d5, d6, d7 and d8 all being securely covered.

Finally, 1.Qf1 is superior to 1.Qe2 because it allows for Rd2 in some variations, increases the pressure down the f-file, and leaves e2 open for a Bf3-e2-c4 maneuver.

1...Qc8 2.h3

Stopping ...Ng4.

2...Nd7

This prepares to trade off Black's dark-squared Bishop for White's powerful Bishop on e3 via 3...Bc5. Karpov points out that 2...Qe6 could be met by 3.Rc1, defending the c2-pawn in anticipation of Be2 which would block the f2-Rook's defense of c2, followed by Be2 and Bc4.

3.Bg4

Pinning the Knight, opening the f-file, and stopping Black's threat of ...Bc5.

3...h5 4.Bxd7 Qxd7 5.Qc4. Now White's Queen is far superior to the Black one and White's dark-squared Bishop is also better than Black's. In fact, the only Black piece that is better than a White one is the Knight on b4. White's advantage is obvious.

Summary of Imbalances and Ideas
[diagram (239)]

➤ White has the two Bishops.

➤ At the moment, Black's Knight on b4 is more active than White's on c3.

➤ White has potential pressure down the half-open f-file.

➤ The c4-square might turn out to be a good home for White's pieces.

➤ Black's pawns on a5 and c6 are isolated and therefore potentially vulnerable.

Problem 96

(240)

Karpov-Spassky, Leningrad 1974.
White to play.

White has a clear advantage, but making this statement and improving your position are two very different things. In fact, it's often in this kind of situation that one's edge, visually so clear, begins to evaporate with each and every move.

What should White do to increase his superiority?

Solution 96

All of White's pieces are doing a good job with the exception of his Knight, to which both b5 and d5 are inaccessible. Just because it's developed doesn't mean it's happy or serving a useful function.

Karpov's move makes perfect sense when you realize that the Knight needs to find a new home.

1.Nb1!

A very powerful retreating move. White defends his Rook and prepares to recycle his Knight to greener pastures. Most importantly, White has freed his c-pawn and can now chase Black's well-placed Knight away with c2-c3.

Never allow an opponent's piece to stay on a great square if you have a simple way of chasing it away.

Note that the pseudo-aggressive 1.Bc5 doesn't accomplish anything at all after 1...Qb7.

1...Qb7 2.Kh2!

Keeping the enemy Bishop off of g3.

2...Kg7 3.c3 Na6 4.Re2!

White avoids an exchange of Rooks and frees the d2-square for the Knight. The horse will now move around to f3 via d2 and attack the Black Bishop and e5-pawn.

4...Rf8 5.Nd2 Bd8

And not 5...Qxb2?? 6.Nf3 when both the Black Queen and Bishop are under attack. Many players wouldn't move their Knight to d2 here for fear of hanging the b-pawn. You can't reject good moves in this fashion. Instead, you have to treat the situation after 5...Qxb2 as the actual position and see if you have any way to take advantage of Black's far-advanced Queen and undefended Bishop on h4.

Unfortunately, it's all too common for a player to say to himself, "I can't play 5.Nd2 since that hangs my b-pawn." If you want to play a move, challenge yourself to make it work! Any thoughts of "I can't" should be erased from your mind.

6.Nf3 f6 7.Rd2 Be7 8.Qe6 Rad8 9.Rxd8 Bxd8 10.Rd1 Nb8 Keeping the Rook off of d7. **11.Bc5 Rh8 12.Rxd8!**, **1-0**. Black's world ends after 12...Rxd8 13.Be7.

Summary of Imbalances and Ideas
[diagram (240)]

➤ Black's Knight is annoying as long as it's allowed to remain on b4.

➤ The only way to chase Black's Knight away is by playing c2-c3. However, White's Knight is blocking this advance.

➤ White's Knight has no future on c3.

➤ Black's pawns on a5 and c6 are isolated and therefore potentially vulnerable.

➤ Black's f7-pawn is under some pressure from White's Queen and the f1-Rook.

Problem 97

(241)

Black to move.

Black has a very comfortable Sicilian position and he can handle this situation in several different ways. There's one move that a good player would choose instantly. However, a less experienced player might never even consider it.

Solution 97

Let's take a moment and discuss the gospel of point-count:

When we learn to play chess we are told that pawns are worth one point, Bishops and Knights are worth three points, Rooks are worth five points, a Queen is worth nine points, and a King is priceless since its loss also means the loss of the game. These point-count comparisons are quite useful at first, but eventually they can actually color our vision when it comes to what pieces are really worth in any given situation.

Probably the most commonly seen argument with point-count tradition is the oft-employed Exchange sacrifice. Grandmasters seem to sacrifice Rooks for enemy Knights and Bishops all the time, but ordinary mortals usually get cold feet when it comes to giving up five points for a mere three.

When I was a teenager in San Diego, I used to be amazed by the play of a gentleman who learned how to move the pieces at the age of 70 and thought that Bishops were better than Rooks. He would give up his Rooks at the first opportunity for enemy Bishops, and often win as a result! The fact that this guy could toss away material for no good reason and still retain a 1900 rating shows us that point-count is not a good master to follow blindly.

If we are going to ignore the dictates of point-count on occasion, then what should we be looking for? Well, point-count is a useful tool, but often the normal values of pieces are warped by positional or tactical considerations. All these must be taken into account before a decision of any kind is made.

The position in the diagram shows a situation that begs for a very common Exchange sacrifice. A grandmaster wouldn't hesitate for a moment to play **1...Rxc3! 2.bxc3 Nxe4** when 3.Qd4 is met by 3...d5 with ...Bf6 to follow. No calculation needed: he would just reach out and do it. For the Rook, he gets a well-placed Knight, a strong central pawn, and a clear structural advantage. True, he's down four points to five, but it's not a mere count that interests a strong player. Instead, he wants to gain as many advantages as possible—material is just one of many different plusses. In the present situation, White's tiny extra point can't make up for Black's many other favorable imbalances.

Summary of Imbalances and Ideas
[diagram (241)]

➤ Black's position is very solid and he has some pressure against e4 and down the c-file.

➤ An experienced player would instantly look at the consequences of ...Rxc3.

➤ Don't worship at the feet of materialism. Other factors, like pawn structure and the activity of the pieces, must also be given full respect.

Problem 98

(242)

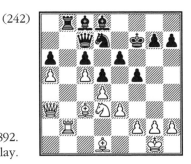

Steinitz-Chigorin, Havana Match 1892.
White to play.

White is much better, but it's very hard to break through and force a win. How would you handle this position?

Solution 98

The position in diagram (242) is very good for White. He has more space, more active pieces, play against the hole on e5 and chances to pressure the Black pawns on a6 and c6. Black has just played ...Rb8, hoping to trade Rooks. This follows the rule that the side with less space should seek exchanges since that will give more room for his other pieces to move about in.

White did not want to avoid the swap by moving his Rook off the b-file. Why turn the file over to Black? Instead, White played a move that increased all of his advantages in a striking way.

1.Rb6!

This powerful use of the support point on b6 attacks both a6 and c6 and sends the following message to Black: "If you want to take my Rook you will have to give me new, advanced squares for my pieces, a powerful passed pawn on b6 and increased pressure against your pawn on c6 and hole on e5."

In other words, White decided that the two points (according to point-count, White will be losing five points for three) lost after 1...Nxb6 would be more than compensated by all the positional plusses he gains. White is not playing for mate. He is not playing for material (of course, White would take a mate or free material if his opponent was kind enough to offer them). He is playing for the acquisition of several small gains that will eventually reap greater rewards. Let's see how this game went.

1...Nxb6 2.cxb6!

Breaking another rule by capturing away from the center (the beginner's books tell us to always capture *towards* the center)! However, in this case White is giving his Knight access to c5 and giving his dark-squared Bishop a chance to get active along the a3-f8 diagonal. Don't blindly follow rules! Every move you play should add to the strength of the rest of your army.

2...Qb7

Black is hoping the Knight will be lured to the c5-square.

3.Ne5+

Placing a Knight on c5 would prevent White's dark-squared Bishop from getting active on the a3-f8 diagonal. Don't let the selfishness of one piece interfere with the activity of the others. By putting the Knight on e5, White sets up a future multiple-attack against c6 by his Knight, light-squared Bishop and Queen.

3...Kg8 4.Ba4

White attacks c6 by bringing all his pieces into play. Chess is a team game. Don't use just one or two pieces and forget about the rest.

4...Qe7

This is desperation but 4...Bd7 5.Qd6 Be8 6.Bb4, threatening 7.Qf8+, is completely hopeless.

5.Bb4 Qf6 6.Qc3 h6 7.Bd6 and Black resigned after a few more moves.

Why did Black lose so badly? Because the only attackable targets on the board were owned by Black, which means that White was attacking and Black was on the defensive. Also important was the fact that Black's Rook had no open files. A Rook is only better than a Bishop or a Knight if it can penetrate into the enemy position on an open file. If such a file does not exist then a well-placed Knight or Bishop can often run rings around the clumsy Rook. Never say that Rooks are better than Bishops or Knights. Ask, "Are Rooks better than Bishops or Knights in *this* particular position?"

Summary of Imbalances and Ideas
[diagram (242)]

➤ White has more queenside space.

➤ White's Knight is eyeing the hole on e5.

➤ Black's pawns on a6 and c6 are targets.

➤ The side with more space usually tries to avoid exchanges. However, if White's Rook moves away from the b-file, Black will gain control of it.

➤ White's pieces are more active than their Black counterparts.

Problem 99

(243)

MacDonnell-Labourdonnais,
London 1834.
Black to play.

Black has a big lead in development and pressure against d4. White has more central space but his King is strangely posted. Who stands better?

Solution 99

If White could maintain his center and develop his forces, he would stand much better. As is usual in positions where one side is ahead in development, the attacker must play as dynamically as possible before his opponent gets the remainder of his forces out.

1...Rxf3+!

This sacrifice of the Exchange destroys the White center and gives Black added control over the f5-square. Though many people might worry about the "loss" of one point (Black gets a Knight and a pawn for his Rook), an experienced master would have no doubts about the wisdom of this decision. Why? Because he achieves his strategic goal. He succeeds in destroying the White center. In other words, this sacrifice was not played with gross threats in mind. It was played so that Black's positional ideals could be achieved.

2.gxf3 Nxd4 3.Bd3 Rf8

This looks like a silly one-move attack against the f3-pawn. Black is well aware that White is going to push it up to f4 but that is just what Black wants! The idea is that the pawn on f4 will permanently block the c1-Bishop. The real purpose behind ...Rf8 is now clear: Black wanted to create a bad Bishop on c1.

4.f4 Bc5

The Bishop was no longer doing anything on b4 so it takes up a new home on c5. Now the Black Queen is staring at b2, the d4-Knight is firmly defended and the line-up on the a7-g1 diagonal is making everything quiver in fear.

5.Rf1 Bb5!

Always be on the lookout for ways to trade off your bad pieces for the enemy's good ones. This move gets rid of the awful Bishop on d7 for White's pride and joy on d3.

6.Bxb5 Qxb5 7.Kh3 Ne2 8.Ng2 Nf5

The f5-square has been beckoning this Knight for a long time. Notice how Black is playing quietly and slowly, showing no fear that White's extra Exchange will play a major role in the coming battle. Why is Black so confident? Because all his pieces are more active than their White counterparts, because White has weak pawns on f4 and h4 while Black has no weaknesses anywhere, and because the Black Knights are better than either White Rook.

9.Kh2 Neg3 10.Rf3 Ne4 11.Qf1 Qe8

Refusing to trade Queens and take some of the heat off the exposed White King. If your opponent's King is more exposed than yours is, keep the Queens on the board!

12.b4 Bd4 13.Rb1 Qh5 14.Rbb3 Rc8

Black doesn't play 14...Nxh4 for two reasons. First, why exchange that beautiful Knight on f5 for White's pathetic one on g2? Second, 14...Nxh4 allows White to play 15.Rh3. Never enter complications when a simple build-up will ensure victory in a safe but sure manner. The logic behind 14...Rc8 is clear: All of Black's pieces are showing maximum activity except that f8-Rook. On c8 the Rook controls the open c-file and threatens to penetrate deep into the White camp. White is so helpless that he can't do anything to stop Black's intentions.

15.Be3 Rc2 16.Kg1 Nxe3

Normally Black wouldn't dream of exchanging his super horse for the silly Bishop but this sets in motion a series of pins and forks that puts a permanent end to White's resistance. As strong as this turns out to be, the family fork with 16...Nd2! is even better.

17.Rfxe3 Nd2 18.Qd3 Rc1+ 19.Kh2 Nf1+! 20.Kh3 Nxe3 21.Nxe3 and White resigned without waiting for his opponent's reply since 21...Qf3+ 22.Kh2 Rh1 is mate.

Summary of Imbalances and Ideas
[diagram (243)]

➤ White has more central space.

➤ White's King is oddly placed and can't be considered completely safe.

➤ Black has a nice lead in development.

➤ Black has pressure against White's pawn on d4.

➤ If White can calmly finish mobilizing his forces, his edge in central territory might amount to something. This means that Black must start a fight now, before White's pieces reach the center.

Problem 100

Some grandmasters pull madly on a locket of hair while pondering their moves. Others shake in their seats or contort their faces in frightful ways. Why are they doing this? Do they have lice? Are they terrified? Do they suffer from delirium tremens?

Solution 100

Chess success depends on willpower, but few seem to really appreciate this important point. When I watch a grandmaster pulling on his nose while he agonizes over a move, I realize that he already knows what he wants to accomplish. His energy is being spent on the method of achieving his goal. To this end, he often won't move until he finds a way to make his desires turn into reality.

Situations involving willpower come up all the time—your opponent tries some idea and you must either let him get away with it or (metaphorically!) slap him in the face and make him take a few steps back. The ability to spot a flaw in his concept, and the desire to impose your own set of views on the situation, is a large part of what makes up chess strength. Thus willpower—a mind that insists on achieving the goals it set—is a major part of every grandmaster's makeup.

VIKTOR KORCHNOI

Problem 101

(244)

Milat-Silman,
National Open 1998.
Black to move.

I had been in agony the whole game (White had missed at least one instant win), and the creation of various perpetual check themes was my last line of defense. After offering my opponent several bottles of free beer which he refused, seemingly intent on winning the game, we reached the position in the diagram.

Black has a choice between two legal moves: 1...Kd7 and 1...Ke7. Is there any real difference between the two? If so, what?

Solution 101

1...Ke7!

This is a very important move, and it shows how selection between seemingly similar choices can have an enormous impact on a game's result. When faced with this kind of decision, you can't take it lightly. It's very important to hunker down and try and discern what the differences are, and how those differences will ultimately affect your chances. In this case, one of the moves draws, while the other simply loses.

The pawn endgame after 1...Kd7?? 2.Qe6+! Qxe6 3.fxe6 is lost for Black because White recaptures with check (this is the difference!). Then 3...Kxe6 4.g4 gives Black a very inferior version of the actual game because his kingside majority would be crippled.

2.Qe6+!?

At the time I was positive that this allowed me to save myself, though much of that view was based on ignorance. I was more worried about 2.Qxh7+ Kd6 3.Qb7 though I was pretty sure that 3...Qd1+ would give me sufficient play. I reasoned that my King was active, White's King was vulnerable, and the White Queen was out of play and unable to stop perpetual check. Whether this really drew didn't matter at the time, the game had been going on for hours and my old, exhausted brain was willing to grab hold of any happy result, real or imagined, that it saw.

2...Qxe6
3.fxe6 f5

My opponent's face fell when I blitzed out this move. He later admitted that he missed it. Now my kingside majority is mobile and it's also keeping his King at bay.

4.b3 Kxe6
5.c3

I began to think that I might even have winning chances! At this point a well-known grandmaster happened to stroll by. He glanced at the position for a couple of minutes and walked away. Later he confided that he also thought that I was on top (two minutes isn't time enough for anyone to figure things out, but it does show that even a world class player won't find these positions easy).

Now I began to think. I thought and thought and thought and became more and more depressed as the minutes ticked by. Finally I convinced myself that I was lost. White can create an annoying outside passed pawn on the queenside. True, Black's King is more active than White's but, during the game, I couldn't see how this was going to save me against best play! Cursing my luck, I struggled to find some saving scheme and finally came up with something. Notice that I didn't say "something good."

5...Ke5

At the time I thought this was very important. The idea is to meet 6.Ke3 with 6...f4+. Later I'll show that this check is a losing blunder. However, during the game I fully intended to play it! Embarrassing but true! 7.Kf3 (7.Kd3 Kd5 8.b4 c4+ 9.Ke2 g4 creates a drawing blockade. This is one of the important points of 5...Ke5) 7...Kf5 8.b4 g4+ 9.Ke2 Ke4 10.a5 bxa5 11.bxa5 Kd5. I really believed I was drawing here since 12.Kd3?? is met by 12...c4+.

I happily rested in my fool's paradise until I got home. Setting up this position on a board, I immediately noticed that 12.c4+! wins: 12...Kc6 13.Kd3 Kb7 14.Ke4 f3 15.gxf3 gxf3 16.Kxf3 Ka6 17.Ke4 Kxa5 18.Ke5! Ka4 19.Kd6 Kb4 20.Kd5 and Black is toast. This classic situation is known as a Trébuchet!

Fortunately, my opponent agreed with my early incorrect assessment and tossed out:

6.g3

Now the game was eventually agreed drawn due to a line I'd worked out when I played 5...Ke5: **6.g3 Kd5 7.Ke3 Kd6 8.Kd2 Kd5 9.Kc2** And not 9.Kd3?? c4+! when Black wins. **9...Kd6 10.Kd3 Kd5 11.b4 Kc6 12.Kc4 cxb4 13.cxb4 b5+! 14.axb5+ Kb6 15.Kd5 Kxb5 16.Ke5 f4 17.gxf4 gxf4 18.Kxf4 Kxb4 19.Kf5 Kc5 20.Kf6 Kd6 21.Kg7 Ke7 22.Kxh7 Kf7** with a basic draw.

At the time I was impressed with myself. As already pointed out, though, my elation turned to self-loathing when I returned home. It seemed (incorrectly, as it turns out) that I was indeed lost after 6.Ke3. In a way, I was lucky to have been deluded. Who knows what I would have done if I'd seen what was "really" going on? In this case, ignorance really was bliss.

Now other voices started to join in on this King and pawn endgame debate. First IM Jack Peters offered up some new ideas from the diagrammed position:

(245)

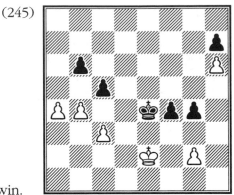

White to move and win.

I have already pointed out that 10.a5 (10.bxc5 bxc5 11.c4 also does the trick) 10...bxa5 11.bxa5 Kd5 12.c4+ wins for White, but Jack noted, quite correctly, that Black can put up a better but ultimately hopeless defense after 12...Kc6 13.Kd3 Kb7 14.Ke4 with, instead of my 14...f3, 14...Ka6 15.Kxf4 Kxa5 16.Kxg4 Kb4 17.Kf3! Kxc4 18.g4 with four possibilities:

✦ 18...Kd5 19.g5 Ke6 20.g6, Queening.

✦ 18...Kb3 19.g5 c4 20.g6 c3 21.g7! when White
  Queens with check.

✦ 18...Kd3 19.g5 c4 20.g6 c3 21.gxh7 c2 22.h8=Q c1=Q
  23.Qd8+ Kc2 24.Qc8+ Kb1 25.Qxc1+ Kxc1 26.h7
  and White wins.

✦ 18...Kb4 19.g5 c4 20.g6 c3 21.Ke2 Ka3 22.gxh7 c2
  23.Kd2 Kb2 24.h8=Q+.

I wasn't too upset by these additions. They basically verified my own conclusions. Then I found a bombshell waiting in my e-mail. A strong grandmaster (who wishes to remain anonymous) claimed that my analysis was completely flawed and that Black was better after all (that makes two grandmasters who were off their rocker!), though a draw would ultimately be the correct result!

Shocked, I glanced at his e-mail "blindfolded" (as the years roll by, I get lazier and lazier and often don't bother looking at a chessboard) and took his word for it (yes, I too am influenced by a high rating!). Sending the analysis to IM John Watson, he lambasted me for listening to anyone (a very wise bit of criticism, by the way!). This prompted me to take a closer look and I immediately saw that the grandmaster was hallucinating.

(246)

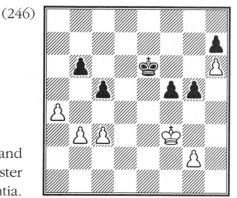

Black to play and
demonstrate grandmaster
dementia.

5...Kd5

The "Unknown Grandmaster" considered 5...Ke5 (the actual game continuation) to be a mistake. As we shall eventually see, it turns out that, in reality, both 5...Kd5 and 5...Ke5 lead to a draw.

6.Ke3 Kc6

Black's idea is to play ...b6-b5. I must admit that I'd never considered such a plan.

7.Kd3

The grandmaster claimed a Black win after 7.b4 Kd5 8.Kd3 f4 9.a5 bxa5 (this analysis is horribly flawed. Here, 9...c4+ is the correct way for Black to ice the game) 10.bxa5 (and now 10.c4+ gives White the better game!) 10...c4+ 11.Ke2 g4, but IM John Watson and Patrick Hummel (2300) pointed out that he was a bit off since 9.c4+ wins easily for White. IM Ron Burnett came back with a challenge: "Just how does White win after 9.c4+?" Fortunately, Mr. Hummel had answered this several days earlier and saved me the trouble of doing any real work: 9.c4+ Kd6 (9...Ke5 10.bxc5 bxc5 11.a5 Kd6 12.Ke4 is easy for White) 10.b5 Ke5 11.Ke2! g4 (also hopeless is 11...Kf5 12.a5) 12.Kd3 and White's King will penetrate to e4 and enjoy a feast.

7...b5 I later discovered that this is a blunder and that Black can still draw with a correct seventh move, though I'm leaving it to the reader to figure this out for himself. Now our mystery GM claims a draw after 8.axb5+ Kxb5 9.Ke2 Kc6 10.g3 Kd5 11.Ke3 Ke5 12.Kf3 Kd5. However, IM Watson once again points out that White wins easily with 8.a5 (instead of 8.axb5+??) 8...b4 9.cxb4 cxb4 10.Kd4 Kb5 11.Ke5 Kxa5 12.Kxf5 Kb5 13.Kf6 Kc5 14.Kg7 and it's time for Black to hang up his Rooks.

So what does this mean? Are IMs better endgame players than GMs (yes, published for the first time! IMs are indeed better than GMs at the endgame!)? Was the GM pulling my leg? Is there any meaning to unearth? I tend to think that the GMs in question were too lazy to give this position a serious look. But it does show that endgames can be very tricky, and that anyone is capable of completely misjudging such a complicated situation.

For those that are interested, the best defense appears to be:

(247)

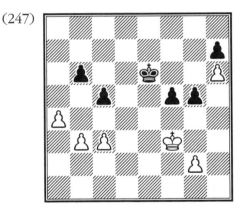

5...Ke5

As played in the actual game. At the last second, I also discovered that 5...Kd5 draws in all lines! A small sample: 6.Ke3 Kc6 7.b4 Kd5 8.Kd3 Kc6 9.Kc4 cxb4 10.cxb4 b5+! 11.axb5+ Kb6 12.Kd5 Kxb5 13.Ke5 f4! and Black draws as in Peters' subsequent analysis to 5...Ke5. I'll leave it up to the reader to figure out all the other details (and there are LOTS of complicated details to figure out!) for himself.

6.Ke3 Kd5

Instead of my original intention of 6...f4+??, which was analyzed earlier.

7.Ke2 Ke4 8.b4 cxb4!

Worse is 8...Kd5 9.Kd3 f4 10.c4+! Kc6 (10...Kd6 11.b5 Ke5 12.Ke2 g4 13.Kd3 isn't any better) 11.b5+ Kd6 12.Ke4 Ke6 13.g3 (or the simple 13.Kf3) and Black's defense breaks down. Analysis by Patrick Hummel.

9.cxb4 Kd4 10.a5 bxa5 11.bxa5 Kc5 12.Kd3

This was given as a White win by Mr. Hummel and John Watson, but Jack Peters points out that the position is a draw.

12...Kb5 13.Kd4 Kxa5 14.Ke5 f4!

This very important, but simple, move was missed by Watson, Hummel and myself. Black's King looks awfully far away, doesn't it?

15.Kf5 Kb6 16.Kxg5 Kc6 17.Kf6

A book draw follows 17.Kxf4 Kd7 18.Kf5 Ke7 since Black's King gets to h8.

17...Kd7 18.Kg7 Ke7 19.Kxh7 Kf7 and now the point of 14...f4! is clear: White doesn't have a tempo move that will enable him to regain the opposition. Thus, the game is drawn.

I gave this complicated analysis—really far outside the scope of the rather basic initial question—for three reasons: 1) Some players will get a lot of enjoyment going over the variations. 2) Some players will learn quite a bit about typical King and pawn endgames. 3) This shows just how difficult King and pawn endgames can be. However, none of this would be possible without an understanding of basics like opposition and outside passed pawns.

Summary of Imbalances and Ideas
[diagrams (244-247)]

➤ At times seemingly simple positions have unplumbed depths to them.

➤ If you have a choice of two moves, make sure you give the position a thorough look before tossing one of them out.

➤ It's impossible to solve a complicated endgame
without a solid understanding of the basics
(opposition for King and pawn endgames,
Lucena and Philidor positions for Rook endings).

Problem 102

(248)

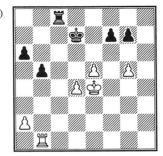

M.Adams-J.Emms, London 1991.
White to move.

White's passed d-pawn and vastly superior King give him a winning
advantage. What's the best way to proceed?

Solution 102

Though a passed d-pawn and a superior King are wonderful things,
possessing them doesn't mean you can stop looking for ways to
gain new advantages.

1.g6!

This move effectively ends the game. Black must choose between 1...f6 2.exf6 (forcing the creation of a monster passed pawn
on g6) 2...gxf6 3.Kf5 (the White King continues to assert itself)
3...Ke7 4.Re1+ Kf8 5.Kxf6 or he can take on g6, as happened in
the actual game.

1...fxg6
2.Rg1

Black's extra pawn is hardly something to be proud of, while
White's newly created connected passers on d4 and e5 are winning possessions.

2...Rc6 3.Kd5 b4 4.Rf1

White's Rook joins the act and the end comes abruptly.

4...Rc2 5.e6+ Ke7 6.Rf7+ Ke8 7.Kd6, 1-0.

Summary of Imbalances and Ideas
[diagram (248)]

➤ Even though you might have several big advantages, never stop looking for ways to add new plusses to your résumé.

➤ By getting rid of Black's f-pawn, White's e-pawn instantly turns into a powerful passer. That only leaves one question: how can White eradicate Black's f-pawn?

Problem 103

(249)

D. Pruess (2200)-P. Ruggiero (2100),
San Francisco 1998.
Black to move.

Black's King is in check, but does the first player have any real winning chances?

Solution 103

This position is hopelessly drawn. Even without the f-pawn, the game could and should be agreed drawn. An understanding of the following basic endgames would turn this into a trivial affair:

✦ LUCENA: Black can't allow White to reach a Lucena position.

(250)

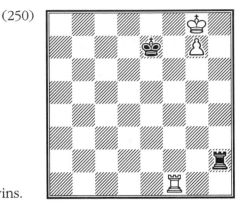

White wins.

This Lucena position wins for White after **1.Re1+ Kd7 2.Re4!**
This is called, "building a bridge." **2...Kd6 3.Kf7 Rf2+ 4.Kg6 Rg2+
5.Kf6 Rf2+ 6.Kg5 Rg2+ 7.Rg4, 1-0**.

✦ PHILIDOR: Even if Black doesn't know the Philidor
   position and misplays the defense, he will still draw
   because White's remaining pawn is a g-pawn.

(251)

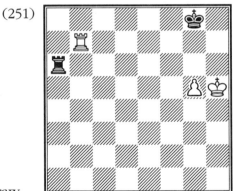

A simple draw.

This basic Philidor position leaves White with no chance to
win. Black just moves his Rook back and forth on the 6th rank
(...Ra6-c6-a6-c6, etc) and White will be unable to make progress.
Eventually White will be compelled to play 1.g6 when 1...Ra1 or
1...Rc1 leaves White open to endless checks via ...Rh1+.

(252)

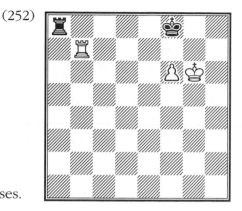

Passive Rook loses.

Black's passive Rook leads to his demise. White plays **1.Rh7 Kg8 2.f7+** and wins instantly. In general, the defender must avoid this type of situation and strive to reach the calm waters of the Philidor position (previous diagram).

(253)

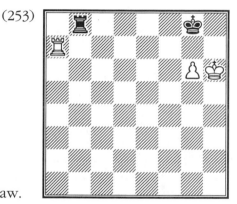

A mindless draw.

In this diagram Black has played horribly and allowed White to milk the position for every possible advantage. Nevertheless, the fact that White's remaining pawn is a g-pawn makes the game uninteresting. The reason lies in the fact that White's Rook can't leap far enough to the other side of the King. 1.Rh7 contains no threat as it did in the previous diagram.

Going back to the position in our original diagram (249), we can appreciate that a Class C player (1400-1599) should draw a master with ease. Unfortunately, a nightmare ensues (I'm not sure if these are the exact moves, but the basic gist is accurate):

1...Kg7

2.Kh5 Rb1?

Preparing to make a bad check. Note the problem she is facing here: Pam desperately wants to be active and fails to realize that passive defense would quickly draw the game.

In general, it's very important to make your Rook active in Rook endgames. However, in the present situation her Rook is needed to defend against mates, stop enemy checks and bother the White King from the side and *not* from the rear, as she is trying to do here.

A very simple draw could have been obtained by 2...f3 or the passive but effective 2...Rb7.

3.Ra7+ Kg8
4.Kh6 Rh1+??

Overlooking the reply!

Seriously, why play a move that helps the opponent? By forcing White's King to g6, Black creates a mate threat against her own monarch. This leads to her King being pushed away from the front of the pawn. In turn, this sets the seeds for the creation of a winning Lucena Position.

One simple way to draw was 4...Rb6+ 5.g6 Rb8 when, with an extra Black pawn, we have the position from diagram (253).

5.Kg6 and White managed to win, though I don't have the concluding moves. Oddly enough, the position still appears to be drawn: **5...Kf8 6.Ra8+** Useless is 6.Rf7+ Kg8 7.Rxf4 Ra1 followed 8...Ra8 with a basic draw, as seen in diagram (253). **6...Ke7 7.Ra4** Or 7.Kg7 f3 8.Ra2 Rg1 9.g6 Rg2 with a draw. **7...f3!** And not 7...Rf1 8.Kg7 f3 9.g6 f2 10.Re4+ Kd6 when 11.Re2! wins. **8.Rf4 Rf1 9.Kg7 f2 10.g6 Ke6! 11.Re4+ Kd5** Even simpler is 11...Kf5 12.Re2 Kf4 13.Kf7 Kf3. **12.Re2 Kd4 13.Kf7 Kd3 14.g7 Kxe2 16.g8=Q** and, though White has managed to Queen, the game still can't be won.

The endgame after 5.Kg6 turned out to be surprisingly interesting!

Summary of Imbalances and Ideas
[diagrams (249-253)]

➤ If you don't possess an understanding of the most basic Rook endings, you are setting yourself up for huge helpings of pain, suffering, and humiliation.

➤ You *must* obtain a thorough understanding of the Lucena and Philidor positions! Don't wait. Study these positions NOW!

➤ Being a pawn down in a Rook and pawn endgame is often no big deal if you know what you're doing. If the opponent has an extra g- or h-pawn then your drawing chances are even greater than usual.

Problem 104

In an endgame, which minor piece dominates if there is a pawn race involving passed pawns on both sides of the board?

Solution 104

The long-range ability of a Bishop makes it far superior to a Knight when running pawns exist on both sides of the board. Make sure you understand the middlegame and endgame implications of a Bishop versus Knight battle.

Problem 105

In an endgame, what can you do to make a Knight superior to a Bishop?

Solution 105

A Knight often rules in closed positions because it's the only piece that can jump over enemy or friendly pawns. A Knight also takes on added value in positions where all the pawns have been traded on one side of the board. By creating a situation where pawns only exist on one side of the board, the long-range abilities of the enemy Bishop are neutralized, and the fact that a Knight can move to any colored square (this means that the enemy King can eventually be checked off of any square, and the enemy pawns will always be vulnerable to attack) suddenly makes the humble horse far superior to a mere Bishop.

Problem 106

(254)

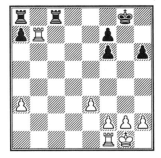

Silman-Nocon (2250),
National Open 1998.
White to move.

White is obviously doing well, but claiming a clear, easy, win is quite another matter. Write down your general observations about this position and then, based on the power and logic of these observations, show a concrete way for White to proceed.

Solution 106

The first thing that White must understand is that most four vs. three Rook endgames where all the pawns are on one side of the board should be avoided like the plague! In fact, the defending side should always try and trade pawns on one side of the board. This leaves him with a much smaller area to defend and less targets to worry about. Rook endgames with pawns on one side of the board are either drawn or are nightmares to win.

With this in mind, we can see that White has no interest in trading off the a-pawns. For example, 1.g3 Rc3 2.Rd1 Rxa3 3.Rdd7 Rf8 4.Rxa7 Rxa7 5.Rxa7 isn't even a consideration for White!

Two White problems are:

✦ He must spend a tempo at some point to parry Black's back rank mate threats.

✦ Black's Rooks are going to get active after ...Rc3.

So White must find a way to end the back rank threat, defend his a-pawn, restrain Black's Rooks and activate his own. No wonder Black thought that he had some real chances to hold the game!

1.Rb4!

A fine move that allows the White Rooks to dominate their Black counterparts. The immediate 1.g3 allows 1...Rc3 2.Ra1 when White's a1-Rook is doomed to a passive life. Making sure your Rooks stay active is one of the most important concepts in Rook endgames!

The point of 1.Rb4 is shown by the fact that this Rook, on b7, previously attacked the a-pawn but it didn't serve any defensive function. From b4, it will move to a4 where it will attack a7 and also defend a3. This frees the other Rook, which can now seek an active role in the game.

1...Rab8
2.Rg4+ Kh7

Now the f-pawn isn't defended. This becomes important in the next couple of moves.

3.g3

Back rank mates no longer exist! Now White is ready to activate his f1-Rook.

3...Rc3
4.Ra4

Better than 4.a4?, which allows 4...a5 followed by 5...Rb4.

4...Rb7

Thanks to White's check on move two, Black can't play 4...Rbb3 because 5.Rxa7 Rxa3 6.Rxf7+ is an easy win for White.

5.Rd1

Threatening 6.Rd6.

5...Rc6
6.Rd5 Re6
7.Rda5 Ree7

8.Ra6

See what a difference active Rooks make? One look at White's dominant towers, compared to Black's cowering pieces, should convince anyone to keep their Rooks hopping! Black can't avoid further material losses.

8...Kg6
9.Rg4+ Kh5
10.Rg8! Re6

Also leading to a quick mate is 10...f5 11.Ra5 when nothing can stop Rxf5.

11.Ra4, 1-0. Black can't stop Rh4 mate.

Summary of Imbalances and Ideas
[diagram (254)]

➤ In general, the player with a material plus wants to avoid pawn up endgames where all the pawns are situated on one side of the board.

➤ Always try your best to ensure that your pieces dominate their enemy counterparts. This means that White must do everything in his power to make his Rooks more active than Black's.

➤ White must give his a-pawn a firm defense.

➤ At some point, White will need to defend against a back rank mate.

Problem 107

(255)

Smyslov-Golombek, London 1947.
White to move.

White is clearly better here, but a forced win is nowhere in sight. Can you formulate a plan that will give you some chances to score the full point?

Solution 107

White is better due to his more active King and his superior pawn structure. To increase his advantage, White must place his Knight on g4 and his Bishop on c3, dominating the enemy Knight. Any trade of White's Bishop for Black's Knight will increase the first player's chances because the Black Bishop has very little mobility while the White Knight can dance to almost any square on the board. Once White gets his Bishop to c3 and his Knight to g4, the threat of Nf6 will force Black's h-pawn to move to h5. This, in turn, weakens the g-pawn. When this is done, White will train his sights on g6 and, if necessary, freeze it in its tracks by h2-h3 followed by g3-g4-g5.

In the game this plan worked out brilliantly, and Smyslov's play is well worth serious study:

1.Nd1!

Making way for the Bishop's relocation to c3, and also preparing to bring the Knight to g4 via Nd1-f2-g4.

1...Bd6

Black wasn't enticed by 1...e5 since, aside from the fact that the d5-square is seriously weakened and made accessible to the White Knight via Ne3-d5, the creation of a kingside pawn majority would be much simpler to achieve after 2.f5.

2.Nf2 Nd8

White wasn't worried about 2...Nd4 since 3.Bc3 would force it into immediate retreat.

3.Bc3 Nf7
4.Ng4

Heading for f6 where it will attack h7.

4...h5?

There was no reason to push this pawn until it was actually attacked. Now White's advantage takes on very serious dimensions.

5.Bf6+!

Smyslov plays very accurately. The Bishop's leap to f6 stops Black from trying any ...g6-g5 ideas.

5...Kd7
6.Nf2 Bc7

Black plays too passively. He had to try 6...Be7 7.Bc3 g5 8.fxg5 Nxg5+ though White would retain a considerable advantage with 9.Kf4.

7.Nd3 Kc6
8.Ne1!

Bad would be 8.Ne5+?? Bxe5 since it wouldn't be possible to attack g6 without the White Knight, while the Black Knight would keep White's King out of e5 and g5.

With 8.Ne1 White intends to swing the Knight around to h4, where it will target g6 for destruction.

8...Nd6+
9.Kd3 Nf5
10.Nf3 Kd7

Black decides against 10...b5 since 11.cxb5+ Kxb5 12.Ng5 would win material.

11.Ke4

Threatening 12.Ne5+ Bxe5 13.Kxe5 followed by a Bishop move and Kf6, when White's King penetrates into the enemy camp.

11...Nd6+
12.Ke3

White's King is heading for f2 where it will defend g3. Then h2-h3 followed by g3-g4 will force the Black Knight into a passive position.

12...Nf5+
13.Kf2 Bd6
14.h3!

Preparing g3-g4, chasing the enemy Knight back and, in many cases, allowing g4-g5, fixing the weakness on g6.

14...Bc7
15.g4 hxg4
16.hxg4 Nh6
17.Kg3 Nf7

White wins easily after this final display of passivity. Black had to try 17...Ke8 when 18.Be5 Bd8 19.Bb8 a6 20.Nc5 g5 21.Nc6 Bf6 22.Be5 Bxe5 23.Nxe5 gxf4+ 24.Kxf4 leaves White with an outside passed pawn in the Knight endgame.

18.g5

The annoying and highly destructive threat of Nh4 is once again "on," and 18...Nd6 loses to 19.Ne5+.

18...Bd8
19.Kg4 Bxf6
20.gxf6 Kd6
21.Ne5! and Black resigned.

Summary of Imbalances and Ideas
[diagram (255)]

➤ White enjoys better King position.

➤ White has the superior pawn structure.

➤ Black's queenside pawns are on the color of his (and White's!) Bishop.

➤ Black's Bishop is an inactive piece. Thus, White isn't adverse to trading his Bishop for Black's Knight because he would then be left with a good Knight versus a poor Black Bishop.

Problem 108

(256)

White to move.

White is a pawn down, his remaining pawn on g5 is weak, and his Knight on g3 is hanging. Things look grim for the first player. Is there any hope of holding this position?

Solution 108

There are several options open to White: He can trade Queens and seek salvation in an opposite colored Bishop endgame with two pawns less (after 1.Qxd6+ Kxd6 Black would also pick up the g-pawn); he can check on a5; and he can calmly play 1.Qe3 and just try to hang on for dear life.

Without some basic endgame knowledge concerning Bishops, this position would prove to be an unsolvable riddle. However, possession of seemingly unimportant knowledge can often make the most mysterious of problems relatively easy to solve.

Let's take a moment and build a foundation that will lead us right to the answer. We have all heard about the infamous Bishops of opposite color. These two pieces rest on different colored squares and will never meet on the chessboard. All very interesting, but what this means is less clear. Are Bishops of opposite colors good or bad? The following rules should prove useful:

Rule 1 — Bishops of opposite colors favor the attacker since he can attack something that the defender's Bishop will not be able to defend.

(257)

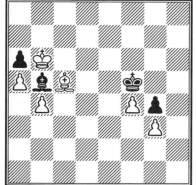

White to move.

White can win immediately by using the combined power of his Bishop and Queen to attack the g7-pawn: **1.Qe5** forces resignation because 1...f6 allows 2.Qxe6+, picking up a pawn and the Rook on c8. If Black's Bishop had been a dark-squared Bishop sitting on e7, then he could have defended easily by ...Bf8 or ...Bf6. However, the light-squared Bishop was unable to assist in the defense of the g7-point.

Rule 2 — In endgames, Bishops of opposite colors are notorious for their drawish characteristics. This is because most pieces have been traded off; the Bishops, bereft of help from other pieces, become defensive. This means that one can defend what the other cannot attack, and an enemy King by itself cannot break down the defense the Bishop gives.

(258)

White to move.

White enjoys a two-pawn advantage but he can't win because Black's Bishop defends his queenside pawn and simultaneously stops both of the White pawns in that sector. The extra pawn on the kingside is also useless because the Black King can't be chased away from f5. Note how White's Bishop plays no part in the action on either side of the board.

Rule 3 — Keeping points one and two in mind, we can say that when opposite colored Bishops exist, the stronger side can optimize his winning chances by retaining as many pieces as possible. In other words, don't exchange pieces without good reason!.

(259)

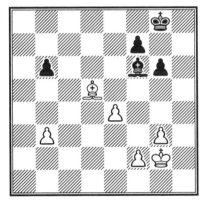

Black to move.

This position is drawn, even though White has an extra pawn. Black's Bishop will go to d4 and his King will move to e7; then White will find it impossible to do anything decisive.

However, give a Rook to each side, as seen in the next diagram, and the picture changes drastically.

(260)

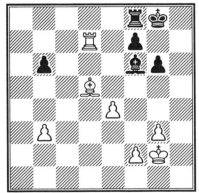

Black to move.

Now Black's King and Rook are stuck guarding the pawn on f7. Add the attacking power of the White Rook into the equation (for example, it threatens 1.Rd6 when 1...Bd8 2.Rxg6+ picks up a pawn, and 1...Bd4 2.Bxf7+ also adds to his spoils), and you can see just how poor the Black position has become.

> **Rule 4 — A one-pawn advantage is not enough to win if no other pawns exist on the board. Moreover, even two pawns may not suffice if the enemy King and Bishop can form a blockade.**

(261)

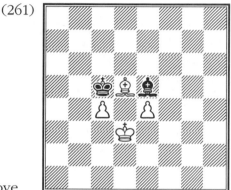

White to move.

White has two extra pawns, but neither of them is going anywhere. If White plays his King to e3, f3, g4 and f5, Black will play ...Bd4 followed by ...Kd6 and the pawns will still be stuck.

> **Rule 5 — In general, a two pawn vs. zero pawn advantage grows in significance if the pawns are far apart. The further apart the pawns, the greater the chance of winning. The reason for this is that the defending King and Bishop are not able to work together to form a blockade as they were in the previous diagram.**

The next diagram shows how easy the win can be if the pawns have enough distance between them.

(262)

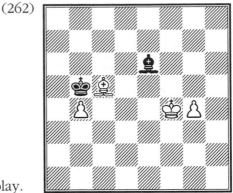

White to play.

White wins by advancing his g-pawn and King, winning the enemy Bishop for this pawn, and then walking to the queenside to help escort his final pawn to the promoting square: **1.g5 Kc6 2.Ke5 Kd7 3.b5 Bc4 4.b6 Kc6 5.Be3 Bb3 6.Kf6 Bd5 7.g6 Kd7 8.g7 Kc6 9.Ke7** followed by 10.Kf8 and 11.g8=Q.

Rule 6 — Two connected passed pawns will not win if the defending side knows how to create the correct defensive set-up.

Diagram (263) shows the correct drawing technique.

(263)

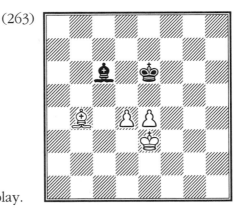

White to play.

White can't hope to win. His King is stuck defending the e-pawn and, if he plays 1.d5+, then 1...Bxd5 ends matters. Also useless is 1.e5 since 1...Bd5 followed by moving the Bishop back and forth creates a complete blockade. If White passes with something like 1.Kf4, then simply 1...Bb7 followed by ...Bc6 shows White the futility of his efforts.

(264)

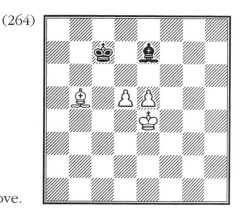

White to move.

Let's clarify the previous point by taking a look at this position. Has Black managed to create the drawing scenario that we learned in diagram (263)? No, he didn't. Though the positions look very similar, Black is actually lost in this example. Of course, if the position of Black's King and Bishop were reversed (Black King on e7 and Black Bishop on c7), then Black would draw easily. However, the position in question is lost because the Bishop is not attacking White's e5-pawn. The defending Bishop needs to attack e5 AND simultaneously prevent d5-d6+. Thus, placing Black's Bishop on g7 is hopeless because it fails to stop d5-d6+. This tiny detail changes the result because now White's King is free to roam to e6 and help his pawns advance: **1.Kf5 Bf8 2.Ke6 Kd8 3.d6 Bh6 4.Kd5 Bg7 5.e6** If the pawns get to the sixth rank they always win. **5...Bf8 6.Ba4 Kc8 7.e7** and the pawn Queens.

Compare this and the previous diagrams carefully until the differences between them become obvious to you.

Now it's time for us to return to our original position and original question. Our newfound knowledge should help us find an easy answer to this enigma. Keeping the Queens on with 1.Qa5+ or 1.Qe3 is possible, but doesn't the presence of the Queens and Knights favor the stronger side? This means that we should trade as many pieces as possible. If we can get rid of the Queens and Knights, we should draw, even if we lose the g-pawn, by using the techniques shown in diagram (263). Clearly, the fact that the two connected passed pawns don't win with Bishops of opposite colors is an important bit of information!

Let's follow our endgame rules and see how easy it is to hold this position: **1.Qxd6+ Kxd6 2.Ne4+ Nxe4 3.Bxe4 Bxg5 4.Kf3 f5 5.Bb1 Ke5 6.Ba2**

This ties the Black King down to the defense of his e6-pawn, thus forcing him to move it. Once this pawn moves we will enter the parameters of our drawing position from diagram 263.

6...Kf6 7.Bb3 e5 8.Bc2! followed by Bd3-c2-d3, etc. The draw is now simple.

So things were pretty easy for us once we acquired some basic knowledge about Bishop of opposite color endgames. Even the hardest problems soften up if we simply go back to basics!

Summary of Imbalances and Ideas
[diagrams (256-264)]

➤ The Bishops are of opposite colors.

➤ Opposite colored Bishops often give the defending side chances to make a draw even if he's a pawn or two down.

➤ In general, the stronger side wants to retain as many pieces as possible so he can highlight the attacking potential of opposite colored Bishops. This means that White should pursue a strategy of exchanges.

Problem 109

(265)

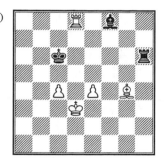

Black to move.

Can Black draw this position?

Solution 109

Black can easily draw this position by trading Rooks and entering a pure Bishops of opposite colors endgame. Remember: when you're two pawns down (in a two to nothing situation), the closer the pawns are, the greater the drawing chances. Why? Because the defending King and Bishop can work together to form a solid blockade, thanks to the fact that the stronger side's Bishop can't challenge the same squares as the defending Bishop.

Black wants to trade Rooks because, in general, the stronger side usually wants to keep as many pieces on the board as possible. In this way, you can make use of the attacking powers of the Bishops of opposite colors.

1...Rd6+!

With the Rooks gone, Black doesn't have to worry about anything but blocking those two White pawns.

2.Rxd6+ Kxd6, =. White will never be able to safely advance either of his pawns.

Summary of Imbalances and Ideas
[diagram (265)]

➤ The Bishops are of opposite colors.

➤ Opposite colored Bishops often give the defending side chances to make a draw even if he's a pawn or two down.

➤ In general, the stronger side wants to retain as many
pieces as possible so he can highlight the attacking
potential of opposite colored Bishops. This means
that Black should pursue a strategy of exchanges.

➤ White is two pawns up, but the pawns are close
together (the further apart the pawns are, the greater
his winning chances). This means that Black has
good chances of effecting a blockade of both enemy
pawns.

Problem 110

(266)

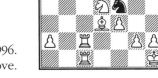

Human versus computer, 1996.
Black to move.

The machine played 1...Bd7. Is this best?

Solution 110

No, it's inferior, but easy to understand. The machine wanted to
develop, and White, supposedly, won't take the Black Knight
because Bishops are better than Knights in the endgame (most
computers have been programmed to believe this drivel). Naturally, there followed:

2.Bxe4!

The truth is that White's Knight is far superior to Black's
Bishop in this position. In fact, the only piece able to challenge
the d4-Knight was the Black horse on e4. The poor computer,
though, is a prisoner of its programming. Of course, many humans are guilty of the same flaw, but that's another story en-
tirely.

2...Rxe4

3.Rb2 and White enjoyed the superior position.

Summary of Imbalances and Ideas
[diagram (266)]

➤ White's Knight is stronger than Black's Bishop.

➤ The only piece that can challenge the White Knight is Black's horse on e4.

➤ By taking on e4, White ensures his Knight a long and fruitful life, and also takes a lot of pressure off of c5. This leaves his Rooks free to place pressure against the b7-pawn.

Problem 111

(267)

Possible endgame from Alekhine-Euwe, London 1922. White to play.

How would you play this position? Take a little time and see if you can figure out a winning plan.

Solution 111

Alekhine claims a forced win (not hard to imagine, considering the fact that every positional factor is in his favor) and gives four phases to secure the victory:

Phase One: 23.h4! followed by g4 and g5 on which Black will have nothing better than ...h5, seeing that the exchange of pawns abandons the square h4 to White's Knight.

Phase Two: b3, followed by Kd3, Nc3 and Ke4.

Phase Three: The maneuvering of the White Knight to d3 after which Black must immobilize his King on d6 in order to be able to defend the doubly attacked e5-pawn.

Phase Four: And lastly f4!, forcing the win of the e5-pawn or the g6-pawn after which the advantages secured will be decisive.

Did that make sense? Let's try to explain things in a clearer fashion: Black is passively placed and can't do anything active; all he can do is sit around and try to stop White from breaking through. This means that you can take all the time you want to set up some ideal position. It's important to understand this!

To win, White must create as many targets as possible. His main targets—pawns that can't be defended by other pawns—are e5 and g6. To make sure that the g6-pawn remains on that vulnerable square, White starts out with 23.h4!.

Next on the agenda is 24.g4 and g5. Now the g6-pawn is stuck on g6 forever.

When this is done, White changes the guard on e4: he will move his King to that square and place his Knight on d3 so both pieces can gang up on e5. To defend the e-pawn, Black must move his King to d6. White then administers the coup de grace: a timely f2-f4 forces ...exf4 when Nxf4 brings the Knight into range of g6. That pawn is lost and White wins the game.

Here's how this plan might develop:

23.h4! Kd7 24.g4 Ke7 25.g5

Now Black's g-pawn is permanently fixed on g6.

25...h5

This makes sure that h4 is off limits to the White Knight. Worse is 25...hxg5 26.hxg5 because then White would easily win by placing his King on e4 and his Knight on f3. After Black defends with ...Kd6, the simple Nh4 picks up the g6-pawn for free.

26.b3

Taking his time and placing the pawn on a safe light square.

26...Kd7 27.Kf3 Ke7 28.Nc3 Kd7 29.Ke4

White begins to swarm around the e5-pawn.

29...Ke7 30.Ne2 Bh8 31.Nc1 Bg7 32.Nd3 Kd6 33.f4! exf4
Far better is 33...Bh8 34.fxe5+ Ke7 though White still wins with
35.b4. White also wins in a long and convoluted manner after
33...a5. **34.Nxf4** and the g6-pawn falls.

Summary of Imbalances and Ideas
[diagram (267)]

➤ White's pawn structure is obviously superior to
Black's.

➤ White's Knight is far stronger than Black's Bishop.

➤ White's King will be able to set up shop on the
powerful c4-square. Black's King can't look forward
to any activity at all.

➤ White wants to place pressure against the weak
Black pawn on e5.

➤ White wants to fix Black's kingside pawns and add
these to his list of attackable objects.

Problem 112

(268)

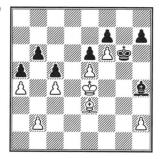

Smyslov-Yastrebov, Moscow 1936.
White to move.

Can White win this position? If so, how?

Solution 112

White wins by using an interesting tactic designed to clear the
way for the a4-pawn's advance. It's based on the fact that Black's
queenside pawns are resting on dark squares, thus making them
vulnerable to attack by White's Bishop.

1.b4!! axb4

This makes things easy for White. Black's best chance was 1...cxb4 2.Bxb6 b3 3.Kd3 b2 (3...Kc5 4.Bd4 followed by c4-c5 wins for White) 4.Kc2 Kf5 5.Bxa5 Kxe5 6.Kxb2 Kd6 7.Bd8 Kc5 8.Kc3 when White has good winning chances. Analysis by Smyslov.

2.Bxc5!

The point. The a4-pawn runs for a touchdown.

2...bxc5
3.a5 b3
4.Kd3 Bxf6
5.a6

Not "falling" for 5.exf6 e5 6.a6 e4+ 7.Kc3 e3, though 5.exf6 is actually the most precise move: 5.exf6 e5 6.Kc3! e4 7.Kxb3 and Black should resign.

5...Bxe5
6.a7 b2
7.Kc2 and White won.

Summary of Imbalances and Ideas
[diagram (268)]

➤ In a Bishop endgame, it's a great advantage if your opponent's pawns stand on the same color as your Bishop since that makes them vulnerable to attack.

➤ Black's Bishop is far from any potential queenside action.

➤ Since White has no quiet ideas that will allow him to break into the enemy camp, a tactical operation is called for that makes use of points one and two.

Problem 113

(269)

M.Adams-J.Emms, London 1991.
White to play.

How should White proceed in this position?

Solution 113

1.Kd2

This move allows the King to give d4 some much-needed support by Ke3. It also connects the Rooks and keeps the enemy Rook from penetrating to c3 after ...Rc8.

1.0-0 is completely incorrect because it takes your King out of play. In fact, one of White's advantages in this position is that his King can take an active part in the game while Black's is a lame duck on g8.

After **1...Rfc8 2.Ne5** Keeping Black off of c4 with gain of tempo. **2...Ba4 3.Rhc1** White prevented any Black counterplay. This left White with a superior position thanks to his strong center pawns.

Summary of Imbalances and Ideas
[diagram (269)]

➤ When an endgame is reached, it's often no longer advisable to castle. In fact, it's usually better to rush your King towards the center. It's a strong piece, so don't hesitate to use it!

➤ White needs to defend his center pawns, but he also wants to guard possible entry points into his own camp—the c3 and c4 squares are two glaring examples.

Problem 114

(270)

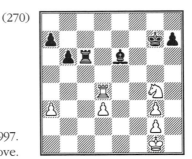

Suveg-Cook, Golden Knights (corr.) 1997.
White to move.

This is an extremely interesting endgame. Who do you think stands better? I'm looking for a general feel of the position rather than a specific move.

Solution 114

Though White is up a pawn, it's doubled, though not completely useless—he can trade the g3-pawn for the h7-pawn and be left with an extra passer. Perhaps the most important imbalance here is that of Bishop versus Knight. Usually a Bishop is superior to a Knight when passed pawns exist all over the board, and this position sees the White Knight going through contortions to stay up with the faster Bishop.

So Black has a superior minor piece and White has an extra pawn. White's a-pawn is also weak while the passed d-pawn might become threatening if Black doesn't use a bit of care. I'd have to assess this very difficult position as being equal. The game continuation appears to verify this:

1.Nf2

The Knight wasn't happy on g4, so it gives itself more options. Now it can jump to e4, or it can maneuver its way to f4 or g5 via h3.

1...Rc1+ 2.Kh2 Kf6 3.g4

Trying to make the extra kingside pawn amount to something. This move also gives White's King access to g3.

3...Ke5 4.Re4+ Kd5 5.Nh3 Kd6 6.Ng5 Bd5 7.Re3 Rc3 8.Nxh7 Rxa3

Usually the Bishop would reign supreme in this kind of pawn race because it covers White's promotion square on g8 and also eyes the queenside. However, White is able to hold the balance by using his g-pawn, Knight, and Rook to badger the Black King.

9.g5 Ra4 10.Nf6 Bf7 11.Ne4+ Kd7 12.Nf6+ Kd8 13.Kg3 b5 14.Ne4 b4 15.Nd6 Bh5 16.Nb7+ Kc7 17.Nc5 Ra3 18.Re6 b3 19.g6 Bxg6 20.Rxg6 a5

Trying to keep things interesting. The obvious 20...b2 is met by 21.Rg7+ Kc6 22.Rb7 Kxc5 23.Rxb2 Rxd3+ with a dead draw.

21.Na6+

White decides that enough is enough and forces a quick draw.

21...Kb7 22.Nc5+ Kc7, drawn.

Summary of Imbalances and Ideas
[diagram (270)]

➤ Black's Bishop versus White's Knight gives him excellent chances in any pawn race. The speedy Bishop can eye both sides of the board in a glance. However, the Knight has real trouble getting across the board quickly.

➤ White's extra pawn goes a long way in making up for the disadvantage of Knight versus Bishop.

➤ White's a-pawn is a target.

➤ White's d-pawn might find itself marching up the board. Naturally, Black must be on the watch for this possibility.

➤ Black's h-pawn is a glaring target.

➤ White must avoid a pure Knight versus Bishop pawn race. Instead, he needs to get his small army to work together, mixing threats to Black's King with dreams of promoting the g-pawn.

Problem 115

(271)

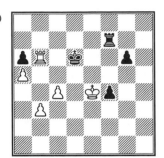

Smyslov-Botvinnik, Moscow World
Championship Match 1958.
Black to move.

Black is in check and must decide where to move his King. Things look
bad no matter what he does. Does the second player have a chance
here?

Solution 115

Black can draw this game by activating his Rook at the last possible moment. He must also avoid a wicked trap, which Botvinnik
fell for in the actual game.

1...Kc7!

Losing immediately is 1...Kc5?? 2.Kd3 when the threat of b4
mate forces Black to resign. Naturally, both 1...Kd7?? and 1...Ke7??
lose quickly to 2.Rb7+ followed by Rxf7 and Kxf4.

2.Rxa6 Rf8

And not 2...f3?? 3.Ra7+, picking up Black's Rook.

3.Rxg6 f3
4.Rg1 Rb8

Black chooses this moment, with White's Rook busy dealing
with the passed f-pawn, to activate his Rook and attack White's
queenside pawns.

5.Rf1

No better is 5.Rb1 f2 with the threat of ...Rxb3.

5...Rxb3
6.Rxf3 Rb1

7.Kd5 Kb7! with a theoretically drawn position. It's well known that Rook and a-pawn and c-pawn (or f-pawn and h-pawn) versus Rook is often drawn, though the method of forcing this is very complicated and far beyond the scope of this book.

Summary of Imbalances and Ideas
[diagram (271)]

➤ Black only has two reasonable moves. Placing the King on c5 looks more active, but then it ends up in a stalemated position, meaning that any lasting check will be mate.

➤ Though Black will lose his a-pawn and be material behind, the strength of his passed f-pawn should not be underestimated.

➤ Black must use his Rook in an active manner if he wants to have any serious hope of surviving.

➤ Black's salvation is based on a possible Rook and a-pawn and c-pawn versus lone Rook position— known to be a theoretical draw.

WALTER BROWNE

Problem 116

Annotate the following game starting after Black's seventh move: Alekhine-Euwe, London 1922. 1.d4 Nf6 2.Nf3 g6 3.Bf4 Bg7 4.Nbd2 c5 5.e3 d6 6.c3 Nc6 7.h3 0-0 8.Bc4 Re8 9.0-0 e5 10.dxe5 Nxe5 11.Bxe5 dxe5 12.Ng5 Be6 13.Bxe6 fxe6 14.Nde4 Nxe4 15.Qxd8 Rexd8 16.Nxe4 b6 17.Rfd1 Kf8 18.Kf1 Ke7 19.c4 h6 20.Ke2 Rxd1 21.Rxd1.

Solution 116

At the time this game was played, this system was new and interesting. Now it's a staple in the repertoires of many amateur players.

8.Bc4!

Alekhine says: "The best square for this Bishop. The reply 8...d5 is clearly not to be feared, as it would merely enhance the prospects of the opposing f4-Bishop."

This little move is quite instructive, because most players would fear the "tempo-gaining" 8...d5. The realization that this push helps activate your other Bishop is something that should be pondered. Don't go to the next move until you completely understand the reasoning behind White's eighth move.

8...Re8

Alekhine says: "Preparing ...e5, which will, however, have the disadvantage of weakening the square d6."

A very interesting moment. Any titled player would instantly recognize two key factors in this position: 1) the potential tactical target on f7 and, 2) the positional target on d6.

The tactical target is easy to notice—the c4-Bishop is striking at f7 and Black's Rook no longer defends that pawn.

The positional target is a lot more esoteric. How is a non-master expected to notice such a thing? Well, the first thing you must ask is, "Why did my opponent play his move and what in the world is this guy up to?" It's only possible to see d6 as a potential weakness when you understand that ...e7-e5 is going to be played (any pawn or square that can't be defended by another pawn is a potential weakness).

Before we go on so that you can see how Alekhine took advantage of these facts, I should point out that a tactical device, like the one Alekhine ultimately employs against f7, is often used as a tool to achieve some positional end. In this game, Alekhine attacks f7 in order to gain enough time to swing his pieces to squares where they can menace d6.

9.0-0

A battle is about to ensue and you *don't* want your King sitting in the center when this occurs!

9...e5

Black follows through with his plan.

10.dxe5

White opens the d-file so that his Rooks and Queen can easily reach d6.

10...Nxe5

Alekhine feels that this might be the decisive mistake. He gives 10...dxe5 11.Bh2 Be6 12.Bxe6 Rxe6 13.Nc4 (hitting d6!) as better for White, but not nearly as favorable as the actual game continuation.

It should be pointed out that, in this last variation, White would be hoping for an ...e5-e4 advance since that would increase the range of the h2-Bishop and bring it to bear on the d6-square.

Alekhine doesn't mention 12.Nxe5, winning a pawn. Black would get some compensation after 12...Nxe5 13.Bxe5 Bxc4 14.Bxf6 Qxf6 15.Nxc4 b5, so perhaps he preferred gaining the initiative with this positional solution (12.Bxe6) to 12.Nxe5 and the pursuit of greed.

11.Bxe5!

A move that perplexes many amateurs and was completely ignored in Alekhine's notes! I suppose he felt that 11.Bxe5 was so obviously good that anyone would easily understand it. If my students are any indication of the chess-playing public, then this is most definitely not the case!

According to my observations, most amateurs would reject 11.Bxe5 and instead consider 11.Nxe5, 11.Be2 or 11.Bb5. Both 11.Be2 and 11.Bb5 waste a tempo and move the Bishop away from its powerful post on c4. Also losing time is 11.Nxe5 since the f4-Bishop would have to move after 11...dxe5. All three of these moves cater to the whims of the opponent—he orders you about and you react.

Alekhine's move forces Black to recapture and, as a result, gives White a moment of peace to do whatever it is he wants to do. In the present case he uses that oasis-in-time to begin his assault against f7 and d6.

11...dxe5

(272)

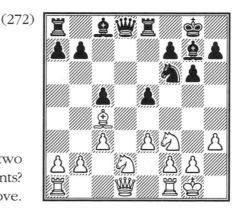

Can you see Black's two weakest points? White to move.

Alekhine would love to place a Knight on d6 but neither of his horses can reach that square at the moment. The following tactical maneuver against f7 allows a Knight to take aim at his real target: the positional hole on d6!

12.Ng5 Be6

Alekhine says: "An heroic resolution, because after the doubling of the pawns, Black's KB is left quite without action."

It looks like the obvious 12...Rf8 is the way to defend, but then White grabs hold of the d6-square by 13.Nde4! Here we see the real point of the attack against f7: White is able to place a Knight on e4 and, once that is attained, another jump places it on the long sought after d6 square. 13...Qxd1 (and not 13...Nxe4? 14.Bxf7+! Kh8 15.Qxd8 Rxd8 16.Nxe4) 14.Rfxd1 Nxe4 15.Nxe4 b6 16.Nd6 with a clear advantage, though any talk of a forced win is still a long way off.

13.Bxe6 fxe6 14.Nde4 Nxe4 15.Qxd8

We've already dragged some opening and middlegame instruction out of this game, now it's time for an endgame lesson! This proves my point about a "total experience." A good master game gives you a taste of just about everything chess has to offer.

15...Rexd8 16.Nxe4 b6 17.Rfd1 Kf8 18.Kf1

As usual, once an endgame is reached, both Kings rush towards the center.

18...Ke7 19.c4

An important move that takes the d5-square away from the Black pieces and also fixes the c5-pawn on a dark square. This makes sure that Black's Bishop remains as blocked in as possible.

19...h6 20.Ke2 Rxd1 21.Rxd1

Now Euwe played 21...Rb8 and lost in the end. However, Alekhine mentions the interesting endgame that occurs after 21...Rd8 22.Rxd8 Kxd8. This position was explored in Problem 111 in the endgame section of this book.

Summary of the Imbalances and Ideas Viewed in this Game

➤ White used a tactical device (weakness on f7) to create positional gains.

➤ White refused to bow to his opponent's wishes. Instead, he happily gave up a Bishop for a Knight in order to gain time and proceed with his own ambitions.

➤ White eventually created a great Knight versus a poor Bishop.

➤ White left Black with a poor pawn structure –and then happily steered the game into a very advantageous endgame.

Problem 117

Play through the following game: Piacenza (1695)-Kuperman (2286), Los Angeles 1999. 1.d4 Nf6 2.Nf3 g6 3.Bg5 Bg7 4.Nbd2 d5 5.e3 Ne4 6.Nxe4 dxe4 7.Nd2 c5 8.c3 cxd4 9.exd4 Qd5 10.Be3 0-0 11.Be2 e5 12.Qb3 Qxb3 13.Nxb3 f5 14.d5 b6 15.Rd1 Bb7 16.Bg5 Bf6 17.Bxf6 Rxf6 18.c4 Nd7 19.0-0.

Annotate these moves and then assess the final position.

Solution 117

1.d4 Nf6 2.Nf3

This is a very common way for amateurs to avoid main line theory while retaining chances for an opening advantage.

2...g6

This tends to sharpen the game and, since Black is much higher rated, this is exactly what the second player wants to do. The classical 2...d5 is often met, at least at the amateur level, by the easy to understand Colle System (3.e3 followed by Nbd2, Bd3, 0-0, c3, and e3-e4).

3.Bg5

White, who desperately wants to avoid theory, has no intention of going into a main line King's Indian Defense or Grunfeld
by 3.c4.

3...Bg7 4.Nbd2

Intending to take the lion's share of the center with 5.e4.

4...d5

This stops White from advancing to e4, though it does give
White some access to the e5-square.

5.e3 Ne4?

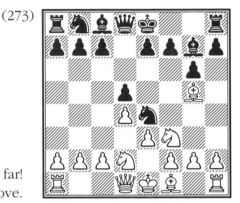

(273)

Black goes a bit too far!
White to move.

A mistake. Black feels he is stronger than his opponent and
wants to create some action. However, it seems that even masters
don't realize that quiet, correct play—the obvious 5...0-0 followed
by central expansion by ...Nbd7, ...Qe8 and ...e7-e5, for example—
will often lead to easy wins with little risk.

6.Nxe4 dxe4 7.Nd2

Now White has the superior pawn structure, and he's already
exerting pressure on the e4-pawn.

7...c5

Black's trying hard to rip open the long black diagonal for his
g7-Bishop.

8.c3 cxd4 9.exd4

Taking back this way is fairly common in this system, but
here I'd have preferred 9.cxd4, fixing the weakness on e4 and
opening up the c-file.

9...Qd5

This guards e4 and attacks the Bishop on g5, but the Queen isn't safe on this square. However, Black's position would have been full of holes after 9...f5 10.Bc4.

10.Be3 0-0 11.Be2?

What's wrong with the obvious, and far more aggressive, 11.Bc4? Black's e4-pawn would then be in serious trouble. For example: 11.Bc4 Qf5 12.Qb1 b5 13.Bb3 Bb7 14.Bc2 and the pawn drops off the board.

11...e5 12.Qb3

White gives his opponent too much credit. I'd have still gone after e4 by 12.Bc4 Qc6 13.d5 Qc7 14.Bb3 when the e4-pawn is ready to be placed in its box.

Apparently, White didn't realize how weak e4 was, and he didn't realize that the Black Queen was very insecure on d5.

12...Qxb3 13.Nxb3 f5 14.d5 b6 15.Rd1

White thinks that his passed d-pawn is destined for great things, but this isn't true. I would have preferred a plan based on a2-a4-a5, which means that White's Rook would want to remain on a1. After White castles, Rfd1 would be the way to go. This could be prefaced by 15.f4, to stop Black from playing ...f5-f4, when 15...exf3 16.gxf3 contains the Black majority, while 15...exf4 16.Bxf4 gives the White Knight access to the d4-square.

White's 15.Rd1 looks nice, but he doesn't really have any detailed plan in mind, just some vague notion of making use of his passed pawn.

Remember: don't just concentrate on what you have, try your best to constantly create new plusses that can be utilized on the path to victory.

15...Bb7 16.Bg5?

White doesn't realize how important this Bishop is. By trading it off, White makes it easier for Black to form a blockade on the c5 and d6 squares.

16...Bf6 17.Bxf6 Rxf6 18.c4 Nd7 19.0-0.

This position favors Black because: 1) White's d-pawn isn't going anywhere. 2) White's Bishop is very bad. 3) Black will be able to blockade the White pawns by playing for control over the c5 and d6 squares. 4) Black's majority of pawns is active, while White's passed d-pawn will soon be static.

Black's advantage turned decisive after **19...a5 20.a4 Kf8 21.Rc1?! Ke7 22.Na1? Nc5 23.b3 f4**.

Summary of the Imbalances and Ideas Viewed in this Game

➤ Black weakened his own pawn formation. This let White create easy pressure against Black's e4-pawn.

➤ Black's Queen was vulnerable, but White never made use of this important fact.

➤ White had a passed d-pawn, but Black was able to completely blockade it. Remember that a passed pawn is only useful if you have play elsewhere (in other words, you use the pawn as endgame insurance) or you have control over the square in front of it, turning the pawn into an active advantage.

Problem 118

Annotate this whole game: 1.d4 d6 2.c4 e5 3.d5 f5 4.Nc3 Nf6 5.Bg5 Be7 6.Bxf6 Bxf6 7.e4 0-0 8.Nf3 Na6 9.Bd3 f4 10.h3 Nc5 11.0-0 a5 12.Na4 Nxa4 13.Qxa4 Bd7 14.Qc2 Kh8 15.c5 Qe8 16.c6 bxc6 17.dxc6 Bc8 18.Rab1 Qg6 19.Kh1 Qh6 20.Qe2 g5 21.Nh2 Rg8 22.Ng4 Qg6 23.b4 axb4 24.Rxb4 Be7 25.f3 h5 26.Nf2 g4 27.fxg4 hxg4 28.Nxg4 Bxg4 29.Qxg4 Qxg4 30.hxg4 Rxg4 31.Rb7 Bd8 32.Bc4 Kg7 33.Rfb1 Kf8 34.Rb8 Rxb8 35.Rxb8 Ke7 36.a4 Rg3 37.Rb3 Rxb3 38.Bxb3 d5 39.exd5 Kd6 40.a5 Kc5 41.a6 Kb6 42.Bc4 Be7 43.Kg1 Bd6 44.Kf2 Ka7 45.g3 fxg3 46.Kxg3.

Solution 118

B.Hall (1482)-M.Piacenza (1695), Los Angeles 1999. **1.d4 d6**

With 1...d6 Black has offered to transpose into a Pirc Defense after 2.e4 Nf6 3.Nc3 g6 (this usually arrives via 1.e4 d6 2.d4 Nf6, etc.).

2.c4

Naturally, 2.e4 is the most principled reply, but 2.Nf3, stopping ...e7-e5, has also proved popular when 2...Bg4 3.c4 Bxf3 4.gxf3 leads to a very interesting position—White's two Bishops versus Black's superior pawn structure.

2...e5 3.d5

To many it would seem very attractive to play 3.dxe5 dxe5 4.Qxd8+ since after 4...Kxd8 Black's King has lost the right to castle. However, the absence of Queens and the fact that Black's King will be quite safe after ...c7-c6 (this takes away the b5 and d5 squares from a White Knight on c3) followed by ...Kc7 makes this method of handling the opening rather innocuous for White. For example: 5.Nf3 (after 4...Kxd8) 5...f6 6.Nc3 Be6 7.b3 c6 8.Bb2 Nd7 9.g3 Kc7 is quite comfortable for the second player.

Since neither 3.dxe5 nor 3.d5 offer White a theoretical advantage, he does best to try 3.Nf3 when 3...e4 4.Ng5 f5 5.Nc3 transposes into a sharp line of the English Opening.

3...f5

Black immediately gains space on the kingside in anticipation of an eventual kingside attack.

4.Nc3 Nf6 5.Bg5

A new move. Presumably, White intends to get rid of Black's key central Knight and initiate a fight for the e4-square.

In Alburt-Miles, USA ch. 1988, White tried the immediate 5.e4 but Black achieved equal play after 5...Nxe4 6.Nxe4 fxe4 7.Ne2 Be7 8.Ng3 0-0 9.Nxe4 Bf5 10.Bd3 Nd7 11.Be3 Bxe4 12.Bxe4 Bg5 (trading his bad Bishop for White's good one) 13.Qh5 Nf6 (changing tack and swapping his Bishop for White's on e4) 14.Qxg5 Nxe4.

5...Be7 6.Bxf6 Bxf6 7.e4 0-0

The first major moment in the game. Does this let White "win" the e4-square? Did either player even consider this important question?

Alternatives are: 7...g6!? (this shows good positional sense) 8.exf5 gxf5 (this pawn gives Black a firm hold over e4) 9.Qh5+ Ke7 (Black's King is quite safe here) and 7...f4, though in this case White would exchange his bad Bishop by 8.Be2 followed by 9.Bg4 (leaving Black with a poor Bishop on f6, though a later ...c7-c6 followed by ...Bf6-d8-b6 might bring it back to life).

(274)

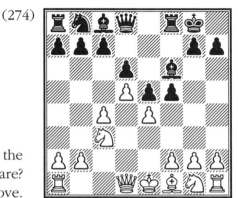

Can White win the
e4-square?
White to move.

8.Nf3

This brings us to the game's second major moment. White could try to turn e4 into a home for his pieces by 8.exf5 Bxf5 9.Bd3. Black would be clearly worse if he meekly traded on d3 and allowed White to follow up with Ne4. However, the fact that he wants to activate his dark-square Bishop, and the fact that White's King isn't castled, prompts the second player into shifting to a higher gear by 9...e4!, opening the position and freeing the f6-Bishop.

Therefore, 8.exf5 isn't sufficient for a White plus.

8...Na6

Heading for c5, but 8...g6, intending to meet 9.exf5 with ...gxf5, should have been given serious consideration.

9.Bd3 f4 10.h3?!

This can't be right. Why make an unnecessary weakening move on the kingside? White would love to exchange light-squared Bishops—his Bishop is bad while Black's is good—so ...Bg4 could always be met by Be2 followed by Nd2 (the Bishop is no longer doing anything on d3).

10...Nc5 11.0-0 a5 12.Na4 Nxa4?!

White's Knight on a4 is poorly placed, while White's "bad" Bishop on d3 can eventually go to e2 and make Black's ...g7-g5-g4 advance harder to achieve. Therefore, 12...Nxd3 13.Qxd3 b6 followed by ...g7-g5, ...h7-h5, and ...g5-g4 with a strong kingside attack, was indicated.

13.Qxa4 Bd7 14.Qc2 Kh8?

White's play will come on the queenside via c4-c5, gaining space and opening lines in that sector, so Black should have tossed in 14...b6, making a break on that side much harder to achieve.

15.c5 Qe8 16.c6

White's heart is in the right place, but 16.cxd6 cxd6 17.Qc7 Be7 18.Qxb7 Rb8 19.Qa6 was very tempting.

16...bxc6 17.dxc6 Bc8

Black wisely reasons that White's own c-pawn will block his Queen, Rooks and Bishop from penetrating into the queenside.

18.Rab1 Qg6?

When the center is closed you must play on the wings with pawns. These battering rams, with the rest of the army following, will gain space and open up lines for the Rooks. With this in mind, we can see that Black should have preferred 18...g5 followed by 19...h5 and 20...g4 with strong threats on the kingside.

19.Kh1 Qh6 20.Qe2 g5 21.Nh2

Now Black's much-needed ...g5-g4 advance will be difficult to achieve.

21...Rg8 22.Ng4?

A very bad move that forces the Black Queen out of the way of the h-pawn. White has to learn to avoid this kind of one-move threat.

22...Qg6 23.b4

White has to open up lines on the queenside and create threats there before Black takes over the game with his kingside attack.

23...axb4 24.Rxb4 Be7

Also playable is 24...h5!? 25.Nxf6 Qxf6 26.Qxh5+ Kg7 27.Qe2 f3! 28.Qxf3 Qxf3 29.gxf3 when both 29...Rf8 and 29...Rh8 give Black adequate compensation for the sacrificed material. However, Black's 24...Be7, intending to gain time on the Knight, seems to be a more promising move.

25.f3 h5 26.Nf2 g4!

Black's attack is now very dangerous.

27.fxg4 hxg4

Every piece should be brought into the attack, so 27...Bh4!? would be the move I would want to play. This prepares to chop off White's main defensive piece with ...Bxf2 followed by ...hxg4 when White will have enormous trouble holding the position. Of course, in such positions, good intentions have to be backed up by tactical analysis since normal positional considerations and rules often fall victim to the harsher truths of brute force calculation.

After 27...Bh4!? 28.Bc4 Rg7 29.Qf3 (things really heat up after 29.Rfb1 hxg4 30.Rb8 f3 31.Qf1 gxh3 and now 32.g3 Qxg3 33.Rxa8 Qg2+ leads to a win for Black. However, 32.g4!! appears to be a draw: 32...Rxb8 33.Rxb8 Kh7 34.Rxc8 Bxf2 35.Qxh3+ Qh6 36.Rh8+ Kxh8 37.Qxh6+ Rh7) 29...hxg4 30.Nxg4 Bxg4 31.Qxg4 Qxg4 32.hxg4 Rxg4 33.Rb7 Rg7 Black, who threatens 34...Bg3, seems to be doing well, but White has the surprising 34.g4!! when he's okay. It wouldn't be a shock if subsequent analysis proved that Black was on top after 27...Bh4 but, at the moment, I have to accept that 27...hxg4 is Black's best chance for an edge.

Why am I luke warm about 27...hxg4? My main gripe is that Black seems to be in a hurry to exchange Queens. It's important to point out that, in general, the side that is attacking the King wants to avoid Queen trades—the Queens offer the attacker a knockout punch. The side playing for a queenside attack is happy to swap Queens because he is usually much better in the endgame—the queenside attack plays for small positional gains that translate to a good endgame while a kingside attack is often a do or die proposition. In the present position, though, Black's attack continues even if he chops the Queens off the board.

28.Nxg4 Bxg4 29.Qxg4 Qxg4

I would have tried 29...Qh6!? followed by 30...Rg3 when Black would retain some serious attacking chances. A sample of what might occur: 30.Qe2 Rg3 31.Rb7 Re3 32.Qd2 Bg5 33.Rfb1 f3 34.Rb8+ Rxb8 35.Rxb8+ Kg7 36.Rb7 Re1! 37.Rxc7+ Kg6 38.Qxd6+ Bf6 39.Qd3 Qf2 and Black wins.

30.hxg4 Rxg4 31.Rb7 Bd8??

Much stronger was 31...Rxa2 (also interesting is 31...d5!?) with a simple yet compelling threat against g2.

32.Bc4 Kg7 33.Rfb1 Kf8 34.Rb8 Rxb8 35.Rxb8 Ke7 36.a4 Rg3 37.Rb3??

White had the game in the palm of his hand, but he throws it away by trading the Rooks. This allows the famous drawing tendencies of Bishops of opposite colors to take effect (in general, the stronger side wants to retain as many pieces as possible to work with his Bishop, thus highlighting the attacking potential of Bishops of opposite colors).

If you look at what each Rook is doing, it becomes clear that White's is tying up Black's King and Bishop, effectively leaving him in a helpless state. Therefore, where's the logic in exchanging a very strong Rook for a passive one?

White could have won with the straightforward 37.a5! Ra3 (37...Rc3 38.a6!) 38.a6 when Black can still squirm with 38...d5 (passive play lets White win mundanely with Ra8 followed by a7, bringing the King to b4, and then Bb5-a4, blocking off the Black Rooks control of a7 and a8), but 39.exd5 e4 40.d6+! cxd6 41.Rb7+ followed by c7 will still award White with the full point.

37...Rxb3 38.Bxb3 d5!

This lets the Black King join in the defense.

39.exd5 Kd6 40.a5 Kc5 41.a6 Kb6 42.Bc4 Be7 43.Kg1 Bd6

There was nothing wrong with 43...e4 followed by 44...e3, but Black's choice also splits the point.

44.Kf2 Ka7 45.g3 fxg3+ 46.Kxg3 and the game was eventually drawn since there is absolutely nothing White can do to significantly improve his position.

Summary of the Imbalances and Ideas Viewed in this Game

➤ Neither side seemed to be aware of the importance of the e4-square.

➤ The game eventually degenerated into a common queenside versus kingside attack, delineated by the closed center, forcing each side to seek his chances on the wings. In such positions, Black must throw everything, including the kitchen sink, at the White King, and he almost always wants to avoid Queen trades because that effectively ends his threat of a knockout.

➤ White must try and hold off the Black attack. If he can successfully do so, his many positional advantages on the queenside will lead to a smooth middlegame or endgame victory.

Problem 119

Annotate the following game:

Piacenza (1713)-Winston (1265), Continental Open 1996.

1.d4 Nf6 2.Nf3 b6 3.e3 Bb7 4.Bd3 e6 5.Nbd2 c5 6.c3 Nc6 7.0-0 Bd6 8.e4 cxd4 9.cxd4 Be7 10.a3 h5 11.b4 Qc7 12.Bb2 Rg8 13.Rc1 a6 14.Re1 g5 15.g3.

Solution 119

1.d4 Nf6 2.Nf3

White's best move is 2.c4 but this solid alternative retains the option of going back into main lines with c4, or of heading for safer, less theoretical, systems with c3.

2...b6

Very sensible. With Nf3, White doesn't do anything to challenge Black's control over the e4-square. Due to this, Black quickly prepares to move his Bishop to b7 where it will join with the f6-Knight in fighting for the key central squares d5 and e4.

3.e3

White could still transpose into the main line Queen's Indian Defense by 3.c4 e6 4.g3 Bb7 5.Bg2.

3...Bb7 4.Bd3 e6 5.Nbd2

It's now clear that White will move his pawn to c3 where it will defend d4 and keep Black's pieces off of b4. In general, White plays c2-c4 if he intends to place the Knight behind it so both pawn and Knight hit d5. If the Knight goes to d2, the pawn usually ends up on c3.

5...c5 6.c3 Nc6 7.0-0

So far both sides have handled the opening reasonably well. White intends to play for central expansion via e3-e4 while Black can try and forestall this by 7...d5. Black's next move, though, gives us the first hint about his true King-hunting psychosis.

7...Bd6??

Awful. Black is so intent in aiming everything at White's King that he ignores such "minor" things as central play and castling. Simply put, play in the center always beats play on the wings. Of course, Black doesn't believe this and decides that it's time to strike out at his opponent.

8.e4

Hitting Black in the center and creating an immediate threat of 9.e5, forking Black's pieces.

8...cxd4 9.cxd4 Be7

Avoiding the fork via e5. Black admits that his seventh move wasn't very good.

10.a3

A very useful move. White keeps the Black Knight out of b4 and prepares to gain queenside space with a later b4 advance.

10...h5??

Black unleashes the full fury of his subconscious! Where he got such hatred for royalty is beyond me, but it's clear that only the White King's head will make him happy.

This move demonstrates the desire to attack without any justification for the decision. In the end, all it really does is weaken the g5-square, waste time, and ignore the center.

11.b4

After adjusting his glasses to make sure he had seen Black's move properly, White ignores his opponent's berserk play and gains some queenside space.

11...Qc7?

Taking aim at h2. Unfortunately, Black's Queen is very vulnerable on the c-file.

12.Bb2

White continues to develop and build in the center and on the queenside. I often see amateurs react to Black's kingside gestures with moves like 12.h3, keeping Black's pieces off of g4. Why waste a tempo on a non-threat and why give Black something to aim at when he advances his pawns by ...g7-g5-g4? Don't give Black's plan more respect than it deserves!

12...Rg8??

Yet another subtle move. I imagine flecks of aggressive foam forming on Black's lips as he looks at his opponent, hoping to see a quiver of terror or eyes wide with fear.

(275)

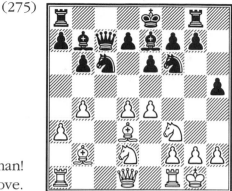

Black's a madman!
White to move.

13.Rc1

White yawns and improves his position. Showing such a lack of respect for your opponent's idea often unnerves him and undermines his confidence.

13...a6??

This stops White from winning a piece with b4-b5, but it loses in another way. Black should have gotten his Queen off the c-file by 13...Qf4.

14.Re1?

A nice buildup move that misses the win of a piece by 14.d5! exd5 15.Bxf6 gxf6 16.exd5.

14...g5??

Black lets out a roar as he jumps into the abyss. He should have played 14...Qb8 and hoped for the best.

15.g3?

White finally shows some fear and makes an unnecessary defensive move. Far stronger was 15.d5! (meeting an attack on the flank with a counterattack in the center) 15...exd5 16.Bxf6 Bxf6 17.exd5+ when Black should quietly resign before rushing off to lick his wounds.

This instructive game shows us that an unsound kingside attack can often be completely ignored in favor of progressing with your own plans, especially if those plans intend to make use of the center.

Summary of the Imbalances and Ideas Viewed in this Game

➤ Black starts out by fighting for the key square e4.

➤ After getting a couple of pieces out, Black shows his true inclinations and starts eyeing the White King without any justification at all for doing so. Remember: you can't attack because you feel like doing so, you attack because the position wants you to!

➤ Central play almost always beats play on the wings.

➤ It's often best to simply ignore your opponent's unsound threats. Never give the enemy more respect than he deserves.

Problem 120

Annotate this whole game. Then see if you can correctly list the strengths and weaknesses of the player (NOT the position, but the player himself) with the White pieces.

1.e4 c5 2.Nf3 d6 3.Bb5+ Nd7 4.c4 a6 5.Ba4 Qc7 6.Nc3 e6 7.0-0 Ngf6 8.Qe2 Be7 9.d4 cxd4 10.Nxd4 0-0 11.Be3 Nb6 12.Bb3 e5 13.Nf5 Bxf5 14.exf5 Rac8 15.g4 h6 16.h4 Nh7 17.g5 hxg5 18.hxg5 Bxg5 19.Bxg5 Nxg5 20.Qg4 Qe7 21.Kg2 Nh7 22.Rh1 d5 23.cxd5 Qg5 24.Qxg5 Nxg5 25.Rh5 f6 26.d6+ Rf7 27.Rah1, 1-0.

Solution 120

Virtually every player finds himself stuck on a rating plateau at some point in his career. You learn the game, you study, you make progress and then, for reasons that aren't clear at the time, you get stuck at a particular strength for months or even years. Naturally, this can be very depressing and has even convinced many players to give up the game.

What's important to understand is that this is a normal stage in one's chess development. You take in information, you pick up experience, your brain quietly (even secretly!) fights to digest all this new material and, suddenly, you wake up one day hundreds of points stronger than when you laid your head on the pillow a few short hours before.

For those that are not able to wake up from their "nightmare of chess inadequacy," the most likely explanation for this all-too-common full stop to chess enlightenment resides in a lack of understanding in some key area of the game.

Do your openings make you a laughing stock? Does the idea of an attack make you fall to your knees and quake in fear? Is positional play your personal cure for insomnia? Does the endgame remind you of the green vegetables your parents forced you to eat during childhood?

If you wish to rise above the quagmire that most of us find ourselves in from time to time, you must figure out the weakest phase of your game and do everything you can to educate yourself in that particular area. The only way to accomplish this in your own play is to go over your games with a fine-tooth comb—if you don't know your weaknesses, you can't do anything to weed them out!

Here we'll use the following game (annotated by you) as a sort of guinea pig. If you can figure out Pam's weaknesses, then you should be able to do the same for your own.

Pam Ruggiero (2100)-D. Pruess (2200), San Francisco 1998.

1.e4 c5
2.Nf3 d6
3.Bb5+ Nd7
4.c4

Pam knows some openings fairly well, but has no knowledge whatsoever of other systems. Here White usually plays 4.d4, trying to take advantage of his lead in development by tearing open the position. However, that would require some book knowledge and she didn't want to go into a sharp opening line unprepared. This is a wise philosophy. By playing for space and keeping things quiet, she hopes to get an interesting middlegame with minimum opening risk.

4...a6

This doesn't seem right. Black lets White's Bishop eventually get back into play on b3 or c2. Sensible alternatives are 4...g6, 4...Ngf6, 4...e6, or 4...e5, shutting down the center.

5.Ba4 Qc7

Black is worried about a possible e4-e5 advance, so he spends a tempo to stop it. Apparently, White's quiet approach to the opening has confused her opponent.

6.Nc3 e6
7.0-0 Ngf6
8.Qe2

White defends c4 before pushing her d-pawn to d4. She wants to play d2-d4 because, on d3, the pawn would doom her light-squared Bishop to everlasting passivity.

8...Be7
9.d4 cxd4
10.Nxd4 0-0
11.Be3 Nb6?

Very ugly. This Knight doesn't have a future on b6. No doubt it's a reaction to 11...b6 12.Nc6, picking up Black's valuable dark-squared Bishop. Instead of 11...Nb6, Black should have tried 11...Ne5 or 11...Nc5, with a perfectly playable position in either case.

(276)

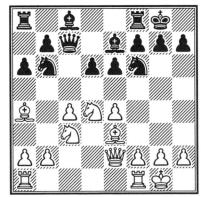

Does Black's Knight
belong on b6?
White to move.

12.Bb3 e5?

Trying to force the issue against a lower-rated opponent, Black loses his grip on the light-squares.

13.Nf5 Bxf5
14.exf5 Rac8
15.g4!?

A "normal" way to handle this position is 15.Rac1 (the best move) when White's two Bishops give her a clear advantage. Note that 15.Rac1 Nxc4?? loses material to 16.Bxc4 Qxc4 17.Qxc4 Rxc4 18.Nd5.

Quiet play isn't Pam's specialty, though. Instead, she loves to increase the tension and declare an all-out war for the initiative, even if it's not completely sound!

15...h6

Black doesn't fall for 15...Nxc4?? 16.g5 Nd7 (or 16...Nxe3 17.gxf6) 17.Nd5.

16.h4 Nh7

The usual recipe for White's kingside expansion. By covering the g5-square and attacking h4, it seems that Black has refuted White's plan. In fact, many strong players would have rejected White's g4-g5 idea due to this well-known remedy, but Pam is rarely a victim of convention.

17.g5!

Bringing her opponent back to reality. By sacrificing a pawn, she retains the initiative and rips open the h-file for her Rooks. It's not clear if White's attack will really work, but the pressure this places on the opponent is far from easy to deal with.

17...hxg5
18.hxg5 Bxg5
19.Bxg5 Nxg5
20.Qg4 Qe7

Note that 20...f6?? fails to 21.c5+ when the b3-Bishop rears it's ugly head!

21.Kg2

Simple and to the point. The threat of Rh1 brings Black to his knees.

21...Nh7??

Hoping that the "threat" of ...Qg5, trading Queens, will slow his opponent down a bit. However, a much better defense was 21...Rc5!, stopping White's threatened c4-c5 in its tracks, 22.Rh1 f6 when White still has to prove the soundness of her attack.

22.Rh1 d5

The immediate 22...Qg5 loses instantly after 23.Qxg5 Nxg5 24.Rh5 Nh7 (once again, 24...f6 fails to 25.c5+) 25.Rah1. Black's 22...d5 clogs up the b3-g8 diagonal.

23.cxd5 Qg5

The Queen exchange fails to put out the flames of the White attack.

24.Qxg5 Nxg5
25.Rh5 f6
26.d6+ Rf7

Sad, but 26...Nf7 also loses to 27.d7! Rc7 28.Rah1 Nc4 29.Nd5.

27.Rah1, **1-0**. A total catastrophe for Black! White's Bishop and d6-pawn join forces with the White Rooks to weave a mating net around the Black King. An impressive display by Pam, who looked like she was the higher rated player disposing of someone far below her in strength.

Pam's Strengths and Weaknesses:

- ◆ Pam is not comfortable in quiet positions, much preferring a more forcing tempo of play. If this describes you, it might prove instructive to study the games of positional players like Karpov, Ulf Anderssen, and Petrosian.

- ◆ Pam is not an opening specialist, but she makes up for this by playing in a logical fashion. This game proves that intelligent, sensible moves and an understanding of your opening's basic ideas far outweigh brute memorization.

◆ Pam has a tremendous grasp of the initiative. If you can't emulate that kind of heat, then a study of the games of Alekhine, Tal, and Kasparov should prove useful.

◆ Pam has good tactical vision. Constantly studying books of tactical quizzes will help you in this phase of the game.

Summary of the Imbalances and Ideas Viewed in this Game

➤ White got more central space right out of the opening.

➤ White got two Bishops. Black eventually missed his guardian of the light-squares.

➤ When her pawn reached f5, she was able to claim more space on the kingside. She decided to translate this advantage in territory into a direct attack against the Black King.

➤ The sacrifice of a pawn left Black in a purely defensive stance and allowed the White Rooks to enter the attack with enormous effect.

Problem 121

Annotate this whole game: 1.c4 Nf6 2.Nc3 g6 3.e4 d6 4.d4 Bg7 5.Be2 0-0 6.Bg5 Na6 7.Qd2 e5 8.d5 Qe8 9.f3 Nh5 10.Be3 f5 11.0-0-0 Nf4 12.g3 Ng2 13.Bf2 f4 14.Bf1 Ne3 15.Bxe3 fxe3 16.Qxe3 Nc5 17.Bh3 Na4 18.Kb1 Nxc3+ 19.Qxc3 Bh6 20.Bxc8 Rxc8 21.h4 c6 22.Nh3 cxd5 23.exd5 e4 24.f4 b5 25.Qb4 bxc4 26.Qxd6 Qb5 27.Qe6+ Kh8 28.Ng5 Rb8 29.Rd2 Bg7 30.Nf7+ Rxf7 31.Qxf7 Bxb2 32.Rc2 Bc3+, 0-1.

Solution 121

R. Musselman-Pam Ruggiero, San Francisco 1998.

1.c4 Nf6
2.Nc3 g6
3.e4 d6

4.d4 Bg7
5.Be2 0-0

The King's Indian Defense fits Pam's style like a glove. It's very important to find openings that suit your tastes and complement your strengths. This opening is also sensible in that it can be used against every opening move other than 1.e4.

6.Bg5

The Averbach Variation is a favorite of GMs Kaidanov, Yermolinsky and Bareev.

6...Na6

A good system. Black will play ...e7-e5 when the c5-square will eventually be available to this Knight. In some lines, the Knight shows its versatility by defending the c7-square.

7.Qd2 e5
8.d5 Qe8

It seems that Pam knows her theory. This move breaks the pin, prepares to move the f6-Knight and, as a result, frees the f-pawn for its key advance to f5.

Note the importance of an eventual ...f7-f5 push. The center is closed so that leaves both players scrambling for domination of the wings. In the present case, Black's pawn chain c7-d6-e5 "points" to the kingside, and so that is where Black's space lies and that is where she should seek her chances.

9.f3

The most accurate response is thought to be 9.Bd3 with Nge2 to follow.

9...Nh5

Knowing the main ideas of your openings is critical. Here, Pam plays for the thematic ...f7-f5 advance as quickly as she can.

10.Be3

Unnecessary. Probably best is 10.Bd1 followed by 11.Nge2.

10...f5
11.0-0-0 Nf4

Yet another thematic KID idea. Black would love White to take on f4 and open up the g7-a1 diagonal. Sacrificing a pawn for control of the dark squares is a small price to pay, though here the f4-pawn turns out to be poison: 12.Bxf4? exf4 13.Qxf4 fxe4 14.Qxe4 Bh6+.

12.g3 Ng2!?

An instructive moment. Many players would try 12...Nxe2+ 13.Ngxe2 fxe4 14.fxe4 Bh3, but Pam decides to intensify the battle by offering a pawn.

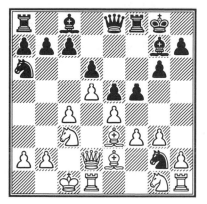

(278)

12...Ng2, a sign of genius
or insanity?
White to move.

13.Bf2 f4

This, her intention when she played 12...Ng2, is the simplest way to save the impudent Knight, but also possible is 13...fxe4!? 14.Nxe4 Bf5 with crazed complications. A sample of the possibilities: 15.Bd3 Qa4 16.Nc3 Qa5 17.Bf1 Nb4 (threatening 18...Qxa2!!) 18.g4 (or 18.a3 Nc2 with the idea of 19...Nb1 followed by ...Nb3+) 18...Bc2 19.Bxg2 Bxd1 20.Kxd1 Nxa2.

14.Bf1 Ne3
15.Bxe3 fxe3
16.Qxe3 Nc5

White is a pawn ahead but Black's pieces will find good squares to live on. An important point is that f3-f4 is always bad for White since that would unleash the now dormant monster on g7.

Whether this sacrifice is sound or not doesn't really matter. Psychologically it's perfect. Pam feels in control while her opponent is disoriented and can't find a plan

17.Bh3 Na4
18.Kb1 Nxc3+
19.Qxc3 Bh6
20.Bxc8 Rxc8
21.h4 c6

Black prepares to open lines on the queenside. This is particularly effective since White can't challenge the c-file because the h6-Bishop is eyeing c1.

22.Nh3?

A good idea played at a bad moment. Much safer is 22.Qd3, while 22.h5 is also tempting.

22...cxd5
23.exd5?

White had to try 23.Rxd5.

23...e4

All of a sudden the a1-h8 diagonal is blasted open and White's game reaches critical mass.

24.f4??

The losing move. White had to try 24.Rde1.

24...b5

From this point on, Pam doesn't give her opponent a moment's rest. Quiet play would allow White to vastly improve his position by Nh3-g5-e6.

25.Qb4 bxc4
26.Qxd6 Qb5
27.Qe6+ Kh8
28.Ng5 Rb8
29.Rd2 Bg7
30.Nf7+? Rxf7

31.Qxf7 Bxb2
32.Rc2 Bc3+, **0-1**.

Summary of the Imbalances and Ideas Viewed in this Game

➤ Black correctly played for kingside expansion by ...f7-f5 once the center became locked.

➤ Black sacrificed a pawn to add tension to the position and to trade off White's dark-squared Bishop for a White Knight.

➤ Black knew that any opening of the h8-a1 diagonal would allow her Bishop to dominate the game.

Problem 122

Annotate this game: 1.e4 c5 2.Nf3 Nc6 3.d4 cxd4 4.Nxd4 Nf6 5.Nc3 d6 6.Bg5 a6 7.Qd2 Nd7 8.Be2 g6 9.Nd5 f6 10.Ne6 Qa5 11.Ndc7+ Kf7 12.Nd8+ Kg7 13.Ne8+, 1-0.

Solution 122

Kruger-Nagy, Budapest 1942. **1.e4 c5 2.Nf3 Nc6 3.d4 cxd4 4.Nxd4 Nf6 5.Nc3 d6 6.Bg5**

This is a popular line in the Sicilian Defense known as the Richter-Rauzer. Fischer used to favor 6.Bc4.

6...a6

More common is 6...e6, but the text is fully playable.

7.Qd2

Preparing for queenside castling.

7...Nd7?

Black wastes a tempo and moves his Knight to a passive square. Losing time isn't a wise idea when the center is open.

8.Be2

This stops Black from chasing away the g5-Bishop by 8...h6 due to 9.Ne6! when 9...fxe6?? runs into 10.Bh5+ g6 11.Bxg6 mate.

8...g6?

Another loss of time that instantly places Black in a critical situation.

(279)

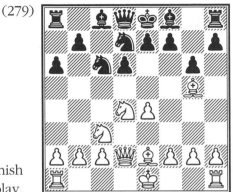

White to move and punish Black's horrible play.

9.Nd5!

Suddenly Black is having trouble moving anything. 9...Bg7? loses mundanely to 10.Nxc6 bxc6 11.Bxe7 trapping the Queen, while 9...h6 10.Bh4 g5 11.Ne6! is crushing.

Note how White is not castling. He wants to castle, but Black's moves are so bad that White feels compelled to punish the guy immediately. Of course, 9.0-0-0 was quite possible but then Black would have been back in the game with 9...Bg7 followed by 10...0-0. If your opponent plays too many mistakes, you become duty bound to punish him for his transgressions against the goddess of chess.

9...f6??

Moves don't come any uglier than this. He had to try 9...Nxd4 10.Qxd6 f6, though that hardly inspires confidence either.

10.Ne6

This forces the win of copious amounts of material and effectively ends the game.

10...Qa5 11.Ndc7+! Kf7 12.Nd8+! Kg7 13.Ne8+, 1-0. Black

will be mated after 13...Kg8 14.Bc4+. One rarely sees two Knights side by side on the eighth rank.

Summary of the Imbalances and Ideas Viewed in this Game

➤ Moving the same piece twice in the opening often leads to a serious lag in development.

➤ Black's refusal to develop a piece after his fourth move virtually begged for some form of retribution. If you're White, why not give him the punishment he so richly deserves?

➤ Black created an enormous hole on e6 with his ...f7-f6 blunder. This led to his instant demise.

Problem 123

(280)

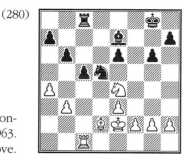

Petrosian-Botvinnik, World Championship Match (5th match game), 1963. White to move.

The position in the diagram came about after Black's 22nd move (22...Be7). Black's game appears to be slightly inferior but solid; true, the pawn on e6 is isolated, but nothing can attack it.

Annotate the following moves and try and explain what White is up to: 23.b4 c4 24.b5 Kf7 25.Bc3 Ba3 26.Rc2 Nxc3+ 27.Rxc3 Bb4 28.Rc2 Ke7 29.Nd2 c3 30.Ne4 Ba5 31.Kd3 Rd8+ 32.Kc4 Rd1 33.Nxc3 Rh1 34.Ne4 Rxh2 35.Kd4 Kd7 36.g3 Bb4 37.Ke5 Rh5+ 38.Kf6 Be7+ 39.Kg7 e5 40.Rc6 Rh1 41.Kf7 Ra1 42.Re6 Bd8 43.Rd6+ Kc8 44.Ke8 Bc7 35.Rc6 Rd1 36.Ng5 Rd8+ 47.Kf7 Rd7+ 48.Kg8, 1-0.

Solution 123

Most of us learned at a very young age that walking into doors or walls was not a good idea. A flattened nose, a lump on one's head—all these little aches and pains began to make sense to us as experience grew and injuries mounted. Strangely enough, these early life lessons don't seem to carry over into our understanding of chess. We charge a solid wall of pawns and end up bouncing off painfully. We dash at an enemy King and wonder why we failed to drag it down. We attack enemy pieces and get agitated when they simply move out of the way or even show the rudeness to attack us back.

Believe it or not, there is a connection between a concrete wall and a solid wall of pawns. Both tend to repel anyone or anything that tries to walk through them; it's also true that doors or holes can be created in both obstructions which allow a human or a chess piece to pass safely to the other side.

Chessically, this means that you should only attack an enemy unit or an area of enemy space if it is weak. Of course, these weaknesses will not just appear out of thin air. As the general who leads his pieces, your responsibility is to first create holes or targets in the enemy position and then to attack or surround these targets with your own army.

In the Petrosian-Botvinnik game, White realized that he couldn't get to the weakness on e6, so he sought to create a target that's closer to home and therefore more accessible.

23.b4!

White makes use of the pin on the c-file and offers to trade his b-pawn for the enemy c-pawn. This exchange would turn the formerly solid c-pawn, well defended by the pawn on b6, into an isolated target that is very vulnerable to any form of persistent attack.

This is how chess should be played. You create as many weaknesses in the enemy camp as possible and then bring your pieces to bear on these targets. You may not be able to win anything right away, but your pieces will clearly be the aggressors while the enemy bits will be passively trying to hold onto life and limb.

23...c4

Naturally, 23...Nxb4?? loses to 24.Bxb4 since 24...cxb4 would lose the Rook to 25.Rxc8+. The move actually played (23...c4) creates an attack on the b4-pawn by the Black Bishop and Knight, keeps the White King out of d3 and tries to show that the Black c-pawn, now passed, is a strength rather than a weakness.

Note that a holding pattern by 23...Rc7 would have left White in control after 24.bxc5 bxc5 25.Kd3 Don't forget that your King is a powerful piece and should be actively employed as soon as an endgame appears. 25...Kf7 26.a5 (to keep the Black Knight off of b6) followed by Kc4 when the White pieces are dominating their Black counterparts and the Black pawn on c5 is in need of constant defense.

24.b5

This move places the White pawns on light-colored squares where they will be safe from the attentions of the Black Bishop.

24...Kf7?!

The Black King prepares to join the battle. It also gives support to the weakened pawn on e6 in case a White piece eventually manages to attack it.

Later it was shown by Grandmaster Averbach that Black could have held the position by using the following active defense: 24...Ba3! 25.Rc2 c3! (sacrificing the pawn so that the Black Rook can reach the White pawn on a4) 26.Bxc3 (26.Nxc3?? Nb4 traps the White Rook!) 26...Bb4 27.Kd2 (avoiding 27.Kd3?? Bxc3 28.Nxc3 Nb4+ forking White's King and Rook) 27...Rc4 28.Bxb4 (28.Kd3 Rxe4! wins material) 28...Rxe4 29.Bd6 Rxa4 (it seems to me that things are not so clear after 30.f3 Ra5 31.e4 Nf6 32.Rc8+ Kf7 33.Rc7+ when Black still has problems to solve).

Notice how Black got out of his difficulties (if indeed he does get out of them!). He used his weak pawn to temporarily tie up the White pieces. This gave him enough time to begin his own attack against White's weak pawn on a4. Black suffered because he had a weak pawn and he saved himself because he managed to get at a weak pawn in the White camp.

25.Bc3

This places the Bishop on an active diagonal and blocks Black's passed pawn. If the opponent has a weak pawn, first block it, then surround it, and finally swallow it.

25...Ba3

Black, not wanting to sit around and wait for White to improve his position, tries to get something going.

26.Rc2

Simply placing the Rook on a safe square.

26...Nxc3+

Black gets rid of the strong Bishop and tries to distract White from surrounding the c4-pawn by Nd2 followed by Bd4.

27.Rxc3

Recapturing his lost piece and threatening both 28.Nd2, winning the pawn, and 28.Rxa3, winning the Bishop.

27...Bb4
28.Rc2 Ke7
29.Nd2

The hunt for c4 begins in earnest.

29...c3

Saving the pawn but giving up the d3-square to the White King. If Black had taken with 29...Bxd2 then White would have still surrounded the pawn by 30.Kxd2 followed by Kc3, Rd2 and Rd4.

30.Ne4 Ba5
31.Kd3

Keeping the enemy Rook off of c4 and threatening to eat the c3-pawn. Notice how White never loses sight of his goal to surround and win the weak c-pawn.

31...Rd8+
32.Kc4 Rd1

Hoping that his active Rook will give him some compensation for the lost pawn. Passive defense by 32...Rc8+ was hopeless since 33.Kb3 followed by Nxc3 still leads to the loss of the pawn, but also leaves Black's Rook passive.

33.Nxc3

The pawn that White made weak on move 23 has finally been conquered! White now has a won game.

33...Rh1
34.Ne4!

White could have held onto his h2-pawn by 34.h3, but instead he begins an attack that allows all his pieces to penetrate deeply into the Black position and harass the Black King.

34...Rxh2
35.Kd4 Kd7
36.g3

A forcing alternative is 36.Nf6+! Ke7 (36...Kd8 37.f3 followed by Ke5) 37.Ke5 Rxg2 38.Rc7+ Kd8 39.Rd7+ Kc8 40.Kxe6 Rxf2 41.Ne4! Rf8 42.Nd6+ Kb8 43.Rb7+ Ka8 44.Rxh7 and Black is completely helpless. Analysis by Louis Morin.

36...Bb4
37.Ke5 Rh5+
38.Kf6 Be7+
39.Kg7 e5
40.Rc6

Preventing the Black King from advancing to e6. When you have control of a game, always do everything in your power to curtail the activity of the enemy pieces.

40...Rh1
41.Kf7 Ra1
42.Re6! Bd8
43.Rd6+ Kc8

Avoiding 43...Kc7?? 44.Ke8 when the Black Bishop has nowhere to run to.

44.Ke8 Bc7 35.Rc6 Rd1 36.Ng5 Rd8+ 47.Kf7 Rd7+ 48.Kg8 and Black resigned because 48...h6 loses to 49.Ne6 Kb7 50.Rxc7+ Rxc7 51.Nxc7 Kxc7 52.Kg7 when all Black's kingside pawns will be eaten.

Summary of the Imbalances and Ideas Viewed in this Game

➤ White enjoyed the superior pawns structure thanks to the weakness on e6.

➤ White's King was better than Black's since it was already placed in the center. When the endgame arrives, you usually want your King to be in the center.

➤ It's usually impossible to force a win if the enemy only has one weakness. Thus, the creation of a second or even third weakness is highly desirable.

➤ Black missed a chance to get back in the game by putting pressure on White's weak link on a4. Usually, active counterplay is more promising than passive defense.

➤ In the end, White's Knight was superior to Black's Bishop, White's King was incredibly active, and White's Rook worked with his teammates while Black's army was in disarray.

Problem 124

1.c4 e6 2.d4 d5 3.Nf3 Be7 4.Nc3 Nf6 5.Bg5 0-0 6.e3 h6 7.Bxf6 Bxf6 8.Qd2 b6 9.cxd5 exd5 10.b4 Bb7 11.Rb1 c6 12.Bd3 Nd7 13.0-0 Re8 14.Rfc1 a515.bxa5 Rxa5 16.Bf5 Ra6 17.Rb3 g6 18.Bd3 Ra7 19.Rcb1 Bg7 20.a4 Qe7 21.Bf1 Ba6 22.h4 Bxf1 23.Rxf1 h5 24.Re1 Raa8 25.g3 Qd6 26.Kg2 Kf8 27.Reb1 Kg8 28.Qd1 Bf8 29.R3b2 Bg7 30.Rc2 Ra7 31.Rbc1 Nb8 32.Ne2 Rc7 33.Qd3 Ra7 34.Qb3 Ra6 35.Nf4 Rd8 36.Nd3 Bf8 37.Nfe5 Rc8 38.Rc3 Be7 39.Nf4 Bf6 40.Ned3 Ra5 41.Qxb6 Rxa4 42.Rc5 Ra6 43.Rxd5 Qxf4 44.Qxa6 Qe4+ 45.f3 Qe6 46.Qc4 Qxe3 47.Ne5 Rf8 48.Rc5 Be7 49.Rb1 Bxc5 50.Rxb8, 1-0.

This is a long, hard game. Can you figure out what was going on?

Solution 124

While there has never been any doubt that the Road Runner is considerably weaker than the ever-persisting coyote, this fact doesn't come into play in the popular cartoon series because the bird is much too fast to be caught.

If we carry this state of affairs over to the chessboard, we begin to understand that a weak pawn is really only weak if it can be fixed in its position (moving targets are hard to hit) and then reached by members of the enemy army.

T.Petrosian-B.Spassky, Moscow 1969 World Championship Match.

1.c4 e6 2.d4 d5 3.Nf3 Be7 4.Nc3 Nf6 5.Bg5 0-0 6.e3 h6 7.Bxf6 Bxf6 8.Qd2 b6

We've reached a position from the early to middle stages of the opening. Many people feel that both sides should be getting their pieces developed before thoughts of any kind of plan begin to emerge. However, this is completely incorrect. In this position, Petrosian sees that Black has the two Bishops and would love to blow the center open with a ...c7-c5 advance. White would like to prevent this because, aside from stopping Black's plan, it would leave the pawn on c7 backward and potentially weak. If the Black c-pawn can't advance to c5 then no other pawn can protect it and it will always require a piece to act as its nursemaid. If Black's b-pawn still stood on b7, Black could play ...c7-c6 when everything is solid and safe.

With all these things in mind, White plays to stop the Black c-pawn in its tracks and create a target that may trouble Black later. White does intend to develop, but this will come after the more important question of the pawn structure has been addressed.

9.cxd5

This simple capture forces a Black pawn to permanently occupy the d5-square. This is usually quite acceptable for Black since the d-pawn covers the important c4 and e4 squares. However, in this case the immobile pawn on d5 has two shady aspects to it: 1) It will block Black's light-squared Bishop when it moves to its home on b7. 2) If Black ever plays ...c7-c5, White can capture via dxc5 and create a discovered attack on the d5-pawn with his Knight and Queen.

9...exd5 10.b4

This gains queenside space and stops the Black c-pawn from moving to c5.

10...Bb7 11.Rb1

This excellent move gets the Rook off the potentially dangerous f6-a1 diagonal (a diagonal that could be ripped open if Black sacrificed a pawn with ...c7-c5), defends the b4-pawn, and completely rules out ...c7-c5 because of bxc5 when the Rook is eyeing Black's Bishop on b7.

11...c6 12.Bd3

Now that White has nipped Black's queenside expansion ideas in the bud, he finishes off his development.

12...Nd7 13.0-0 Re8 14.Rfc1

The White Rook also finds a half-open file. On c1 the Rook defends the c3-Knight and begins to stare in greedy fashion at the pawn on c6.

It's important to note that White has not tried any kind of attack thus far. Instead, he has been content to gain a bit of queenside space, restrict the Black Bishops, create some potential targets and develop his pieces to good squares where they can assist in placing pressure on the Black position.

This style of play might surprise some of you when you realize that White virtually had to win this game if he wanted to retain any chances of keeping his title (which Spassky ultimately took from him in this match). Instead of throwing himself upon his opponent in a do-or-die effort, Petrosian calmly builds his position and waits for the right opportunity to present itself.

14...a5

This position had been reached in an earlier game of this same match. In that instance, Petrosian answered with 15.a3 when 15...axb4 16.axb4 b5 followed by 17...Nb6 and 18...Nc4 created a powerfully placed octopus which covered up the backward pawn on the c-file.

15.bxa5!

The prepared improvement which opens up lines for both White Rooks. Now the Black pawns on b6 and c6 come under pressure.

15...Rxa5

The White pawn on a2 is vulnerable but Black has two potentially weak units on c6 and b6. All the other White pawns are as solid as rocks.

16.Bf5

Threatening to win the b-pawn by Bxd7.

16...Ra6 17.Rb3

This prepares to double Rooks on the b-file, increasing the pressure against the Black pawns.

17...g6 18.Bd3

A tempting move that gains a tempo by attacking the Black Rook on a6. However, White no longer is placing pressure on the Black Knight, and after the game it was agreed that 18.Bh3 was somewhat superior to the move actually played.

18...Ra7 19.Rcb1

(281)

Black to move and put up maximum resistance.

19...Bg7

This was given a thumbs-down by critics. Do you see a better way for Black to place his pieces? How about 19...Kg7, giving support to h6, followed by ...Be7-d6-c7 when Black's b-pawn is firmly defended.

20.a4

This places the White a-pawn in a slightly more vulnerable position, but it also stops Black from ever entertaining ideas of a ...b6-b5 advance.

This type of restrictive move was very typical of Petrosian. He loved to take away every possible active option from the opponent. He preferred to strike when the enemy was drooling and helpless.

Black now has a fairly solid but passive position.

20...Qe7 21.Bf1

Since Black is helpless, White takes his time and places his pieces on the safest possible squares. From f1 this Bishop can go to h3 after g2-g3. It also frees the d3-square for a Knight.

21...Ba6?

Not good. Black gives up his Bishop pair (two Bishops have the potential to be strong. One Bishop is not so troublesome) and also leaves c6 without proper support.

22.h4

Suddenly White turns his attention to the kingside. Of course, if allowed he might create some weaknesses in that sector with h4-h5. His real intention, though, is to set up a firm kingside formation which will end any thoughts of Black kingside counterplay before continuing his queenside play. This setup will be achieved by g2-g3 and Kg2 when everything is solid and defended.

22...Bxf1 23.Rxf1 h5 24.Re1

After this, Black must always take a possible e3-e4 advance into account.

24...Raa8 25.g3 Qd6 26.Kg2

Now the kingside light-squares and the f3-Knight are well defended.

26...Kf8

Black can't see any way to improve his position so he begins to go back and forth in the hope that White won't be able to make any progress.

27.Reb1 Kg8 28.Qd1 Bf8 29.R3b2 Bg7 30.Rc2

After some boring cat and mouse play which serves to wear out the defending side, White turns his attention to that other weakness on c6.

30...Ra7 31.Rbc1 Nb8 32.Ne2

This Knight is ultimately heading for d3 where it will eye the b4, c5 and e5 squares. Petrosian always took the time to ensure that every one of his pieces was placed at its best possible post.

32...Rc7

Avoiding 32...Rxa4 33.Rxc6 Nxc6 34.Qxa4.

33.Qd3 Ra7 34.Qb3 Ra6 35.Nf4 Rd8 36.Nd3 Bf8 37.Nfe5

The pressure mounts on c6. Notice how Petrosian makes sure that every one of his pieces is doing a job. His King defends the holes on h3 and f3, his d3-Knight is ready to join the attack against c6 via Nb4, his e5-Knight is already bearing down on c6, his Queen attacks b6, eyes d5 and defends a4, and his Rooks both charge down the c-file and attack c6.

37...Rc8 38.Rc3 Be7 39.Nf4 Bf6 40.Ned3

The threat of Nb4 is winning for White. Another method was 40.Nxc6! Rxc6 41.Rxc6 Nxc6 42.Qb5 Nb8 43.Rc8+ Kg7 44.Rxb8.

40...Ra5 41.Qxb6

Simple and good was 41.Nb4, threatening to take advantage of the unprotected state of the c8-Rook by 42.Nbxd5. The move played by Petrosian begins a tactical sequence that utterly destroys the Black position.

41...Rxa4 42.Rc5! Ra6 43.Rxd5! Qxf4 44.Qxa6 Qe4+ 45.f3 Qe6 46.Qc4 Qxe3 47.Ne5 Rf8 48.Rc5 Be7 49.Rb1 Bxc5 50.Rxb8!, 1-0 since 50...Qxd4 51.Qxf7+! ends the game.

Summary of the Imbalances and Ideas Viewed in this Game

➤ Black gained the two Bishops but the central situation left them inactive.

➤ Black's c-pawn is a long-term weakness. To keep it that way, White will stop it from advancing to c5 by pushing his b-pawn to b4. Remember: a moving target is hard to hit. Thus, stop it in its tracks and then batter away at it all day long.

➤ You don't need to attack to win a game. A slow buildup that enables you to gain space and create enemy weaknesses is often extremely effective.

➤ Black's 19...Bg7 was lazy, in that it didn't address the weaknesses on the queenside. He should have brought this Bishop over to c7 where it would have given b6 some firm support.

➤ It's instructive to see how White always took time to ensure that all his pieces were placed on their very best squares.

Problem 125

In this game both players were ten-year-old girls with ratings in the 1400 range. Do their moves make sense and, when a mistake is played, can you recognize it?

1.e4 e5 2.Nf3 Nc6 3.Bc4 Nf6 4.d3 Be7 5.0-0 0-0 6.c3 d6 7.Re1 Bg4 8.h3 Bh5 9.Nbd2 Re8 10.Nf1 a6 11.Ng3 Bxf3 12.Qxf3 Na5 13.Bg5 Nxc4 14.dxc4 Qd7 15.Nf5 Qe6 16.b3 Bd8 17.Bh6 gxh6 18.Qg3+ Ng4 19.Qxg4+ Qg6 20.Nxh6+ Kf8 21.Nf5 Qxg4 22.hxg4 Bg5 23.Rad1 Rad8 24.g3 Rd7 25.Kg2 Red8 26.Rh1 Kg8 27.Rh5 f6 28.Rhh1 c6 29.Rhf1 and White won a piece and the game.

Solution 125

During the 1995 Youth Festival in Brazil, I was going over a game with ten-year-old Cindy Tsai when I pointed out a possibility that would have led to her having doubled pawns. Looking at me as if I was demented, she said, "Doubled pawns are always bad."

Thinking about this, it struck me how many beginner books and many deluded chess teachers pass on this inaccurate gospel from one generation to the next. Of course, doubled pawns can be bad, but they can also be a very positive addition to one's position.

Deciding that I had to set things right, I immediately began to lecture Cindy about the more positive features of our doubled friends. I didn't really expect her to make use of this information for a long time since one little lesson is usually not nearly enough to change the bad habits of a lifetime. Imagine my surprise when, just a few days later, Cindy played the following game in which she made wonderful use of the plusses of doubled pawns.

Cindy Tsai-S.Ananya, World Youth Festival, Brazil 1995.

1.e4 e5 2.Nf3 Nc6 3.Bc4 Nf6

The Two Knights Defense. Black invites 4.Ng5 when great complications arise after 4...d5 5.exd5 Na5 6.Bb5+ c6 7.dxc6 bxc6 with a lead in development for the sacrificed pawn. Since Cindy didn't know the theory, she wisely avoided this path and quietly developed her pieces.

4.d3 Be7 5.0-0 0-0 6.c3

A useful move that keeps the d4-square under control, thus ending any future threats based on ...Nd4. 6.c3 also prepares to gain central space with d3-d4.

6...d6 7.Re1 Bg4 8.h3 Bh5 9.Nbd2

Starting a well-known maneuver that destroys the pin on the f3-Knight and brings the b1-Knight into contact with the juicy f5-square.

9...Re8 10.Nf1 a6

Taking the b5-square away from the White Bishop and preparing to surround it by ...Na5.

11.Ng3

A good move. However, if White wanted to retain her light-squared Bishop she could have tossed in 11.Bb3 when 11...Na5 would be met by 12.Bc2.

11...Bxf3 12.Qxf3 Na5 13.Bg5!

A very fine move that has a couple of important points. First, White is happy to have her pawns doubled since these particular pawns add to her control of the center. Second, White has no intention of taking the Black Knight on f6. She is hoping that Black will play ...h6 when a Bishop retreat to e3 will show that the pawn on h6 is a weakness that is vulnerable to attack via Nf5. Advanced stuff from one so young!

13...Nxc4 14.dxc4

This is Cindy's first purposeful usage of doubled pawns and she is right on the mark! These doubled pawns control key squares on d5 and d4 and give the White Rooks a half-open d-file. Finally, nobody could possibly call these pawns weak; with b2-b3 the c4-pawn will be as solid as a rock. So what's wrong with these doubled pawns? The answer, obviously, is nothing!

14...Qd7?

Much better was 14...Nd7 (hoping to trade her bad Bishop for White's good one) 15.Be3 Bg5!. Another idea is 14...b5! 15.cxb5 axb5 when Black has weakened White's grip on d5 and has also opened the a-file for her Rook.

15.Nf5 Qe6 16.b3 Bd8?? 17.Bh6!

This unexpected move forces the win of at least a pawn.

17...gxh6

17...g6 18.Ng7 forks the Queen and e8-Rook.

18.Qg3+ Ng4 19.Qxg4+ Qg6 20.Nxh6+ Kf8 21.Nf5!

White brings her Knight back to its wonderful post and allows Black to give her a new, and favorable, set of doubled pawns. The inferior 21.Qxg6? hxg6 would fix Black's pawns and would also deprive the White Knight of the f5-square.

21...Qxg4?

Black jumps at the change to give White more doubled pawns but this just makes White's position even stronger since now she will be able to make use of the half open h-file.

22.hxg4

The pawn on g4 gives White added control over f5 and h5.

22...Bg5 23.Rad1

This excellent move places the Rook on a nice half-open file and also keeps the Black Bishop out of d2. Cindy is trying her best to deprive her opponent of any active play.

23...Rad8?

Correct was 23...b5! when 24.cxb5 axb5 gives Black counterplay against White's a2-pawn. Black's refusal to generate some play with ...b5, here or on subsequent moves, leads to her downfall.

It's interesting to note that Black's only hope was to undouble White's c-pawns! Keep in mind that labeling something good or bad won't help you win games. Instead, create attackable targets in any and every way possible.

24.g3

This takes away the f4-square from the enemy Bishop and gives the White King a nice home on g2.

24...Rd7 25.Kg2 Red8 26.Rh1 Kg8 27.Rh5

Attacking g5 and also preparing to double on the h-file. Note that all this play on the h-file is due to the doubled pawn on g4.

27...f6

Black defends her h7-pawn laterally with the Rook and also gives her Bishop the support it needs. 27...Bf6 would have lost quickly to 28.Rdh1.

(282)

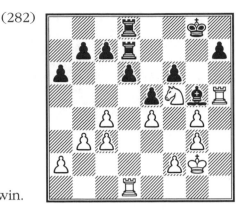

White to move and win.

28.Rhh1!!

The subtle point of White's play. By forcing ...f7-f6, White has taken away a route of retreat from the Black Bishop. White now intends to win the Bishop with Rhf1 and f4. There is no defense against this threat.

Note that 28.Rdf1? would have allowed the Bishop to escape with ...Bd2.

28...c6 29.Rhf1 and White won a piece and the game. Learn to love your doubled pawns!

Summary of the Imbalances and Ideas Viewed in this Game

➤ White avoided being sucked into a sharp theoretical discussion where her opponent would have had the upper hand thanks to her pre-game preparation.

➤ White broke the pin on her f3-Knight by the well-known but very useful maneuver Nb1-d2-f1-g3.

➤ White allowed her c-pawns to become doubled. These pawns gave her more central space and use of a half open d-file.

➤ A tactic based on the powerful position of her f5-Knight forced the win of material.

➤ White allowed the doubling of her g-pawns. This gave her access to the half-open h-file.

Problem 126

The following game is given without notes. Try to list the names of the main themes. For example, if one side tries for a smothered mate, say so. If we see one side making use of an unprotected piece, list that.

1.e4 c5 2.Nf3 Nc6 3.d4 cxd4 4.Nxd4 g6 5.Nc3 Bg7 6.Be3 Nf6 7.Be2 0-0 8.Qd2 d5 9.Nxc6 bxc6 10.e5 Ng4 11.Bxg4 Bxg4 12.h3 Bf5 13.g4 Be6 14.Qd4 f6 15.f4 Qc7 16.exf6 Bxf6 17.Qc5 Bh4+ 18.Ke2 Bc8 19.Nxd5 Ba6+ 20.c4 Qb7 21.Nb4 e5 22.Nxa6 exf4 23.Bd4 Rae8+ 24.Kf3 Re3+ 25.Kg2 f3+ 26.Kf1 Rfe8 27.Kg1 Bg3 28.Rf1 Re1 29.Bc3 Qxb2, 0-1.

Solution 126

Everyone loves to sacrifice huge quantities of material for a nice mate. However, though we all find it satisfying to give up a couple of pieces or even our Queen, few of us know how to go about it in over-the-board play. Are the legendary combinations based on a mixture of talent and inspiration, or is some other factor at work? Tal, one of the greatest attacking geniuses in history, was once asked where the inspiration for all his combinative blows came from. He said, "Most certainly in the black coffee I drink before every game!"

It turns out that most combinations, no matter their complexity or seeming originality, are based on a knowledge of tactical and combinative patterns. These patterns are picked up from isolated master games, being the whipping boy in countless blitz sessions and, more commonly, from books that discuss these things in great detail. In other words, with a little work it's remarkably easy to assimilate most of these tactical ideas.

The first step is to convince the amateur that everyone can create a work of combinative art. EVERYONE! To prove this point, let's glance at a game played between two Class C players (1400-1599) which actually won the tournament brilliancy prize ahead of several grandmasters and international masters. In fact, it was even used in a Russian book of great brilliancies!

Catig-Mills, San Francisco 1974.
1.e4 c5 2.Nf3 Nc6 3.d4 cxd4 4.Nxd4 g6

This line is known as the Accelerated Dragon.

5.Nc3 Bg7 6.Be3 Nf6 7.Be2 0-0 8.Qd2?!

This gives Black instant equality. White's best move is 8.Nb3.

8...d5 9.Nxc6 bxc6 10.e5 Ng4 11.Bxg4 Bxg4 12.h3 Bf5

After the game, Mills said that he was "goading" his opponent into the weakening 13.g4.

13.g4 Be6 14.Qd4 f6 15.f4 Qc7 16.exf6 Bxf6 17.Qc5 Bh4+ 18.Ke2 Bc8!

Starting a series of beautiful sacrifices. This clearance-move switches the Bishop around to a6 and prepares ...e7-e5, ripping the center wide open.

19.Nxd5 Ba6+ 20.c4 Qb7

Threatening both 21...cxd5 and 21...Qxb2+. Theme: Double attack and breaking a pin.

21.Nb4 e5!

Theme: Opening the center so that the Black pieces can get to the vulnerable enemy King. It also clears the e7-square and threatens to win a piece by 22...Be7.

22.Nxa6 exf4

Themes: Creating lines of attack for the Black army and double attack on e3 and a6.

23.Bd4 Rae8+ 24.Kf3 Re3+!

Themes: Retaining the initiative by working with threats at all times; Playing against the overworked piece (White's Bishop on d4 must defend the e3-square and the b2-pawn); Sacrificing material to open more lines for the rest of the Black forces.

25.Kg2

Also hopeless was 25.Bxe3 fxe3+ when 26.Kxe3 Bf2+ picks up the White Queen. Themes: Discovered check and skewer.

25...f3+ 26.Kf1 Rfe8!

Threatening mate on e1. Theme: Making use of the overworked d4-Bishop which is covering both e3 and b2. Now 27.Bxe3 Qxb2 wins immediately for Black.

27.Kg1

Trying to give the White King a place to run to on h2.

27...Bg3!

Theme: Building a mating net by taking away the squares that the enemy King can run to.

28.Rf1 Re1

Threatening 29...Rxf1+ followed by 30...Re1 mate.

29.Bc3

Covering the e1-square and stopping the threat of mate. White would also have lost if he had tried 29.Qa5. Do you see the win? It's 29...Rxf1+ 30.Kxf1 Qe7! and mates.

(283)

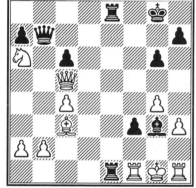

Black to move and win brilliantly.

29...Qxb2!!

Theme: Making use of an overworked piece (the poor Bishop is covering both b2 and e1).

White resigns since 30...Qg2 mate is threatened and 30.Bxb2 Rxf1+ 31.Kxf1 Re1 is mate.

Amazing! How could such a low-rated player have found all this? The answer is shocking: Mills told me that he really wasn't able to calculate most of the variations; instead, he simply followed the advice given in Vukovic's book, *The Art of Attack in Chess*. It turns out that he was studying this book before the tournament. Having memorized the basic themes and patterns, he was delighted to have an opportunity to make use of them in an actual game.

Summary of the Imbalances and Ideas Viewed in this Game

➤ Black opened up the center when he realized that White's King was trapped in that sector.

➤ Double attack.

➤ Pin.

➤ Opening up files for the Rooks.

➤ Playing against an overworked piece.

➤ Sacrificing material to open more lines for the rest of the Black forces.

➤ Discovered check and skewer.

➤ Building a mating net.

Problem 127

Take a look at this bare game score.

1.e4 Nc6 2.d4 e5 3.d5 Nce7 4.c4 Ng6 5.Bd3 Bb4+ 6.Nc3 Nf6 7.Bd2 0-0 8.Nf3 Bxc3 9.Bxc3 Nf4 10.0-0 Nxd3 11.Qxd3 d6 12.h3.

Play through all twelve moves, then go back and annotate all of them to the best of your abilities. Also take a guess as to the strength of both players.

Solution 127

I'm constantly getting letters and e-mails from every strata of society: doctors, lawyers, convicted criminals, priests, construction workers. The list goes on and on. Everyone asks the same thing (if we discount the hate-mail), and nobody wants to deal with the answer when they get it. The question is, "How do I get better at chess?" The answer, short and to the point, is, "Hard work!"

Sadly, the chessic equivalent to Viagra hasn't been invented yet, and chess-photosynthesis (holding a chess book to your head in the hope that the knowledge will seep into your skull) just doesn't seem to work (I've tried!). Thus, we're left with long hours of study, strained eyes, and the weight of countless defeats resting on our rapidly slumping shoulders.

I'm constantly shocked by tournament players who, after twenty years in the trenches, still don't know what a support point (or any basic bit of chess knowledge) is. They all dream of making master, they all imagine themselves beating up on grandmasters, but, evidently, they think the skill is going to be inherited, or that Zeus will toss a lightening bolt their way filled with the combined chess knowledge of the last 300 years.

To become a good chess player, you have to be willing to play, to lose (often!), and to work hard (very, very hard) at ironing out all the holes in your understanding. There are many ways to begin this journey: study openings and the typical middlegame plans that arise from the systems you wish to employ; read any one of the many middlegame books that have flooded the market; pick up an endgame book and learn the basics in this phase of the game; look at annotated master games (always a good idea); and finally, find a chess teacher who will look at your own games and rip you apart (if you can't handle the criticism, may I suggest taking up solitaire?).

Having a teacher look over your games is extremely useful. He can spot your overall shortcomings, he can patch your openings back together, and he can point out and mend bits of erroneous thinking you take with you to one game after another. Why repeat the same errors over and over again? Why not let a teacher surprise you as he fingers all the errors you've made in a game you felt was one of your very best?

The twelve moves I had you look at might seem pedestrian, but they are actually filled with hard decisions, tension, and errors. This exercise will help you in the following ways:

+ It will make my instructive comments much more personal, since you have already looked at the position and done your best to plumb its depths.

+ It might show you where your weaknesses lie, since you can now compare your own observations with my own.

+ It will whet your appetite for hard work during study (or it will make you swear never to attempt such an exhausting feat again, thereby destroying your chess future in the small space of one tiny problem!).

+ Having a teacher go over a game, or looking at master notes after you've annotated the game yourself, often brings the moves to life in ways that you normally wouldn't experience. This enriches your understanding of chess strategy, and also allows you to embrace the human side of the game. You see its ups and downs, the psychological moments that often bridge the distance between victory and defeat, and the pathos that always comes with any creative/combative endeavor.

+ It might shock you to realize how much is going on in a mere twelve moves! This, in turn, might convince you that there's a lot going on behind your back (and who wants to be oblivious to what's going on around them?).

Now it's time to compare your notes with my own annotations. By the way, the players were both in the 1600-1700 range.

1.e4 Nc6

If you are White, this might prove to be annoying. You've spent days going over the intricacies of the Lopez (1.e4 e5 2.Nf3 Nc6 3.Bb5), you've destroyed your marriage by locking yourself in the garage with 50 books on the Sicilian (1.e4 c5), you've memorized the French Defense (1.e4 e6) until it's coming out of your ears, and you took time off from your job to work out antidotes against the solid Caro-Kann Defense (1.e4 c6), Alekhine's Defense (1.e4 Nf6), and the Pirc Defense (1.e4 d6).

Feeling empowered and ready for anything, you toss out 1.e4 with a flick of your wrist and a deadly gleam in your eyes. And, horror of horrors, 1...Nc6 appears on the board—a move that has clearly descended to Earth from some nether region of hell!

2.d4

This move follows a sane bit of advice: after playing 1.e4, if your opponent lets you take the whole center with 2.d4, why not oblige?

Well, 2.d4 can't be bad, of course. But let's take a look at the guy sitting across from us: when we played 1.e4 he instantly banged down 1...Nc6. When we looked at his face, a malicious death-grin leaped at us from the other side of the table, and a drop of saliva fell from the corner of his mouth onto his soiled shirt sleeve.

What does all this mean? It tells us that he's either completely insane or that he is mirroring our own excitement over being completely prepared. In other words, while you were studying all those openings, he was devoting his life to the study and understanding of the positions arising after 1.e4 Nc6 2.d4.

With this in mind, is it really wise to walk into his preparations? That's a decision only you can make, but most players (even at the grandmaster level) avoid any pre-studied lines by the opponent by simply replying with 2.Nf3. Then 2...d6 3.d4 severely cuts down on Black's options, and 2...e5 takes us back into familiar territory. It's as if the game went 1.e4 e5 2.Nf3 Nc6.

2...e5

The alternative is 2...d5, but Black was still moving at break-neck speed and clearly had prepared this move before the game.

3.d5

An enormous decision! Theory recommends 3.dxe5 Nxe5 4.Nf3, but the text might seem better to many of you because it annexes central space and hits the enemy Knight with gain of tempo. However, such a simplistic view isn't sufficient when deciding on this kind of advance. Instead, you have to look at the change in pawn structure and realize that the closed center, created by 3.d5, means that play on the wings will be called for. Was this apparent to you when you saw 3.d5?

In a nutshell, White's pawns will be pointing towards the queenside (this gives him a spatial plus in that sector) and, as a result, that's where he should strive to open lines so that his

Rooks and other pieces can eventually penetrate into the hostile camp. This is usually done by a c2-c4-c5 advance.

Black's pawns (c7-d6-e5) are pointing at the kingside, and he will strive to gain kingside space via ...Nce7 followed by ...d6 (in the game, he chooses an alternate plan), ...g6, ...Bg7 and an eventual ...f7-f5 advance.

To sum up, White has to be confident that his queenside play is more real than Black's kingside play before he pushes his pawn to d5!

3...Nce7 4.c4

White shows that he's aware of his queenside responsibilities! A move like 4.Nc3, though it looks "pretty," just develops and doesn't take any plan into account. Don't develop without a plan!

If you liked 4.f4, did you take the negative factors of the move into consideration? After 4...exf4 5.Bxf4 Ng6 6.Bg3 d6 Black hopes to claim control over e5 and eventually place pressure against White's backward e-pawn by ...Bf8-e7-f6, ...Nh6, ...0-0, and ...Re8. You can't be aggressive just for the sake of aggression! If you saw all this and thought that ultimately you would win the fight for e5, then well and good. But if you didn't notice that you were creating a weak square on e5 and a backward pawn on e4, then a weakness in your understanding of the game has been revealed and steps have to be taken to strengthen that area of your chess knowledge.

4...Ng6

I've already mentioned that 4...d6 followed by 5...g6, 6...Bg7, 7...Nf6 and 8:..0-0, with an eventual ...f7-f5 to follow, leads to a kind of position normally found in the King's Indian Defense.

The move Black chose in the game makes perfect sense: he frees the f8-Bishop, intending to get it outside the pawn chain with ...Bc5 or ...Bb4, and places his Knight on a square where it threatens to leap into f4 at any moment.

5.Bd3

White had a lot of ideas here: 5.Be3 prevented Black from

placing his Bishop on c5; 5.g3 dominates the g6-Knight and even allows White to entertain ideas like h2-h4-h5. White's choice, though, is quite sensible.

5...Bb4+

Sharp. Black is trying to gain control over f4 and sees that 6.Bd2 Bxd2+ gets rid of White's main defender of that square (though this is hardly bad for White!). Naturally, 5...Bc5 was a perfectly good alternative.

6.Nc3

Of course, 6.Bd2 was possible, as was the odd-looking 6.Nd2 Nf4 7.Bf1 with g2-g3 to follow. White's choice gives Black a possibility that both sides appear to ignore.

6...Nf6

I would have been very tempted to play 6...Bxc3+ 7.bxc3 d6, leaving White's pawn structure compromised and eventually allowing a Black Knight to take up residence on c5 via ...Ng8-f6-d7. In time, Black could also consider ...c7-c6, opening up the c-file so that the Black army could get within reach of White's c-file weaknesses.

The striving for long-term structural plusses is a very important aspect of every master's game, but it's often overlooked by players who can't see beyond the world of simple threats and tactics.

7.Bd2

White decides to prevent the doubling of his pawns, but 7.Nge2 was a much better way to do this, guarding c3 and bringing another piece to bear on f4.

7...0-0 8.Nf3

Once again, I would have preferred 8.Nge2.

8...Bxc3?

Very odd. Instead of showing patience, Black decides that he can take the game by storm. Much better was the obvious 8...d6, freeing the c8-Bishop and giving e5 some much-needed support.

9.Bxc3 Nf4??

Losing the game, but this blunder allows us to take a look into the sordid world of chess psychology—Black tells White a lie and the first player buys into it!

(284)

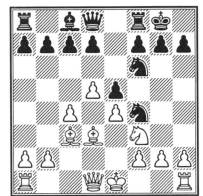

Black pretends that he knows what he's doing. White to move.

10.0-0??

White said to himself, "If I capture on e5, he captures with check on g2. I can't allow that!"

Sadly, the word "can't" should be eradicated from the vocabulary of every serious chess player. Instead, White should say, "What happens after 10.Bxe5 Nxg2+?" An unemotional look will convince you that 11.Kf1 traps the Black Knight and leads to a winning game after 11...Ng4 12.Kxg2 (not 12.Bg3?? due to the fork on e3) 12...Nxe5 13.Nxe5 Qg5+ 14.Ng4 h5 15.h3.

10...Nxd3?

And what is this about? Black has gone to extremes to get his Knight to f4, and now he voluntarily exchanges it for White's poor Bishop on d3. Once again, 10...d6 was called for.

11.Qxd3 d6 12.h3?

Useless. White shouldn't fear ...Bg4 because his Knight isn't doing anything on f3 anyway! Instead of wasting time preventing a non-threat—Black's ...Bg4 can always be met by Nd2 when the Knight is ready to join its comrades on the queenside—White should continue his earlier plans (started with 4.c4) of queenside expansion by 12.b4, while an immediate 12.c5 advance is also very tempting.

This game continued its ups and downs before a draw was agreed.

Summary of the Imbalances and Ideas Viewed in this Game

➤ Don't stop a threat unless it's really a threat!

➤ Bishops are not necessarily better than Knights. Don't trade a good Knight for a bad Bishop!

➤ Every pawn advance seriously effects the position as a whole. Make sure you understand what the ramifications of your intended pawn advance are!

➤ If your opponent's move tells you that up is down, don't take his word for it! Challenge every dictate that the other player makes!

➤ Often psychology plays an important role in the opening choices you make. Try to avoid walking into something he knows and you don't.

Problem 128

Annotate the following game (White tipped the scales at 1842, Black was rated 1695). Don't forget to add an assessment of the final position: 1.e4 e6 2.d4 d5 3.e5 c5 4.c3 Nc6 5.Nf3 cxd4 6.cxd4 Qb6 7.Nc3 Nge7 8.Na4 Qd8 9.g4 Ng6 10.Bd2 f6 11.h4 fxe5 12.h5 Nge7 13.dxe5 Bd7 14.Nc5 Qc7 15.Ng5 Nd4 16.Rc1 Qxe5+ 17.Be3 Nec6 18.Nd3 Qf6 19.f4 Bd6 20.Nf3 Nxf3+ 21.Qxf3 0-0-0 22.Bxa7 Bc7.

Solution 128

1.e4 e6 2.d4 d5 3.e5 c5

The usual recipe, though 3...Bd7 4.Nf3 a6, intending 5...Bb5, is an interesting sideline that would take you out of White's book rather quickly.

4.c3 Nc6 5.Nf3 cxd4?!

Too early. Black should play 5...Qb6, 5...Nge7, or 5...Bd7. After 5...cxd4?! White's b1-Knight will have access to the c3-square. Why hand a square like that over to your opponent for no reason?

6.cxd4 Qb6

A normal move in the French that stops the c1-Bishop from developing. Black's Queen takes aim at b2 and adds to the pressure on d4.

7.Nc3 Nge7

Sensible. This Knight is headed for f5 where it will bring enormous pressure to bear against d4. It's important that all your pieces work together towards a unified goal. The Queen on b6, combined with Knights on c6 and f5, is a nice illustration of this concept.

8.Na4

White decides that the Queen has to be removed from its bothersome b6-perch. An important question now is: will the Knight be useful on a4?

8...Qd8 9.g4?

Bad. This pawn advance uses up an important move to accomplish a rather nebulous weakening of the f4 and h4-squares.

White has a strong center, and he should be doing everything possible to strengthen it.

9...Ng6?!

This signifies an important moment. White has weakened his kingside with g2-g4 but also sent a message: he told Black that his intended ...Nf5 would not be tolerated. Black answers this with 9...Ng6, giving up on his ...Nf5 idea once and for all. Why bow to White's wishes? Far more thematic in this kind of position is 9...h5! when 10.h3 isn't possible due to 10...hxg4, making use of the pin along the h-file, while 10.gxh5 or 10.g5 cedes the f5-square to Black.

10.Bd2?

A horrible move. White is worried about the check on b4 and stops it by wasting a critical tempo to bring his Bishop to the passive d2-square.

10...f6

Black finally begins to play with some energy. He has to generate counterplay against White's center, and ...f7-f6 hits it squarely in the face.

11.h4

White thinks he's attacking, and it soon becomes apparent that Black believes him! The first player has long ago abandoned all thoughts of defending his center.

11...fxe5 12.h5 Nge7

Rather odd. After twelve moves neither side has developed anything but Knights and pawns, unless you want to consider that hideous thing on d2 a developed piece!

13.dxe5 Bd7 14.Nc5

White tries to prove that the Knight on a4 is well placed by making another one-move threat. Naturally, Black diffuses this with ease.

14...Qc7

Defending b7 and continuing to increase the pressure against e5.

15.Ng5??

It's now clear that White doesn't know how to do anything but make one-move threats.

15...Nd4!

This is a good move that creates a discovered attack on c5 and defends the e6-pawn. White's pawn on e5 isn't going anywhere since 16.Nd3 fails to 16...Nc2+.

16.Rc1 Qxe5+ 17.Be3 Nec6

This calmly defends d4 and frees the f8-Bishop. White has been completely outplayed.

18.Nd3 Qf6 19.f4 Bd6 20.Nf3 Nxf3+ 21.Qxf3 0-0-0?!

I would have preferred 21...0-0, instantly bringing the h8-Rook to a half-open file. Then 22.g5? is hammered by 22...Qxg5.

Black might also have considered 21...e5, ripping open the center in an effort to drag White's King to its knees.

Black said that he didn't castle kingside because he felt it was walking into White's attack. Where, may I ask, is this mystery attack? Having some far-advanced pawns doesn't give White the right to claim an attack, and you shouldn't fear such shadows if you can give him a central slap. Remember that central play almost always beats play on the wings.

22.Bxa7 Bc7

(285)

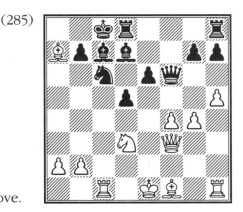

White to move.

Black simply missed 22.Bxa7; fortunately, his reply, 22...Bc7, is excellent. It unpins the Knight and creates an attack against a7. Now a Bishop move, 23.Be3, for example, is met by 23...e5! when Black's counterattack in the center is made all the stronger due to the White King's presence there. Black would then have a clear advantage.

Summary of the Imbalances and Ideas Viewed in this Game

➤ White built a central space advantage and then allowed Black to tear it down. Usually the player with the large center should do everything in his power to protect it.

➤ Black's ability to blast open lines in the center should beat any wing action that White has in mind. An attack in the center usually refutes play on the wings.

➤ If your opponent seemingly prevents an idea that you intended to play, don't believe blindly that he's succeeded. Look for a way to make your plan work anyway.

Problem 129

Annotate the following game. Aside from noting the tactics, try to figure out why Black got into trouble. What important rule did he violate that ultimately led to his demise?

1.e4 e5 2.Nf3 d6 3.d4 Bg4? 4.dxe5! Bxf3 5.Qxf3 dxe5 6.Bc4 Nf6 7.Qb3! Qe7 8.Nc3 c6 9.Bg5 b5? 10.Nxb5! cxb5 11.Bxb5+ Nbd7 12.0-0-0 Rd8 13.Rxd7! Rxd7 14.Rd1 Qe6 15.Bxd7+! Nxd7 16.Qb8+!! Nxb8 17.Rd8 mate.

Solution 129

Black's disaster was caused by his failure to castle in an open position, and his failure to get his whole army involved in the game. Let's discuss these things in more detail.

When we first learn how to play chess, we are told to develop our pieces as quickly as possible and get our Kings out of the center. A few of us follow this advice but many would-be champs don't understand why it is necessary to "waste time" moving all the men when they can go for the throat right away! To prove their point, they bring their Queen and Bishop out and go for a quick mate with just these two pieces. A typical example is 1.e4 e5 2.Bc4 Nc6 3.Qh5, threatening 4.Qxf7 mate.

On occasion, these quick-fix attackers meet opponents who fall for these transparent threats. More commonly, though, we see the berserkers start to lose as they climb up the rating ladder or stand transfixed on the same rung of that ladder. Their flimsy two-piece attacks are pushed back with greater and greater frequency. Having no choice but to make some sort of adjustment (unless he enjoys being violently thrashed), the crazed berserker quiets down and begins to get a few more men out each game until he finally gives in to his original teacher's pleas. Why should we develop all our pieces and castle as quickly as possible? Allow me to answer these two questions in as straightforward a manner as possible.

WHY DEVELOP?

If you were starving on a desert island and knew that sixteen rabid trolls on the other side had copious quantities of hot fudge and ice-cream, would you challenge them alone, or would you create a large raiding party to even up the odds?

If the answer to this question is as obvious as it appears to be, why is it that so many chess players insist on attacking sixteen chess pieces with just two of their own?

WHY CASTLE?

Was George Bush leading our troops down the sandy slopes of Iraq? Did Johnson or Nixon crawl through the steaming jungles of Vietnam? Of course not! Smart rulers stay in a safe place while their loyal subjects are battered into oblivion.

Why is chess any different? On e1 or e8 the Kings get in the way of their Rooks and become fodder for the enemy pieces if central files get opened. Isn't it smarter to rush your monarch to a safe hiding place until the danger of a pitched battle subsides? Remember that a lost piece or two doesn't to prevent you from playing on. A lost King ends the game immediately, irrespective of the material or positional balance.

In the game that follows, note how Black commits two horrible sins: He never moves his King-Bishop or King-Rook, and he never gets his King out of the center. Hopefully, Black's pain will prevent you from suffering in a similar manner.

Paul Morphy-Duke of Brunswick (in consultation with Count Isouard), Paris 1858
Philidor's Defense

1.e4 e5
2.Nf3 d6

This opening, called Philidor's Defense, has never been popular because it fails to develop a piece and restricts the action of the Black Bishop on f8. Most logical is 2...Nc6, a move that would defend e5, develop a piece, and continue the fight for the central d4-square.

3.d4

Morphy immediately gains central space and frees his Bishop on c1. He also prepares to open central files because he knows that an undeveloped opponent can best be punished in a wide open position—a position that has few or no central pawns. Why? Because the lack of central pawns gives Bishops free diagonals and Rooks open files. Don't forget that you can only overrun an unprepared enemy force by maximizing the activity of your pieces and by creating roads which allow your army to penetrate into the enemy position.

3...Bg4?

A poor move that allows White to acquire the two Bishops. Superior tries are 3...Nf6, meeting the threat on e5 with a counter-attack against e4, or 3...exd4, a move that gains time by forcing White to spend a move to recapture his pawn.

4.dxe5!

Extremely unpleasant for Black. Normally this exchange of pawns would make Black happy because it frees the Bishop on f8. However, in this case Black is forced to capture on f3 and bring the White Queen to an aggressive post because 4...dxe5?? 5.Qxd8+ (breaking the pin with tempo) 5...Kxd8 6.Nxe5 simply leaves White with an extra pawn.

4...Bxf3

Not what Black wanted to do, but this is the only way to avoid the loss of material.

5.Qxf3

Most of us have heard that it's not a good idea to develop your Queen too early. This is because the enemy minor pieces can gain time by attacking it. Rules are made to be broken, though. A Queen is a very strong piece and if you can place it on a safe, active post then you should be happy to do so. Note the word safe: a Queen that is immune from the attack of enemy pieces and works in an aggressive manner with the rest of its army is a very valuable commodity.

5...dxe5

6.Bc4

This develops another piece and threatens a one-move mate on f7. I've often lectured students on the uselessness of a two-piece Queen and Bishop attack on f7. Why is this case any different? Though an obvious threat is useless by itself because the opponent will see it and take defensive measures to nullify your attack, in this case White is bringing his Bishop to a wonderful post. Thus, White isn't after the threat, he's just trying to place his pieces on their best squares.

Note that an opening like 1.e4 e5 2.Bc4 Nc6 3.Qf3? is very different. The same mate is looming, but now White has created an obvious threat by placing his Queen on a poor post where it blocks the g1-Knight and is vulnerable to attack via ...Nc6-d4. In the Morphy game, the f3-Knight has already been developed so the Queen isn't blocking anything at all.

6...Nf6

Black develops his Knight and blocks the threat to f7 at the same time. Very commendable, but it falls victim to a bothersome double attack against f7 and b7 because the early development of the c8-Bishop took away the b7-pawn's natural protector. Better was 6...Qd7.

7.Qb3!

Hitting both b7 and f7.

7...Qe7

The best of a bad deal. This defends f7 and intends to trade Queens after 8.Qxb7 Qb4+, though White would be a solid pawn up with a winning game.

8.Nc3

Morphy decides to ignore the win of a "lowly" pawn. I must admit that I would probably have eaten that b7-pawn with glee and happily gone into the pawn-up endgame. In fact, the strong 8.Bxf7+ Qxf7 9.Qxb7 would have been hard to resist. Instead, Morphy keeps developing his forces in an attempt to highlight his advantage in development and crush Black as quickly as possible.

8...c6

This keeps the White pieces out of b5 and d5 and it also allows the Black Queen to protect both b7 and f7.

9.Bg5

White develops his final minor piece and prepares to castle. Notice how White's lead in development is getting greater with each passing move.

9...b5?

This move turns a terrible position into a resignable one. While Black's desire to chase the powerful White Bishop to a less active square is easy to understand, it is rarely correct to lunge forward when you are already off balance. 9...Qc7 followed by the development of the f8-Bishop made more sense.

10.Nxb5!

Seeing that he is way up in development and also seeing that the Black King is doomed to remain in the center for the rest of the game, White is willing to do almost anything to open lines of attack so that his pieces can reach the enemy King. Remember that a lead in development becomes more and more potent as the position becomes more and more open.

10...cxb5
11.Bxb5+ Nbd7
12.0-0-0

Getting the White King to safety and bringing a Rook to the open d-file. Now the two pinned Knights on d7 and f6 are under tremendous pressure and the Black position is starting to creak and groan. Of course, White is a piece down, but this is more illusion than reality because the inactive state of the Black pieces on f8 and d8 give White a superior working force. This means that White is, in effect, material ahead—he has five attacking units (two Bishops, two Rooks, and a Queen) to Black's four defensive units (two Bishops, two Knights, and the Rook on a8).

12....Rd8

White threatened to win material by taking on either d7 or f6. This move gives the d7-Knight some much-needed support.

(286)

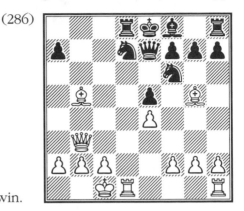

White to move and win.

13.Rxd7!

White must strike while the iron is hot or Black will bring his remaining forces out with ...Qb4 followed by ...Be7. Never forget that a lead in development is not a permanent advantage. If you don't make immediate use of your mobilized army, the opponent will eventually bring his own pieces out and catch up.

This sacrifice of the White Rook makes room for the other Rook and does not give Black the opportunity to carry out any of his own plans.

13...Rxd7
14.Rd1

Throwing his final piece into the attack and bringing more pressure to bear against d7. Black could safely resign here but instead he allows a very pretty finish.

14...Qe6

Following the rule which states that the defender should strive for a trade of Queens.

15.Bxd7+!

Most picturesque. A mundane win would be 15.Bxf6 when 15....Qxb3?? would be mashed by 16.Bxd7 mate.

15....Nxd7

Black may have felt that he had escaped at this point, but White's next move shatters any such illusions.

16.Qb8+!!

A surprising Queen sacrifice that forces the complete opening of the d-file and creates a direct route to the Black King.

16....Nxb8

17.Rd8 mate. Black's f8-Bishop and h8-Rook never took part in this game.

Summary of the Imbalances and Ideas Viewed in this Game

➤ Rapid development is extremely important in open positions.

➤ If the center is open and you're not castled, you should be aware that danger lies around every corner!

➤ If the enemy King is in the center, do everything you can to reach it with your own army. If this entails a sacrifice, then don't be shy about giving it a try.

Problem 130

Annotate this game, starting after Black's 8th move: 1.g3 g6 2.Bg2 Bg7 3.e4 c5 4.Nf3 Nc6 5.0-0 Nf6 6.d3 0-0 7.Re1 d6 8.Nbd2 Rb8 9.a4 b6 10.Nc4 Bb7 11.h4!? Qc7 12.Bd2 Rbd8 13.Qc1 d5 14.Bf4 Qc8 15.exd5 Nxd5 16.Bh6 Rfe8 17.Bxg7 Kxg7 18.h5 Nf6 19.h6+ Kg8 20.Qf4 Nh5 21.Qd2 f6 22.a5! b5 23.a6! Ba8 24.Na5 e5 25.Qc3 Nd4 26.Nb7! Bxb7 27.axb7 Qxb7 28.Nxd4 cxd4 29.Bxb7 dxc3 30.bxc3 Re7 31.Rxa7 Kf8 32.Rb1.

Solution 130

Larsen-Gligoric, Vinkovci 1970. **1.g3 g6 2.Bg2 Bg7 3.e4 c5 4.Nf3 Nc6 5.0-0 Nf6 6.d3 0-0 7.Re1 d6 8.Nbd2 Rb8 9.a4**

A standard move that stops ...b7-b5 and, as a result, gives White's pieces access to the c4-square.

9...b6 10.Nc4 Bb7 11.h4!?

(287)

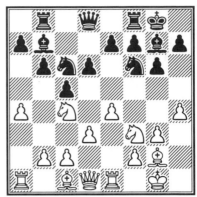

Making use of those
Rook-pawns!
Black to move.

A shock since it really has nothing to do with a kingside attack. The idea of this move is that 11...d5 can now be met by 12.exd5 Nxd5 13.h5! when the h-pawn has become very annoying for Black. The further course of the game saw the h-pawn continue to play an important role.

Though few players would have made this move, Larsen always had a deep love for Rook-pawns, and even said, "When in doubt, push your Rook-pawns!"

11...Qc7 12.Bd2 Rbd8 13.Qc1 d5 14.Bf4 Qc8 15.exd5 Nxd5 16.Bh6 Rfe8 17.Bxg7 Kxg7 18.h5 Nf6 19.h6+

Now Black's King will always feel a bit uncomfortable.

19...Kg8 20.Qf4 Nh5 21.Qd2 f6 22.a5!

Suddenly the other Rook-pawn begins to bite into the queenside. Black must have been feeling a bit confused at this point.

22...b5 23.a6!

An odd sight. Both Rook-pawns have reached the sixth rank.

23...Ba8

Black should have accepted the pawn sacrifice by 23...Bxa6 24.Na5 Nb8 though White would have had strong pressure after 25.Qc3.

24.Na5 e5 25.Qc3 Nd4 26.Nb7! and Black's whole army was in a state of shock. After **26...Bxb7 27.axb7 Qxb7 28.Nxd4**

cxd4 29.Bxb7 dxc3 30.bxc3 Re7 31.Rxa7 Kf8 32.Rb1 White
was winning and eventually scored the full point.

Summary of the Imbalances and Ideas
Viewed in this Game

➤ White created an artificial support point on c4 with
a2-a4.

➤ The advance of the other Rook-pawn to h4 kept
Black occupied with thoughts of an h4-h5-h6 advance if the f6-Knight moved.

➤ White used the typical Qd1-c1&Bh6 maneuver to trade
off Black's g7-Bishop. This weakened the enemy King
and also deprived Black of his most active piece.

➤ When Black played ...d6-d5, White was happy to
exchange by exd5 since that activated the e1-Rook
and instantly placed pressure against the e7-pawn.

➤ When White's h-pawn reached h6, the Black King
knew it would never feel completely safe since mate
threats on g7 would be looming for the rest of the
game. The pawn on h6 also fixes the h7-pawn and
labels it as a potential weakness if an endgame is
reached.

➤ The advance of the other Rook-pawn on a4 to a5
created weaknesses in Black's queenside structure.

Problem 131

Annotate this game. White missed a wonderful opportunity, see if you can spot that moment.

1.e4 e5 2.f4 exf4 3.Nf3 Be7 4.Bc4 Nh6 5.d4 c6 6.Bxf4 d5 7.exd5 cxd5 8.Bb5+ Nc6 9.0-0 Nf5 10.Nc3 0-0 11.Qd2 Bf6 12.Ne2 Nd6 13.Bd3 Ne4 14.Qe1 Re8 15.c3 a6 16.Qb1 Na5 17.Ng3 Nxg3 18.Bxg3 h6 19.Be5 Be6 20.Qc2 Rc8 21.Qf2 Nc4 22.Bxc4 Rxc4 23.Nd2 Bxe5 24.Nxc4 Bxh2+ 25.Kxh2 dxc4 26.Rae1 Qd7 27.Re3 Bd5 28.Rxe8+ Qxe8 29.Re1 Qd7 30.Qe3 Kf8 31.Qe5 f6 32.Qg3 Kf7 33.Qh3 Qxh3+ 34.Kxh3 Be6+ 35.Kg3 Bd5 36.Kf2 Be6 37.g3 Bd5 38.Ke3 Ke6 39.Rb1 Kd6 40.b3 b5 41.bxc4 Bxc4 42.a4 Kd5 43.axb5 Bxb5 44.Rf1 Bxf1, 0-1.

Solution 131

Unlike computers, that look at virtually every move no matter how stupid the move might be, humans depend on past experience and recognition of important patterns to unconsciously eliminate many possibilities. Interestingly, this is both our advantage and disadvantage over chess playing programs. On the one hand, this ability to cut to the chase or play "by feel" saves time, but on the other hand this same ability sometimes lets us down because we sift out key ideas that don't have a place in our overall understanding of the game.

(288)

White to move.

For example, the position in diagram (288) would prove fairly simple to analyze. A human wouldn't bother looking at anything but 1.b4 to discourage Black's eventual ...c6-c5 advance, 1.Rac1 with the same point as 1.b4, 1.Rfd1 (ditto), or 1.Rad1 discouraging ...c6-c5 and intending a possible central advance by e3-e4 when the f1-Rook might wish to be placed on e1.

The human would cut his options down because he sees that Black has two Bishops and that the only way these Bishops could become active is to achieve ...c6-c5 at some point. Thus, a move like 1.b4 stops ...c5, keeps the enemy Bishops contained, and prepares to target c6 as a weakness by placing the Rooks on the c-file.

Though a computer would look at all sorts of rubbish, including 1.Bh7+, a carbon-based life form would automatically ignore this check since it doesn't bother the enemy King at all after 1...Kh8, when the Bishop is suddenly threatened with extinction by 2...g6. In other words, the only thing Bh7+ does is to place the Bishop in a precarious position.

This is where the study of tens of thousands of master games comes in. A player conversant with the classics would be aware of the following contest between Petrosian and Taimanov (Moscow 1955): 1.d4 d5 2.c4 e6 3.Nf3 Nf6 4.Nc3 c6 5.e3 Nbd7 6.Bd3 Bb4 7.0-0 0-0 8.Qc2 Bd6 9.b3 dxc4 10.bxc4 e5 11.Bb2 Re8 12.Ne4 Nxe4 13.Bxe4 h6 14.Rad1 exd4 and now White tossed in the astute 15.Bh7+! (forcing Black's King onto the vulnerable b2-h8 diagonal, and also leaving the f7-pawn without a defender). Black was destroyed after 15...Kh8 16.Rxd4 Bc5 17.Rf4 Qe7 18.Re4! Qf8 19.Rh4 (threatening Rxh6) 19...f6 20.Bg6 Re7 21.Rh5 Bd6 22.Rd1 Be5 23.Ba3! c5 24.Nh4 and Black resigned because he doesn't have a defense to 25.Bh7 followed by 26.Ng6+.

Knowledge of this game, or any memorable game featuring the Bh7+ pattern, would alert a player to the possibilities that a well-timed Bh7+ might harbor. If you're not familiar with it, though, some nice opportunities might be squandered. Our feature game starkly illustrates this.

Joseph (1742)-Yeung (1445), Los Angeles 2000.

1.e4 e5 2.f4 exf4 3.Nf3 Be7 4.Bc4 Nh6

Joseph loves to play the King's Gambit, even though his positional skills outweigh his attacking powers. With 4...Nh6 Black shows that he doesn't know the opening.

5.d4 c6 6.Bxf4

White has effortlessly achieved an excellent position.

6...d5 7.exd5 cxd5 8.Bb5+

Lulled into thinking that his opponent doesn't have a clue as to what's going on, White makes a poor move. The Bishop proves to be vulnerable on this square (try not to place your pieces on undefended squares). The straightforward 8.Bd3 followed by the tightening c2-c3 should have been preferred.

8...Nc6 9.0-0 Nf5 10.Nc3?

A bad idea. White's d-pawn now comes under a lot of pressure. The solid 10.c3 was still very nice for White, leaving Black with nothing to attack in White's camp. It's important that you always be aware of your weakest points and take steps to fix them.

10...0-0 11.Qd2 Bf6 12.Ne2 Nd6

Black begins to show an unfortunate preference for useless one-move attacks, and though there's nothing wrong with this move, I suspect his idea behind it was way off. I doubt that he noticed the potential weakness of d4 and b2.

He was wise to avoid 12...Ncxd4? 13.Nexd4 Nxd4 14.Nxd4 Qb6 since 15.Be3 Bxd4 16.Bxd4 Qxb5 17.Rae1 gives White strong pressure on the dark squares for the sacrificed pawn. Note that 17.Qg5? f6 18.Rxf6?? loses to 18...Rxf6 19.Bxf6 Qb6+.

13.Bd3?

White also seems to be unaware of the problems brewing on d4.

13...Ne4

Another good move, but not played for the right reason.

14.Qe1

White didn't like the look of 14.Qc1 Nb4.

14...Re8?

Missing his chance. If he had been aware of the weaknesses on b2 and d4, he would have had no problem finding 14...Qb6, hitting both targets at the same time.

15.c3

White finally manages to tighten his pawn chain, and the advantage slowly shifts back to its rightful place.

15...a6?

I think Black was confused. He should have kept life and limb together with the solid 15...Bf5 16.Qb1 Bg6.

16.Qb1 Na5?

It still wasn't too late for 16...Bf5, fortifying both e4 and the kingside.

17.Ng3 Nxg3 18.Bxg3?

White becomes lazy. He saw 18.Bxh7+, but thought that Black intended to trap him with 18...Kh8 19.hxg3 g6. A serious look would have convinced him that 20.Bxg6 fxg6 21.Qxg6 with the threat of 22.Kf2 and 23.Rh1+ would have given him a crushing attack.

18...h6 19.Be5 Be6

(289)

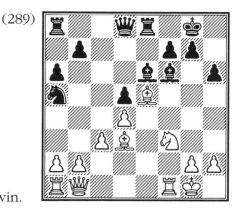

White to move and win.

20.Qc2??

Missing a chance to score a pretty victory. Correct was 20.Bxf6 Qxf6 21.Bh7+! (there is our "Petrosian" check! Of course,

White thought that such a move was completely useless.) 21...Kh8 (21...Kf8 22.Ne5 Qg5 23.Ng6+ ends the game quickly) 22.Ne5 Qe7 and now 23.Bg6 Rf8 24.Bxf7! crashes through: 24...Bxf7 25.Rxf7 when the threat of Ng6+ gives White the full point.

20...Rc8??

Still allowing 21.Bxf6 followed by 22.Bh7+!.

21.Qf2??

And the unseen chance vanishes forever. The rest of the game saw White, after various errors, achieve a dead won endgame only to make a blunder so bad that it thins the blood and brings a scream of anguish to one's lips.

21...Nc4 22.Bxc4 Rxc4 23.Nd2 Bxe5 24.Nxc4 Bxh2+ 25.Kxh2 dxc4 26.Rae1 Qd7 27.Re3 Bd5 28.Rxe8+ Qxe8 29.Re1 Qd7 30.Qe3 Kf8 31.Qe5 f6 32.Qg3 Kf7 33.Qh3 Qxh3+ 34.Kxh3 Be6+ 35.Kg3 Bd5 36.Kf2 Be6 37.g3 Bd5 38.Ke3 Ke6 39.Rb1 Kd6 40.b3 b5 41.bxc4 Bxc4 42.a4 Kd5 43.axb5 Bxb5 and here White, obviously in a giving mood, uncorked **44.Rf1?? Bxf1, 0-1**.

Summary of the Imbalances and Ideas Viewed in this Game

➤ The study of master games plays a key part in any serious student's chess development.

➤ The old saying, "Always check, it might be mate." shouldn't be taken too seriously. However, every check does need to be examined. Hopefully, the possibility of Bh7+ will now become a part of your chess armament.

➤ Don't place your pieces on undefended squares.

➤ Avoid useless one-move attacks! Instead, learn to train your sights on the opponent's structural weaknesses.

GATA KAMSKY

JOHN DONALDSON

Active An aggressive move, line of play, or position. When mentioned in terms of a player's style, it denotes a preference for sharp, tactical or vibrant types of play.

Advantage Having a superiority in position based on a particular imbalance or series of imbalances. See *Imbalance*.

Analysis The calculation of a series of moves in a given position. This can be done in actual tournament conditions (in which you are not allowed to touch the pieces) or in a calmer scenario in which the pieces can be moved about (such analysis is often written down for future study or reference). The purpose of analysis is to discover the best move or plan. There is no limit to its length.

Annotation Written comments (prose, chess symbols or actual moves) about a position or game.

Attack To make a threat or threats against a specific piece or area of the board.

Backward Pawn A pawn that has fallen behind its comrades, and thus no longer can be supported or guarded by other pawns of its own persuasion.

In the diagram, Black has backward pawns at d6 and f7. The pawns on h6 and b7 are not backward because they can safely advance.

Bind To have such a vise-like grip on a position that useful moves are difficult for the opponent to find. One often speaks of a crushing space advantage as a bind.

The diagram shows an extreme example of a bind; Black is bound hand and foot and can undertake nothing positive at all.

Bishop Pair To possess two Bishops versus the opponent's Bishop and Knight or two Knights. Two Bishops work extremely well together and are usually an advantage in open positions.

Bishops of Opposite Color A situation in which each player has only one Bishop, each being of a different color, and thus the Bishops can never come into contact. This is usually a good attacking imbalance for the middlegame, since one can't defend what the other attacks. However, these Bishops are known to be rather drawish in the endgame, due to the fact that the defender can place his pawns and King on the opposite color of the enemy Bishop, whereupon they are impervious to harm.

From an attacking point of view, a general rule for Bishops of opposite colors is that they are at their best with other pieces to back them up. On their own, they are often impotent.

Blockade Conceptualized and popularized by Aron Nimzovich (1886-1935), it refers to the tying down or immobilization of an enemy pawn by placing a piece, particularly a Knight, directly in front of it.

In the diagram, the Knight on d6 is blockading the pawn on d5.

Blunder A horrible mistake that hangs material or makes enormous positional or tactical concessions.

Book Published opening theory. A "book player" is one who relies on memorization of published analysis rather than on his own creative imagination. "Taking someone out of book," refers to sidestepping published analysis by playing a new or unorthodox move. This denies him the chance to make use of a good memory and forces him to find good moves on his own.

Break The gaining of space (and thus more freedom of movement) by the advance of a pawn.

In the diagram, White intends to open lines of attack on the queenside by the break c4-c5, prepared by b2-b4. Black will strive to attack White on the kingside by a ...f7-f5 break.

Breakthrough A means of penetrating the enemy position. This can be accomplished by a pawn break or by a sacrifice involving pieces or pawns.

White to play.

In the diagram, both sides are attacking each other's King. At the moment White is safe, since ...gxf3 can be safely answered by Bxf3. So White uses the time given him to effect a breakthrough on the queenside by 1.bxc5 dxc5 2.Nxc5! bxc5. If Black does not capture the Knight, White will simply retreat it to d3 and rip Black open by c4-c5, Qb2 and Black will be mated.

Brilliancy A game that contains a very deep strategic concept, a beautiful combination or an original plan.

Calculation The working out of variations without moving the pieces physically. Though this book has taught you to talk or reason your way through a game, there are many positions that have a purely tactical nature. In such situations, the player's ability to calculate variations accurately takes on great importance.

In such situations, the player's ability to calculate variations accurately takes on great importance.

The way to train your combinative (calculative) vision is to study the games of attacking players like Alekhine, Tal, or Kasparov. Follow their opening moves and then cover up the rest of the game score. At this point you should endeavor to figure out all the imbalances, the plans, candidate moves, etc. When this is done, calculate each candidate move as deeply as you can, writing down all this information as you go. All these things must be done without moving the pieces around. When you have done all that's possible (take as much time as you need, we are looking for accuracy; speed will follow with practice), look at the move played, make it on your board and keep repeating the process until the game is complete.

Center Usually considered to be the e4-, d4-, e5-, and d5-squares, though the territory within the c4-, c5-, f4-, and f5-parameters can also be thought of as central.

Centralize The central placing of pieces and pawns so they both control the center and extend their influence over other areas of the board. A piece will usually reach maximum maneuverability and power when centrally placed.

Checkmate See *Mate.*

Classical A style of play, sometimes called a school, that is concerned with forming a full pawn center. The strategic concepts that go with it tend to be viewed as ultimate laws and thus are rather dogmatic. A classical opening is an opening based on these views. See *Hypermodern.*

Closed Game A position locked by pawns. Such a position tends to lessen the strength of Bishops and other long-range pieces simply because the pawns get in their way. Knights, not being long-range pieces, can jump over other pieces and pawns and thus are very useful in such closed situations. A typical series of opening moves that leads to a closed position is 1.d4 Nf6 2.c4 c5 3.d5 e5 4.Nc3 d6 5.e4, etc.

Combination A tactical move or series of moves based on the opponent's weakened King, hanging or undefended pieces or inadequately guarded pieces. Usually involving a sacrifice, it is a calculable series of moves leading to material or positional gains. It is important to note that a combination cannot exist if at least one of the above factors is not present.

Though several players have attempted to create a clear definition throughout the years, the following definition by Silman and Seirawan is the most accurate: "A combination is a sacrifice, combined with a forced sequence of moves, that exploits specific peculiarities of the position in the hope of attaining a certain goal."

Compensation An equivalent advantage in one imbalance that balances the opponent's advantage in another. For example: material versus development or space versus a superior minor piece or three pawns versus a Bishop.

Connected Passed Pawns Two or more pawns of the same color on adjacent files. See *Passed Pawn.*

Control To dominate or have the sole use of a file, a square or group of squares, an area of the board, etc. Having the initiative would also put one in "control."

Counterplay When the defending side starts his own aggressive action, he is said to have or be initiating counterplay. However, there are varying degrees of counterplay—some equalizing the chances, some not being quite adequate and some leading to the capture of the initiative and subsequently an advantage.

Cramp A disadvantage in space that leads to a lack of mobility.

Critical Position That point in a game when the evaluation will clearly turn to one side's advantage or stabilize down to equality. In such a position the scales are delicately balanced and the slightest error can lead to disaster.

Defense A move or plan designed to meet an enemy's attack or threats. It is also used in the names of various opening initiated from the Black side. For example: Petroff Defense, Caro-Kann Defense, etc. These Black systems are called defenses since White has the first move and thus Black is considered to be defending. The usual flow from Black's point of view would be: defense leading to equalization followed, only then, by the switch over to a counterattack. This is the classical approach. More modern openings are often designed to create immediate imbalances in an effort to s eize the initiative as Black. Strange as it may seem, even these counterattacking openings are usually given the title of defenses: Nimzo-Indian Defense, Sicilian Defense, Grunfeld Defense, King's Indian Defense, etc.

Development The process of moving one's pieces from their starting posts to new positions where their activity and mobility are enhanced. It must be remembered that one's pieces should be developed to squares where they work with the rest of their army towards a particular goal. If an individual piece is providing a useful service on its original square, then there may be no reason to move it.

Doubled Pawns Two pawns of the same color lined up on a file as the result of a capture. Such pawns are generally considered to be weak, though quite often their ability to control certain squares makes them very useful.

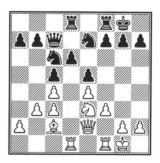

The diagram shows doubled pawns in a favorable light. The doubled pawn on c3 is guarding the critical d4-square, while the other pawn on c4 increases White's control over the important d5-square. Also note how doubled pawns give their owner an extra file to use. Black's position in the diagram would be considerably improved if he could double his own pawns by placing the d6-pawn on e6.

Dynamic The word "dynamic" symbolizes the aggressive potential in any given position or move.

Elo Rating A mathematical system, now used worldwide, devised by Professor Arpad Elo to rank chess players.

En Passant A French term that literally means "in passing." When a pawn advances two squares (something it can only do if it has not

yet moved) and passes an enemy pawn on an adjacent file that has advanced to its fifth rank, it may be captured by that enemy pawn as if the advancing pawn had moved only one square. This optional capture may be made only on the first opportunity else the right is permanently lost.

In the diagram, if Black plays 1...c7-c5, White, if he wishes, may capture the pawn as if it had moved to c6. Thus, 2.dxc6. If after 1...c7-c5 White declines to capture and instead plays 2.c4, then after 2...e7-e5 White could no longer capture the c5-pawn. However, he could capture the e5-pawn by dxe6 if he so desired. In chess notation an En Passant capture is labeled by the letter e.p.

En Prise A French term meaning "in take." It describes a piece or pawn that is unprotected and exposed to capture.

Endgame When most of the pieces have been exchanged, usually leaving both sides with one to three pieces each (plus any amount of pawns), the game is said to have entered the final phase, known as the endgame.

Equality A situation in which neither side has an advantage.

Exchange To trade pieces of equal worth. See *Point Count*. Trading a piece for something of lesser value is called a *Blunder* or a *Sacrifice*.

Exchange, The A comparison of value between a Rook versus a Bishop or Knight. Thus, if you have won an enemy Rook for your Bishop, you have won the Exchange.

Fianchetto An Italian word meaning "on the flank." Though you will hear many different pronunciations, the correct is fee-an-ket-to. When a Bishop is developed on QN2 or KN2 (b2 or g2 for White and b7 or g7 for Black), it is called a fianchettoed Bishop. This term applies only to Bishops.

FIDE An acronym for Federation Internationale des Echecs, the World Chess Federation.

File A column of eight squares. An open file is a file that is not blocked by either side's pawns.

Fish A derogatory term denoting a weak chess player.

Flank The sides of the board—the kingside and queenside. Flank Openings are openings that deal with flank development. Typical starts for such systems are 1.c4, 1.Nf3, 1.b3, 1.g3, etc.

Force All pieces and pawns are units of force. For example, if White has four attacking units on the kingside to Black's two, White is said to have an advantage in force in that sector of the board.

Forced A move or series of moves that must be played if disaster is to be avoided. Two examples: 1) You face a forced move when your checked King only has one legal move to get out of check. 2) A Knight or any other piece is attacked and has only one safe square to go to. Moving it to that safe square is also considered to be forced, even though other moves could legally be played.

Gambit A voluntary sacrifice of a pawn or a piece in the opening with the idea of gaining the initiative, a lead in development or some other compensating factor.

General Principles Basic rules of play designed to serve as guidelines for less advanced players. As one's experience grows, one learns that rules are meant to be broken. For example: the old rule of "always capture with a pawn towards the center," is widely followed, but a good 30% of the time it is correct to capture away from the center. Other rules such as, "avoid doubled pawns," "castle as early as possible," "develop Knights before Bishops," etc., are also just as suspect. The simple fact is that every situation must be looked at with an open mind. Dogma is not something to be nurtured in life or in chess.

Ghosts Threats that exist only in your own mind. A fear of your opponent or a lack of confidence will often lead to the appearance of ghosts and the cropping up of blunders in your play.

Grandmaster   The highest chess title, aside from World Champion, that one can achieve. Conferred by FIDE, it is awarded to players who meet established performance standards. Other titles, in order of importance, are International Master and FIDE Master. Once earned, these titles cannot be taken away.

Grandmaster Draw   This label, originally used to describe a quick, uninteresting draw between grandmasters, is now employed to describe a fast draw between virtually any class of players.

Hack   A derogatory chess term meaning a state of chess ineptitude.

Hanging   An unprotected piece or pawn exposed to capture is said to be hanging.

Hanging Pawns   Two adjacent friendly pawns on their fourth rank, separated from other friendly pawns, and subject to frontal attack on two half-open files. Though often objects of attack, they also possess a certain dynamic potential. Thus, the battle rages around the question, "are they strong or weak?"

The diagram shows a common hanging pawns situation. The hanging pawns on c5 and d5 give Black an edge in space, good control of the central squares and pressure down the half open b-file. However, they are also exposed to attack.

Hog   See *Pig*.

Hold   A defensive term meaning to "hang on." "Such and such a move would have held out longer," means that the move would have offered tougher resistance, but would most likely have ultimately failed. "Such and such a move would hold," means that the mentioned move would have allowed a successful defense.

Hole   A square that cannot be defended by pawns. Such a square makes an excellent home for enemy pieces, especially Knights. For example, the opening 1.c4 c5 2.Nc3 Nc6 3.e4 is playable, but leaves a hole on d4 that, after 3...g6 and 4...Bg7, can easily be used by a Black piece.

Hutch   A special room set aside for players in a tournament to analyze their games and play *skittles*. Such a room allows various kinds of activity to go on without disturbing the unfinished games in the tournament. Usually used by the non-masters (called Rabbits), the term hutch becomes easily understandable. See *Rabbit* and *Skittles*.

Hypermodern A school of thought that insists that indirect control of the center is better than direct occupation. In particular, Reti and Nimzovich successfully propagated the idea of central control from the flanks. Unfortunately, they took their ideas to extremes, just as the classicists did. Today it is recognized that both schools of thought are partially correct, and a blending of the two is the only truly balanced method.

Imbalance Any difference between the White and Black positions. Material advantage, superior pawn structure, superior minor piece, space, development, and the initiative are all typical imbalances.

Initiative When your opponent is defending and you are attacking or putting pressure on him, it is said that you have the initiative.

Innovation A new move in an established position or opening.

Intuitive Usually a sign of experience, it enables a player to choose a move or plan by feel or common sense as opposed to detailed analysis.

Isolated Pawn A pawn with no friendly pawns on either adjacent file. A common opening that allows an isolated pawn is 1.e4 e6 2.d4 d5 3.Nd2 c5 4.exd5 exd5 5.Ngf3 Nc6 6.Bb5 Bd6 7.dxc5 Bxc5 8.0-0 Nge7 9.Nb3 Bd6 10.Nbd4. The negatives of an isolated pawn are its inability to be guarded by a friendly pawn and the fact that the square directly in front of it usually makes a fine home for an enemy piece since no pawns can chase it away. On the positive side, it offers plenty of space and the use of two half-open or open files on either side of it, with the result that one's pieces usually become active.

Kingside The half of the board originally occupied by the King, K-Bishop, K-Knight and K-Rook. The kingside is on the right of the player with the White pieces and on the left of the player with the Black pieces.

Liquidation A series of exchanges that are initiated to quell an enemy attack or to trade off to a drawn or won endgame.

Luft Literally meaning "air." In chess it describes a pawn move in front of one's King that prevents back rank mate possibilities.

Major Pieces Also called heavy pieces. The term applies to Queens and Rooks. See *Minor Pieces* and *Pawns*.

Maneuver A series of quiet moves that aim to favorably reposition one's pieces.

Master A player becomes a master when he reaches an Elo rating of 2200, though he will lose this title if his rating drops below that point.

Mate Short for checkmate. It means that you are threatening to capture the enemy King and nothing your opponent can do will prevent its loss. When this happens, you have won the game.

Material The pieces and pawns, excluding the King. A material advantage is obtained by winning a piece of greater value than the one you gave up. For example, giving up a pawn to win a Rook means that you have an advantage in material.

Mating Attack An attack on the King that is expected to lead to a checkmate.

Middlegame The phase of the game that sits between the opening and the endgame. Subtle plans and exciting attacks are generally seen in the confines of the middlegame. Grandmaster Tarrasch once said, "Between the opening and the endgame, the gods have placed the middlegame."

Minor Pieces The Bishops and the Knights.

Minority Attack A plan based on the use of two or more pawns (the minority) to act as battering rams against the opponent's three or more pawns (the majority) in order to create a weakness in the opposing camp.

　　Here is the most common opening sequence by which a minority attack is reached: 1.d4 d5 2.c4 e6 3.Nc3 Nf6 4.Bg5 Be7 5.cxd5 exd5 6.Nf3 0-0 7.e3 c6 8.Bd3 Nbd7 9.Qc2 Re8 10.0-0 Nf8 11.Bxf6 Bxf6 12.b4 Be7 13.b5 Bd6 14.bxc6 bxc6. White has carried out his minority attack and has left Black with a weak pawn on c6 and a weak square on c5. After a further Rfc1, Rab1 and Na4, White will have great pressure against Black's queenside. This plan is very important to understand, and situations for its use constantly arise.

Mobility To have freedom of movement for one's pieces.

Mysterious Rook Move A move with a Rook that seems to have no threat or purpose, but which actually discourages the opponent from a certain type of action (see Prophylaxis), or sets up a very deep, well-concealed plan.

Occupation When a Rook or Queen controls a file or rank, that file or rank is said to be occupied. Occupation of a square occurs when a piece is safely placed upon it.

Open A type of position (see Open Game) or file (see Open File). This term also refers to a type of tournament in which any class of player can participate. Though a player often ends up with opponents who are much higher or lower rated than himself, the prizes are usually structured around classes and, for this reason, opens are attractive to players of every rating. The open tournament is extremely popular in the United States and is beginning to be seen more and more in Europe.

Open File A column of eight squares that is free of pawns. It is on open files (and ranks) that Rooks come to their maximum potential.

Open Game A type of position that is characterized by many open lines and few center pawns. A lead in development becomes very important in positions of this type.

Opening The beginning phase of a game. This usually encompasses the first dozen moves but it can easily go much further. It is often written that the main opening objectives are: 1) develop your pieces in a quick and efficient manner; 2) occupy as much of the center as possible; 3) castle early (King safety).

   While I can say that these objectives are basically correct, the real purpose of the opening is to create an imbalance and develop your pieces in such a way that they all work together in making the imbalance a favorable attribute.

Opposition In the endgame, a fight between Kings often occurs that ultimately determines which one is stronger. This face-off between the two monarchs is known as the opposition.

Outflanking An endgame maneuver with Kings which makes forward progress on the board while: 1) Simultaneously preventing your opponent from taking direct opposition; or 2) Temporarily giving up the opposition for a higher goal.

Overextended When a player tries to gain some advantages by starting a major advance or offensive, and then this offensive fails, he is often left with various weaknesses and nothing to compensate for them. His position is then said to be overextended.

Overprotection A term coined by Nimzovich. It refers to defending a strong point more times than appears necessary. The idea is that a certain pawn or square may be causing the opponent considerable problems. When the overprotector focuses the energy of several pieces on it, the opponent would be unwise to break that point because that would unleash the latent energy of the overprotector's army.

In the diagram, White is overprotecting the e5-pawn. The reason for this is that the e5-pawn spearheads a kingside attack by White. Normally Black might wish to close lines there by ...f7-f5, but now White would answer this and ...f7-f6 with exf6 when all of his pieces have increased their scope and have become extremely active. Thus Black is unable to do anything that would allow White to remove the e5-pawn. As a consequence, his defensive resources are greatly reduced. Also see *Prophylaxis*.

Passed Pawn A pawn that has passed by all enemy pawns capable of capturing it.

In the diagram, White has connected passed pawns on g5 and h6. Black has a passed pawn on a7 and a protected passed pawn on e4.

Passive An inactive move that does nothing to fight for the initiative. A passive position is a position without counterplay or active possibilities.

Patzer A derogatory term that denotes a hopelessly weak player.

Pawn The least valuable unit of force in a chess game. Pawns are not considered to be pieces, they are simply called pawns.

Pawn Center Pawns placed in the center. White pawns on f4, e4 and d4, for example, would constitute a large pawn center. A common opening that allows White to build such a center, with Black hoping to attack it later, is 1.e4 d6 2.d4 Nf6 3.Nc3 g6 4.f4, etc.

Pawn Chain Two or more like-colored pawns linked diagonally. The weakest point of a pawn chain is the base because that is the one pawn in the chain that cannot be defended by another pawn.

Pawn Island A group of connected friendly pawns. In the diagram, Black has three pawn islands to White's two. It is usually considered to be advantageous to have fewer pawn islands than the opponent.

Pawn Structure The positioning of the whole pawn mass. Also re ferred to as the pawn skeleton. This positioning of the pawns is what usually dictates the types of plans available in a given position due to open files, space, pawn weaknesses, etc.

Pig A slang for Rook. "Pigs on the seventh" is a common term for Rooks doubled on the seventh rank. Also known as "Hogs on the seventh."

Plan A short or long-range goal on which a player bases his moves.

Point Count A system of figuring out the worth of the pieces by giving each of them a numerical value. King = priceless; Queen = 9 points; Rook = 5 points; Bishop = 3 points; Knight = 3 points; pawn = 1 point. The flaw in the system is that it does not take into account other factors such as position, tactics, etc., that often drastically change the relative value of an individual piece.

Poisoned Pawn Any pawn that, if captured, would lead to serious disadvantage is considered to be poisoned.

Positional A move, a maneuver or a style of play that is based on an exploitation of small advantages.

Post Mortem A Latin term borrowed from medicine that literally means, "after death." In chess it refers to the sessions that often take place after a tournament game has finished. Both players discuss the game and attempt to find the reason why someone lost—the "cause of death." In particular, those with huge or delicate egos love post mortems because they can show that they saw much more than the opponent, who was undoubtedly lucky to gain the victory. For those of a more open nature, if you have played a stronger player than yourself, you can sit back, ask what you did wrong and hope that the mysteries of the universe will unfold.

Premature A hasty move, maneuver or plan—to take action without sufficient preparation.

Prepared Variation A deeply researched opening variation that is often strengthened by new moves. It is a common practice to prepare certain lines and new moves for particular opponents, refusing to use it against anyone other than its intended victim.

Problem Child A reference to a Queen's Bishop that is trapped behind its pawns. For example, the French Defense (1.e4 e6 2.d4 d5) is an attractive opening. Its one flaw is the Queen's Bishop, which is blocked by its own pawns and unable to reach an active square.

Prophylactic Move See *Prophylaxis.*

Prophylaxis A strategy explored by Nimzovich. Taken from the Greek word *prophylaktikos,* meaning to guard or prevent beforehand, prophylaxis (or a prophylactic move) stops the opponent from taking action in a certain area for fear of some type of reprisal. Overprotection is a form of prophylaxis.

Promotion Also called Queening. When a pawn reaches the final rank it's usually turned into a Queen. However, the pawn can be promoted into a Bishop, Knight, or Rook (it cannot be turned into a King). When a pawn is turned into something other than a Queen, the pawn is said to have underpromoted.

Protected Passed Pawn A passed pawn that is protected by a friendly pawn. See *Passed Pawn.*

Queening See *Promotion.*

Queenside That half of the board made up of the four files originally occupied by the Queen, Q-Bishop, Q-Knight and Q-Rook. The queenside stands to White's left and Black's right.

Quiet Move A move that is neither a capture, a check, nor a direct attack.

Rabbit A humorous (slightly insulting) term for a non-master.

Rank A horizontal row of eight squares. The seventh rank in particular is the subject of much activity, especially when a Rook settles there. Control of the seventh rank is considered to be an important advantage.

Rating See *Elo Rating.*

Refutation A move or series of moves that demonstrates a flaw in a game, move, variation, analysis, or plan.

Resigns Realizing the hopeless nature of a position and not wanting to insult the intelligence of the opponent, a player can surrender the game—resign—without having to wait for a checkmate.

Resignation occurs in the vast majority of tournament games. Actual checkmates are quite rare.

Risk A double-edged sword. A move, plan or opening variation that aims for advantage while carrying the danger of a disadvantage.

Romantic The romantic era (macho-era) of chess was a time when sacrificing and attacking was considered to be the only manly way to play. If a sacrifice was offered, it was a disgraceful show of cowardice to refuse; thus, many beautiful sacrificial games were recorded simply because proper defensive techniques were not understood. That was in the 1800's. Today, a player who is termed romantic is one who has a proclivity for bold attacks and sacrifices, often throwing caution to the winds.

Sacrifice The voluntary offer of material for the purpose of gaining a more favorable advantage than the material investment. Unlike a combination, a sacrifice is not a cut-and-dried affair. There is usually an element of uncertainty associated with it. Though a combination always has one or more sacrifices, a sacrifice need not be associated with a combination.

Semi-Open Game A position with some closed and some open qualities. Typically, 1.e4 e6, 1.e4 c6 and 1.e4 d6 lead to semi-open games. See *Open Games* and *Closed Games*.

Sharp A bold, aggressive move or position. A sharp player is one who enjoys dynamic, explosive situations.

Shot A strong move that the opponent didn't expect.

Simplify An exchange of pieces to reach a won ending, to neutralize an enemy attack or simply to clarify a situation.

Skittles Chess played in an offhand manner, often at a chess club or after a tournament game.

Sound An analytically correct move or plan. A safe, solid position.

Space The territory controlled by each player. Thus, whoever controls the most territory has a spatial advantage.

Speculative An unclear or risky move or plan.

Strategy The foundation of a player's moves. The way to achieve a particular plan. See *Plan*.

Style The preference for certain types of positions and moves. It is typical to have one player who enjoys open, tactical positions while his opponent may cherish semi-closed structures of a positional nature. Thus, the first part of the battle will be to determine who gets the type of position at which he excels.

Support Point A square that acts as a home for a piece (usually a Knight). A square can only be considered a support point if it cannot be attacked by an enemy pawn or if the enemy pawn advance (attacking the support point) would severely weaken the enemy position.

Swindle A trick from an inferior position.

Symmetry A situation in which both armies are identically placed on their respective sides of the board. For example, 1.c4 c5 2.Nc3 Nc6 3.g3 g6 4.Bg2 Bg7 5.Nf3 Nf6 6.0-0 0-0 7.a3 a6 8.Rb1 Rb8 9.b4 cxb4 10.axb4 b5 11.cxb5 axb5 is a well-known symmetrical position that comes from the English Opening.

Tactics Traps, threats and schemes based on the calculation of variations (at times rather long-winded). A position with many combinative motifs present is considered tactical.

Tempo The unit of time represented by one move. For example: 1.e4 d5 2.exd5 Qxd5 3.Nc3 gains a tempo, as the Queen must move again if it is to avoid being captured.

Territory See *Space*.

Theory Known and practiced opening, middlegame and endgame variations and positions. Opening theory is also referred to as *book*.

Threat A move or plan that, if allowed, would lead to the immediate depreciation of the enemy position.

Time Can be used in several contexts. One meaning is the amount of thinking time as measured by special clocks (see Time Control) It is also used in reference to the ability to stop a particular action by the opponent, i.e., "Black does not have time to coordinate a successful defense against the coming attack." Thus time also measures development (an advantage in time being a lead in development) and the rate at which an attack is pursued or defended.

Time Control The amount of time given to reach a certain number of moves. In international competition this is usually 40 moves in 2 1/2 hours (extra time is given after 40 moves have been played). If a player uses up his 2 1/2 hour allocation and he has not yet made 40 moves, he will lose the game by forfeit no matter what the position on the board is like.

Time Pressure That period of the game when one or both players have used up most of their time and must make many moves with little deliberation. Naturally, this should be avoided since it often leads to mistakes or game-losing blunders.

Transitions The changing of one phase of the game into another—the opening into the middlegame and the middlegame into the endgame.

Transposition Reaching an identical position by a different sequence of moves. For example, the Dutch Defense (1.d4 f5) can be reached by 1.d4 e6 2.c4 f5 or by 1.c4 f5 2.d4 e6.

Trap A hidden way to lure an opponent into making an error. A trap should only be laid if it is part of the overall strategic plan. This way, it does not matter if your opponent falls for it or not; you will still be improving your position.

Unclear An uncertain situation. Some players never use this assessment, insisting that every position is either equal or favorable for one side or the other. It has even been said that "unclear" is a lazy way to avoid figuring out what's really going on in a position.

Variation The first two to five moves of a game lead to the bare bones structure of a particular opening. All divergences from that point on are known as variations. Variations also occur in analysis of middlegame and endgame positions.

Weakness Any pawn or square that is difficult or impossible to defend.

Wild Extremely unclear. A sharp situation or move with unfathomable complications.

Zugzwang "Compulsion to move." A German term referring to a situation in which a player would like to do nothing (pass), since any move will damage his game.

Zwischenzug "In-between move." A German term for an often unexpected reply thrown into an expected sequence of moves.